SHADOW SHOW

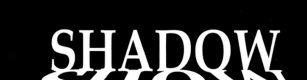

cover by Charles Paul Wilson III
series edits by Carlos Guzman
collection edits by Justin Eisinger & Alonzo Simon
collection design by Gilberto Lazcano

www.IDWPUBLISHING.com
IDW founded by Ted Adams, Alex Garner, Kris Oprisko, and Robbie Robbins

ISBN: 978-1-63140-267-8   18 17 16 15   1 2 3 4

Ted Adams, CEO & Publisher
Greg Goldstein, President & COO
Robbie Robbins, EVP/Sr. Graphic Artist
Chris Ryall, Chief Creative Officer/Editor-in-Chief
Matthew Ruzicka, CPA, Chief Financial Officer
Alan Payne, VP of Sales
Dirk Wood, VP of Marketing
Lorelei Bunjes, VP of Digital Services
Jeff Webber, VP of Digital Publishing & Business Development

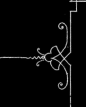

Become our fan on Facebook facebook.com/idwpublishing
Follow us on Twitter @idwpublishing
Check us out on YouTube youtube.com/idwpublishing
Tumblr http://tumblr.idwpublishing.com/
Instagram instagram.com/idwpublishing

HOMECOMING

Mr. Bradbury's letter channeled by Sam Weller and Mort Castle

From: Ray Douglas Bradbury
Date: April 15, 20150
To: All My Family

Since I passed away on June 5, 2012, many people have kindly inquired about both my welfare and whereabouts. As to the latter, can it be any great surprise that I am presently on Mars? The very first stories I wrote as a boy were of Mars. Years later, I said I wanted to be buried here, the first departed person to reside on this red-dusted world. I can say now that, on this fabled, mythical Mars-of-the-wildest-imaginings-and-so-sublime-hopes... Without irony, Mars is Heaven.

Mars is a world most civilized. The art of Edward Hopper, Van Gogh, and Dean Ellis hangs in prominent galleries. Berlioz is much admired, as are the films of Walt Disney, and the motion picture palaces of Mars, with their grand marble staircases, their golden-eyed uniformed ushers, and the best, most lavishly buttered popcorn I've tasted since I saw *The Valley of the Giants* at the opening of the Genesee Theatre back in Waukegan. The funnies section of the Sunday *Martian Tribune* covers half the living room carpet and you can see every hinge of the siege machine in this week's adventure of *Prince Valiant*.

I'll confess, there were moments prior to my "departure" from Earth in 2012 when I was not totally confident of my taking up a new residence. Death? Death doesn't exist. It never did, it never will. But we've drawn so many pictures of it, so many years, trying to pin it down, comprehend it, we've got to thinking of it as an entity, strangely alive and greedy. All it is, however, is a stopped watch, a loss, an end, a darkness. Nothing.

I was prepared in what I now know are wrongly called the "final moments" for the ultimate cessation. *Adieu* and farewell and endless *nuit* ... Perhaps I imagined it, but I thought I heard at my bedside a lyrically sad voice with an Hispanic accent, saying, "I see you never."

And then, just as it happens in good movies and bad, I was watching my life rewind until it came to Labor Day Weekend of 1932. A dingy and dusty carnival had arrived and pitched tents along the rocky shoreline of Lake Michigan in Waukegan, Illinois. It was a gray, gauzy day and a soft rain was falling.

I was 12 years old, in love with carnivals and circuses and sideshow freaks. I wandered into a tattered magician's tent and took a seat alongside a dozen other children on a sawdust-covered floor. The lights dimmed. Mr. Electrico emerged from behind a curtain wearing a black cape. He was wielding a heavy Excalibur sword. The mysterious magician with his great shock of white hair took a seat in an electric chair and an assistant strapped him in. Then at a nod, the assistant pulled a lever from stage-left sending 50,000 volts of pure, unfettered electricity coursing through the magician.

Mr. Electrico's teeth chattered. His eyes glowed. His hair stood on end. Then the assistant pushed the lever back in place and the thunder and lighting show ended as quickly as it began. The assistant unstrapped the magician and Mr. Electrico picked up his sword and slowly walked up to all the children sitting before him. One by one he began tapping his sword on their brows as their hair stood up on end, electricity charging from magician through the sword and into the kids. The members in the audience were incredulous.

Then, finally, Mr. Electrico approached one last child, none other than me. He tapped the sword on my left shoulder, then my right, then gently touched the tip of the sword to my nose. I could feel electricity triggering through every cell in my body and then the magician and I locked eyes.

"LIVE FOREVER!" Mr. Electrico cried.

"Live Forever!"

I thought that a *wonderful* idea, but how did you do it?

With the help of libraries and librarians, and the guidance of clowns and carnivals and teachers of all sorts, and by the act of writing and writing and writing, of following my imagination wherever it might lead to places dangerous and exalted—and to Mars, to Mars!—I set off upon a path that I hoped would enable me to pursue Mr. Electrico's "suggestion"—or obey his command. This writer fell in love with writing. Motivation? The key word is love. You have to get up in the morning and write something you love, you have to write something to live for.

And of course there are the readers, so many of you, God bless, you who have kept alive these visions of a Green Town home boy expatriate, and if your dreams yet live, how can you not live?

So, let us say it has all worked out. I abideth on Mars ...

And as you might imagine, I am not alone. There are writers, my idols, my colleagues, my friends: Mr. Tom Wolfe, who wrote of "Forever and the Earth," and Mr. Hemingway, Papa, who told us "Nobody Ever Dies." And there is upon this sacred and awesome planet another writer from Illinois with whom I have had many good talks over a glass or two of wine, Mr. Edgar Lee Masters, who wrote *Spoon River Anthology*.

I quote that memorable work now:

> Immortality is not a gift,
> Immortality is an achievement;
> And only those who strive mightily
> Shall possess it.

Mightily? Perhaps that is the way, but with love, always with love, and so

With Love,
Live Forever!
Yours,

Ray Bradbury

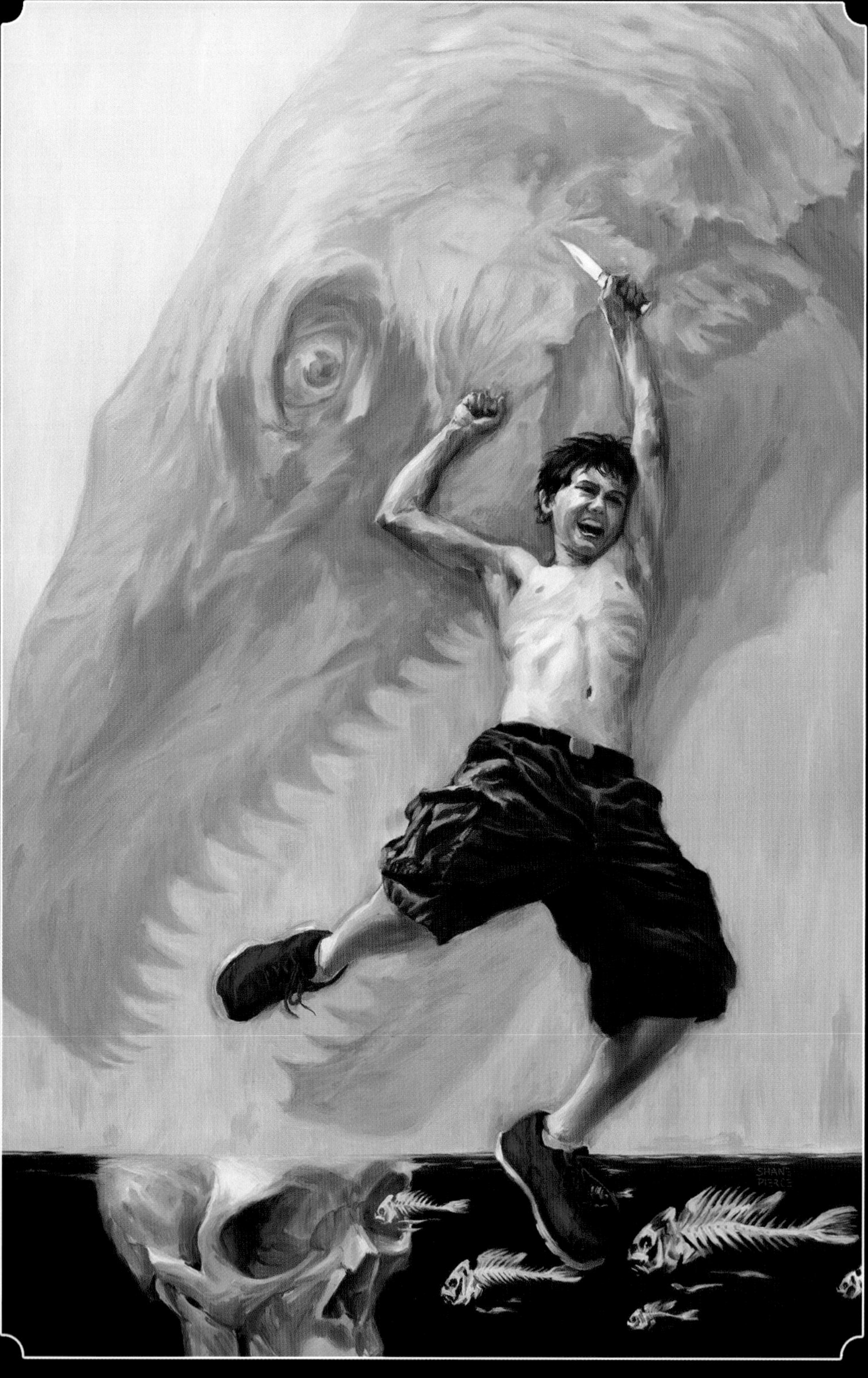
SHANE
PIERCE

art by SHANE PIERCE

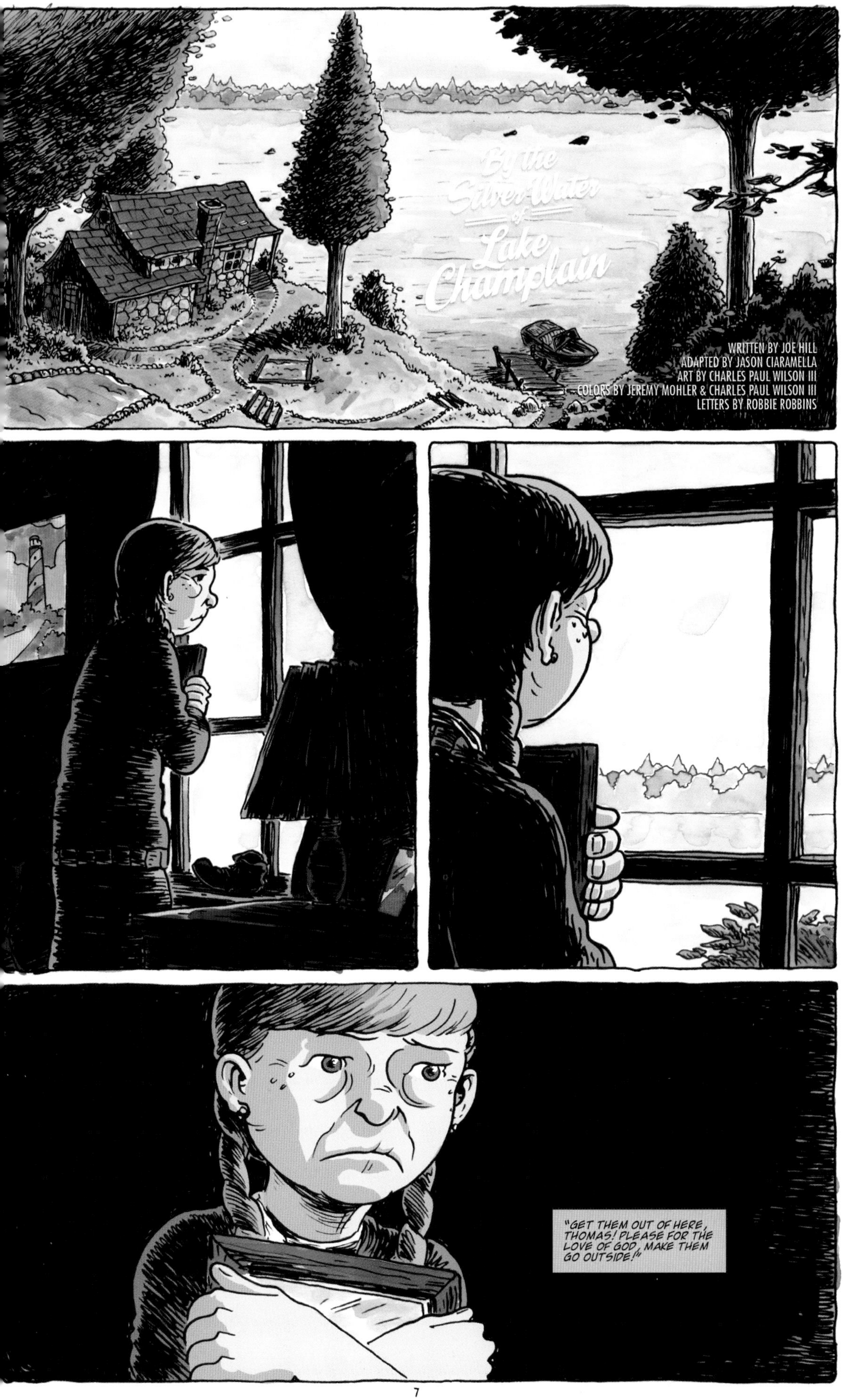
By the Silver Water of Lake Champlain
WRITTEN BY JOE HILL
ADAPTED BY JASON CIARAMELLA
ART BY CHARLES PAUL WILSON III
COLORS BY JEREMY MOHLER & CHARLES PAUL WILSON III
LETTERS BY ROBBIE ROBBINS
"GET THEM OUT OF HERE, THOMAS! PLEASE FOR THE LOVE OF GOD, MAKE THEM GO OUTSIDE!"

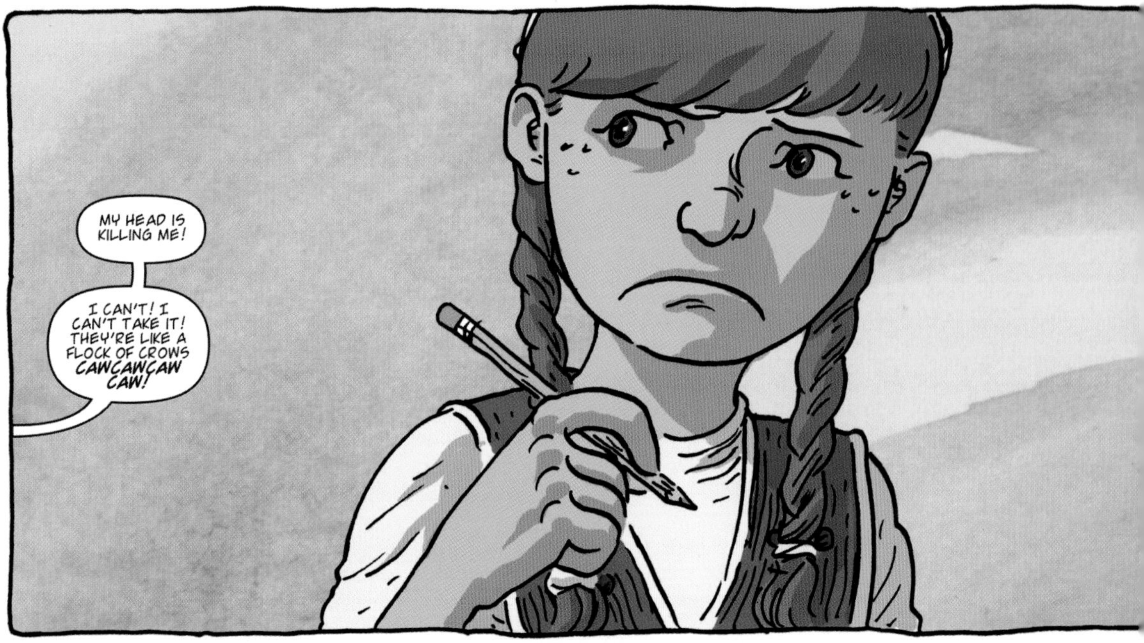
MY HEAD IS KILLING ME!
I CAN'T! I CAN'T TAKE IT! THEY'RE LIKE A FLOCK OF CROWS *CAWCAWCAW CAW!*

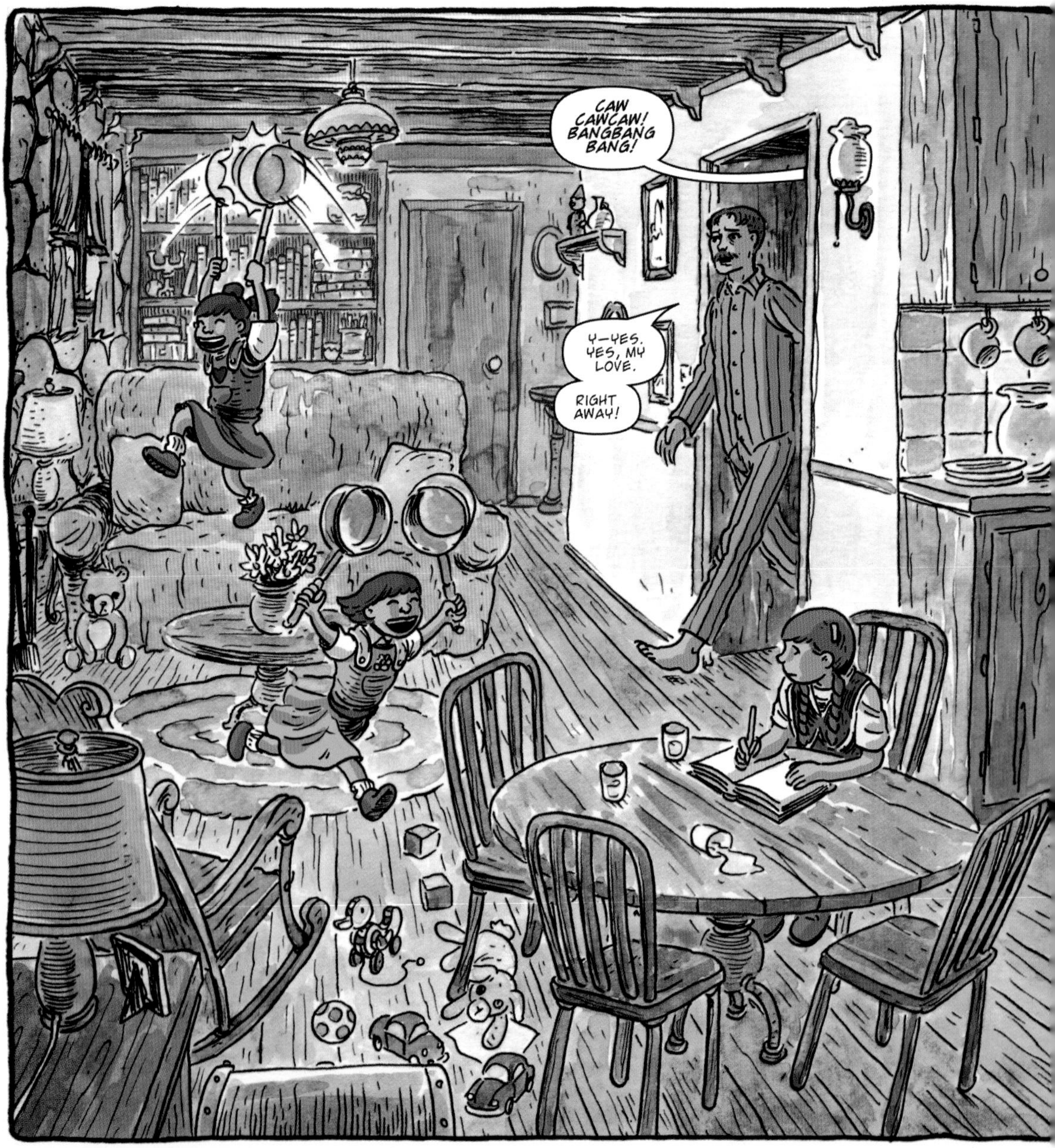
CAW CAWCAW! BANGBANG BANG!
Y-YES. YES, MY LOVE.
RIGHT AWAY!

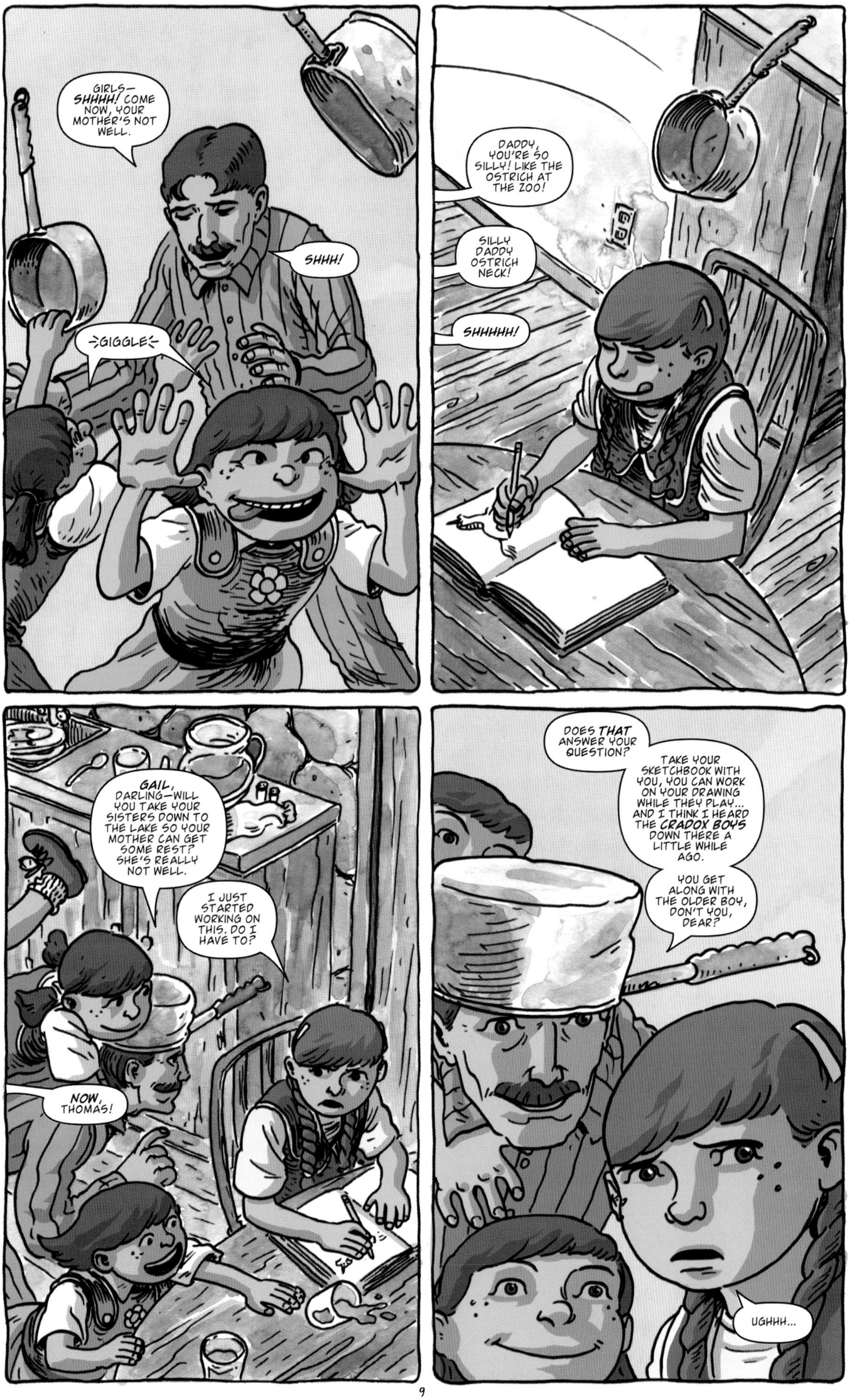
GIRLS— SHHHH! COME NOW, YOUR MOTHER'S NOT WELL.
SHHH!
GIGGLE
DADDY, YOU'RE SO SILLY! LIKE THE OSTRICH AT THE ZOO!
SILLY DADDY OSTRICH NECK!
SHHHHH!
GAIL, DARLING—WILL YOU TAKE YOUR SISTERS DOWN TO THE LAKE SO YOUR MOTHER CAN GET SOME REST? SHE'S REALLY NOT WELL.
I JUST STARTED WORKING ON THIS. DO I HAVE TO?
NOW, THOMAS!
DOES THAT ANSWER YOUR QUESTION?
TAKE YOUR SKETCHBOOK WITH YOU, YOU CAN WORK ON YOUR DRAWING WHILE THEY PLAY... AND I THINK I HEARD THE CRADOX BOYS DOWN THERE A LITTLE WHILE AGO.
YOU GET ALONG WITH THE OLDER BOY, DON'T YOU, DEAR?
UGHHH...

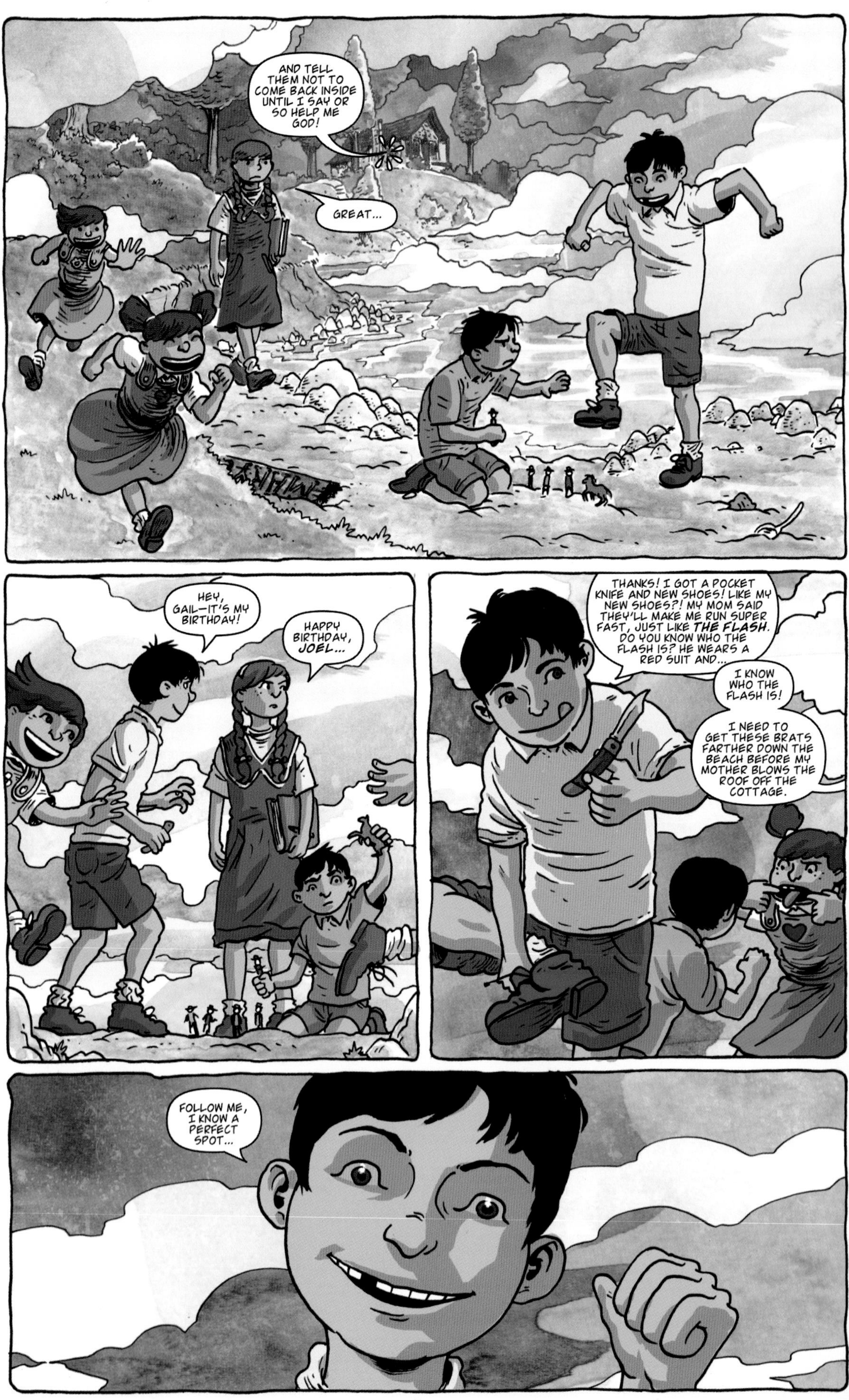
AND TELL THEM NOT TO COME BACK INSIDE UNTIL I SAY OR SO HELP ME GOD!
GREAT...
HEY, GAIL—IT'S MY BIRTHDAY!
HAPPY BIRTHDAY, JOEL...
THANKS! I GOT A POCKET KNIFE AND NEW SHOES! LIKE MY NEW SHOES?! MY MOM SAID THEY'LL MAKE ME RUN SUPER FAST, JUST LIKE THE FLASH. DO YOU KNOW WHO THE FLASH IS? HE WEARS A RED SUIT AND...
I KNOW WHO THE FLASH IS!
I NEED TO GET THESE BRATS FARTHER DOWN THE BEACH BEFORE MY MOTHER BLOWS THE ROOF OFF THE COTTAGE.
FOLLOW ME, I KNOW A PERFECT SPOT...

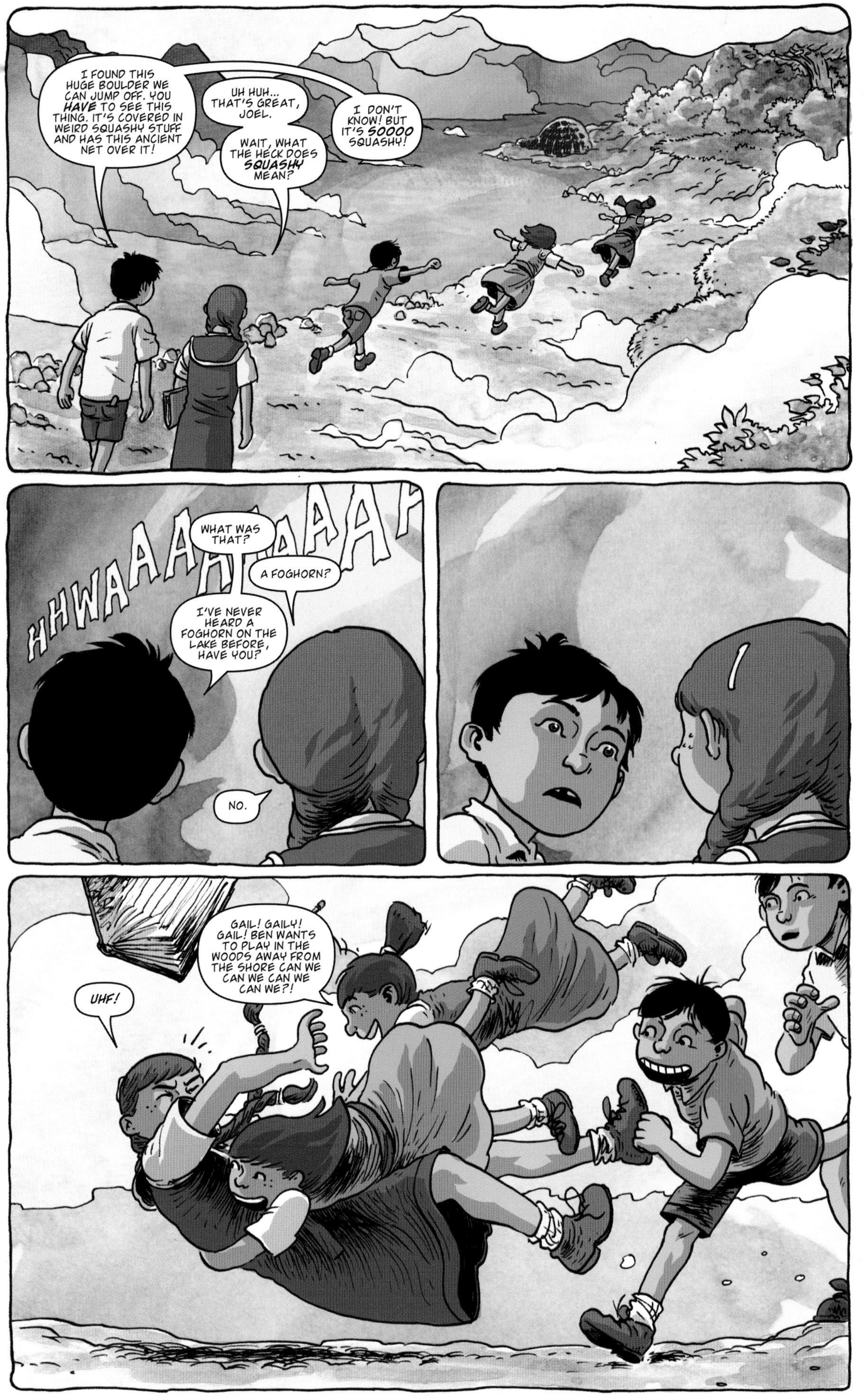
I FOUND THIS HUGE BOULDER WE CAN JUMP OFF. YOU HAVE TO SEE THIS THING. IT'S COVERED IN WEIRD SQUASHY STUFF AND HAS THIS ANCIENT NET OVER IT!
UH HUH... THAT'S GREAT, JOEL.
WAIT, WHAT THE HECK DOES SQUASHY MEAN?
I DON'T KNOW! BUT IT'S SOOOO SQUASHY!
HHWAAAAAAAAAH
WHAT WAS THAT?
A FOGHORN?
I'VE NEVER HEARD A FOGHORN ON THE LAKE BEFORE, HAVE YOU?
NO.
GAIL! GAILY! GAIL! BEN WANTS TO PLAY IN THE WOODS AWAY FROM THE SHORE CAN WE CAN WE CAN WE?!
UHF!

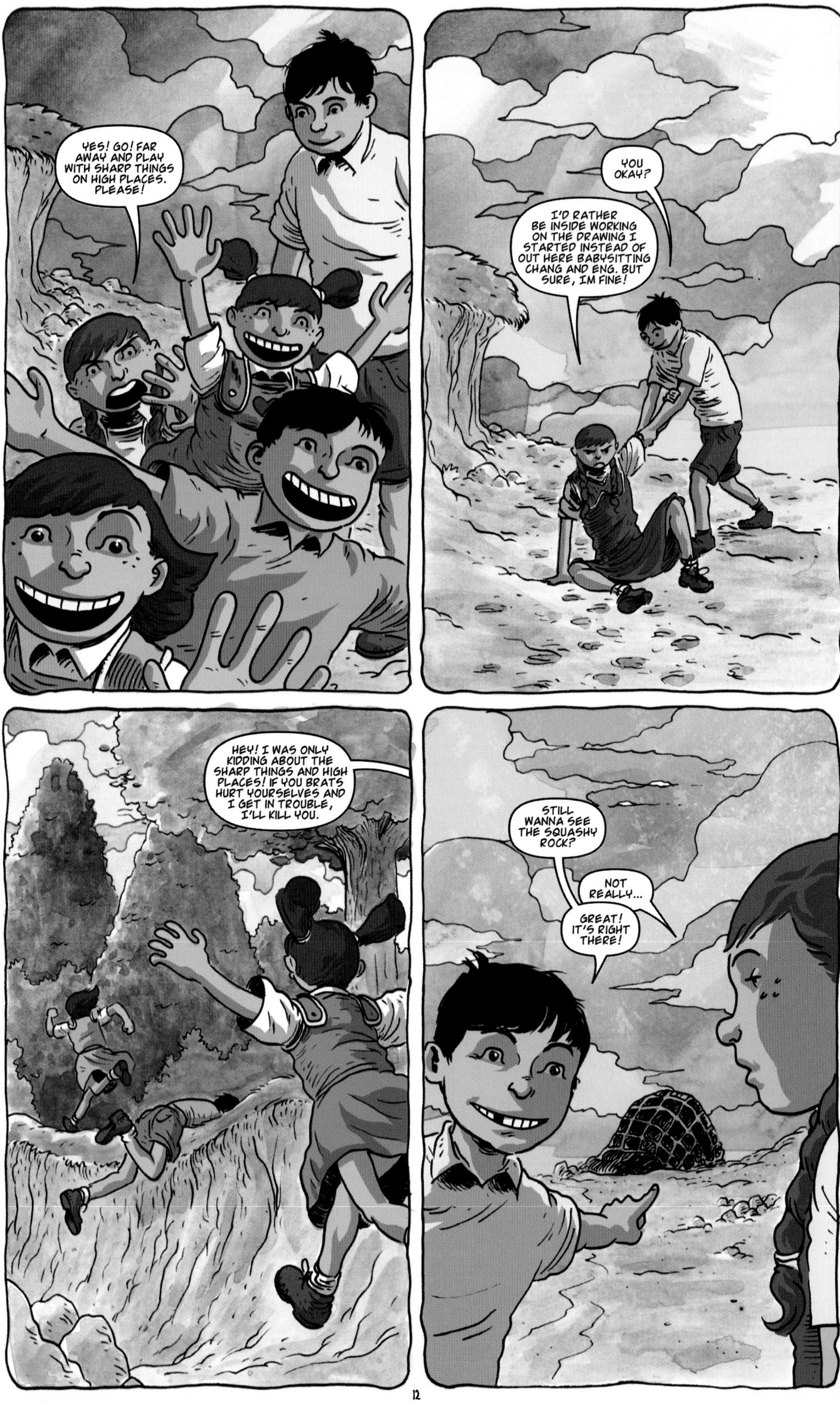
YES! GO! FAR AWAY AND PLAY WITH SHARP THINGS ON HIGH PLACES. PLEASE!
YOU OKAY?
I'D RATHER BE INSIDE WORKING ON THE DRAWING I STARTED INSTEAD OF OUT HERE BABYSITTING CHANG AND ENG. BUT SURE, IM FINE!
HEY! I WAS ONLY KIDDING ABOUT THE SHARP THINGS AND HIGH PLACES! IF YOU BRATS HURT YOURSELVES AND I GET IN TROUBLE, I'LL KILL YOU.
STILL WANNA SEE THE SQUASHY ROCK?
NOT REALLY...
GREAT! IT'S RIGHT THERE!

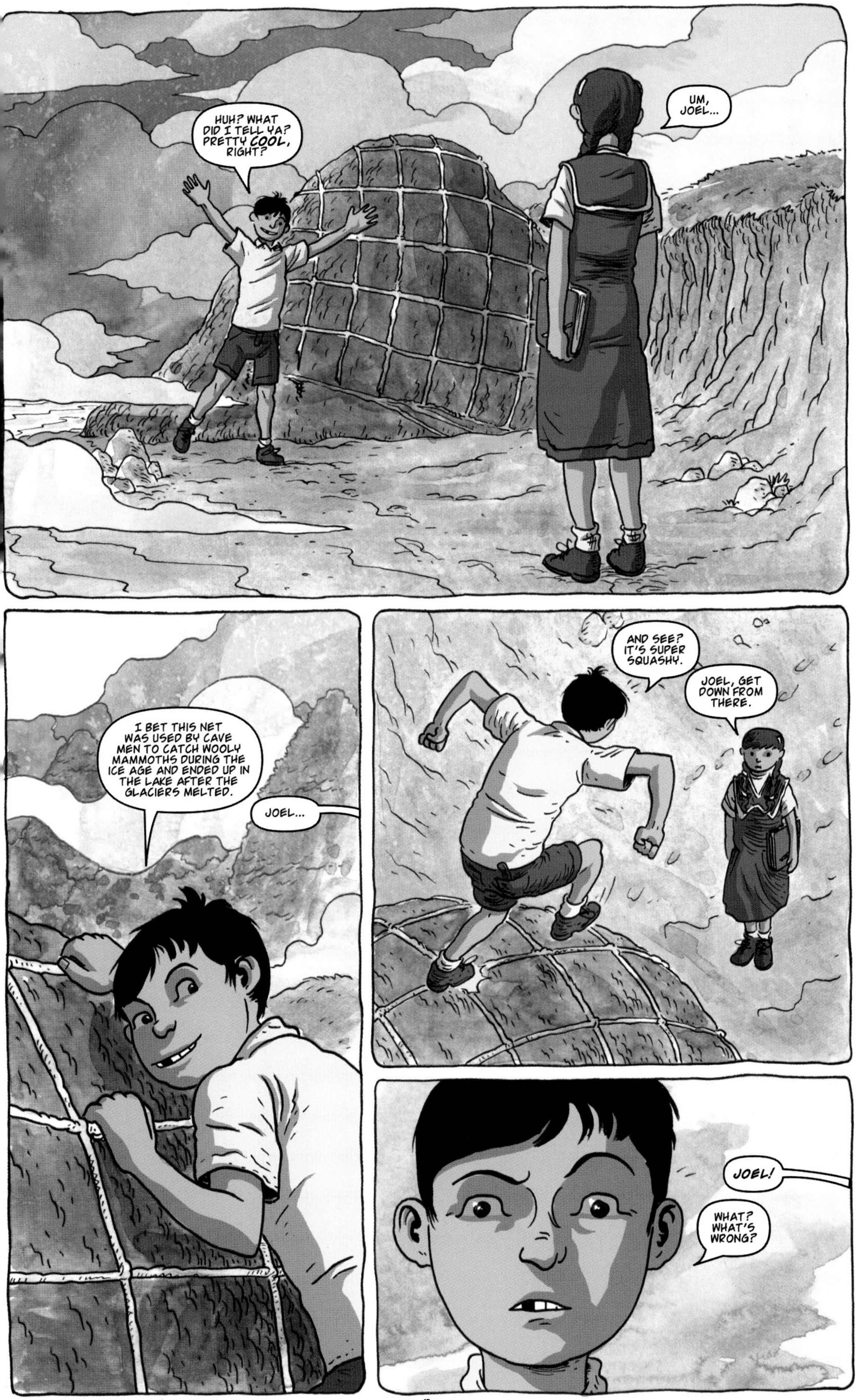
HUH? WHAT DID I TELL YA? PRETTY COOL, RIGHT?
UM, JOEL...
I BET THIS NET WAS USED BY CAVE MEN TO CATCH WOOLY MAMMOTHS DURING THE ICE AGE AND ENDED UP IN THE LAKE AFTER THE GLACIERS MELTED.
JOEL...
AND SEE? IT'S SUPER SQUASHY.
JOEL, GET DOWN FROM THERE.
JOEL!
WHAT? WHAT'S WRONG?

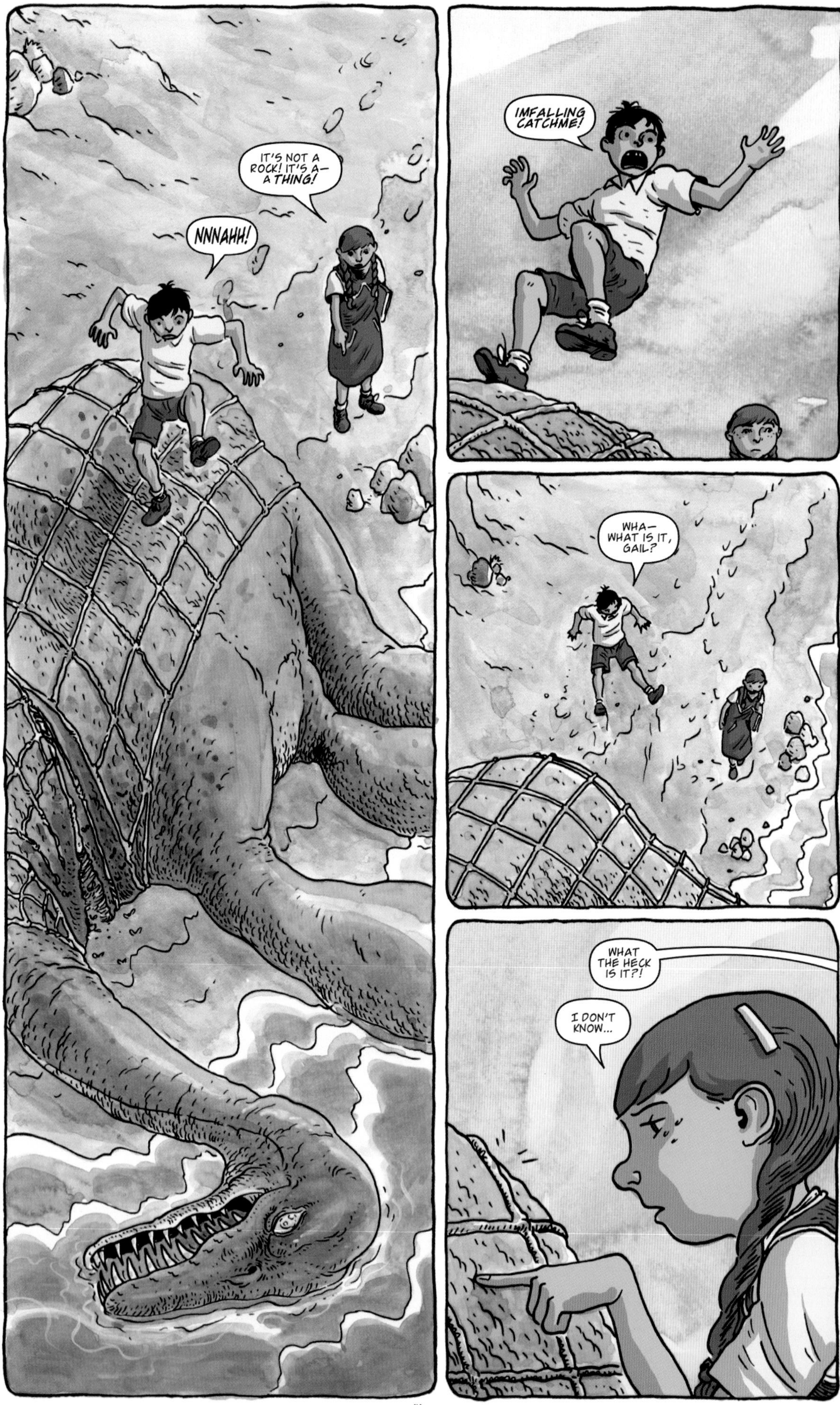
IT'S NOT A ROCK! IT'S A— A THING!
NNNAHH!
IMFALLING CATCHME!
WHA— WHAT IS IT, GAIL?
WHAT THE HECK IS IT?!
I DON'T KNOW...

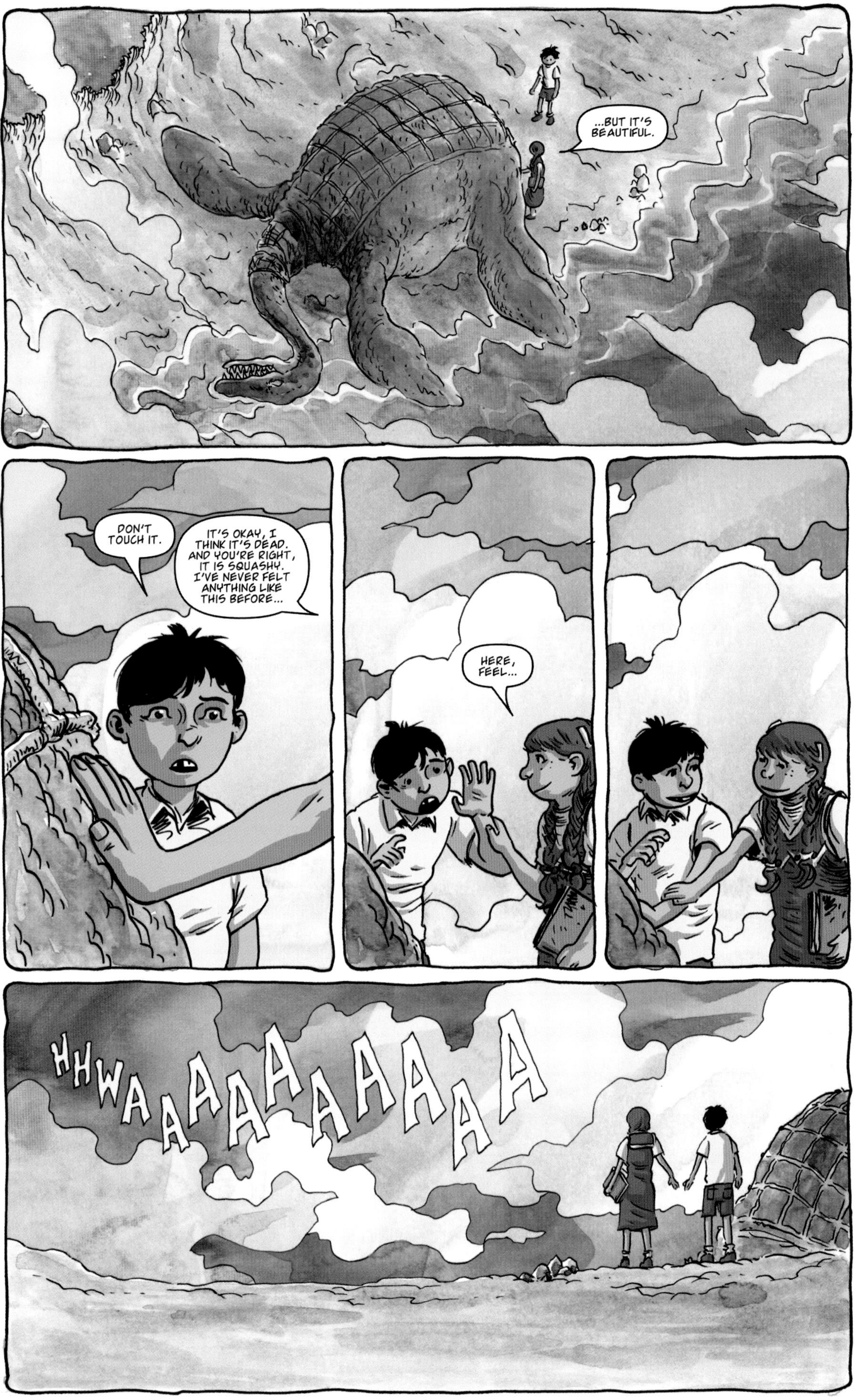
...BUT IT'S BEAUTIFUL.
DON'T TOUCH IT.
IT'S OKAY, I THINK IT'S DEAD. AND YOU'RE RIGHT, IT IS SQUASHY. I'VE NEVER FELT ANYTHING LIKE THIS BEFORE...
HERE, FEEL...
HHWAAAAAAAAAAA

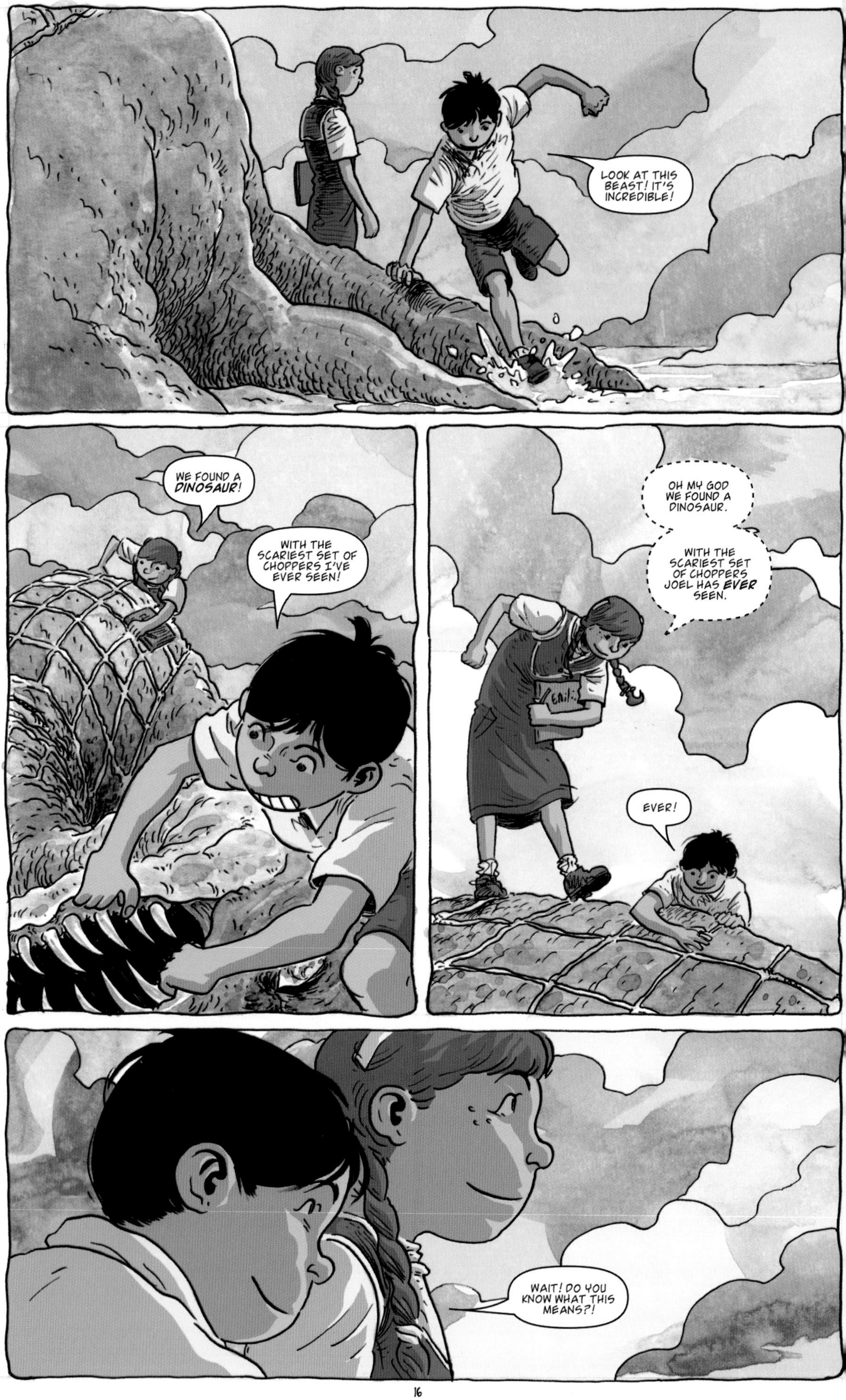
LOOK AT THIS BEAST! IT'S INCREDIBLE!
WE FOUND A DINOSAUR!
WITH THE SCARIEST SET OF CHOPPERS I'VE EVER SEEN!
OH MY GOD WE FOUND A DINOSAUR.
WITH THE SCARIEST SET OF CHOPPERS JOEL HAS EVER SEEN.
EVER!
WAIT! DO YOU KNOW WHAT THIS MEANS?!

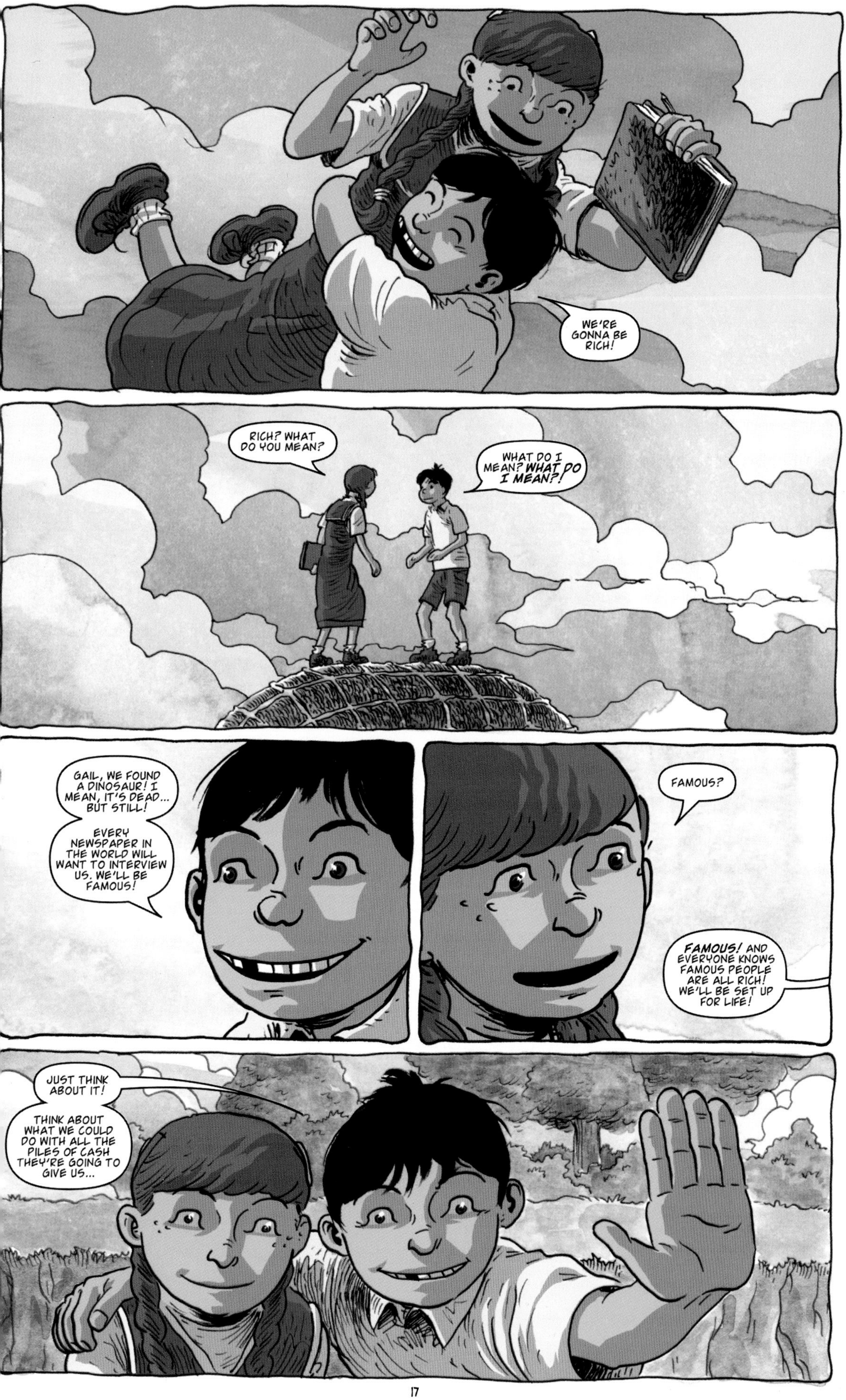
WE'RE GONNA BE RICH!
RICH? WHAT DO YOU MEAN?
WHAT DO I MEAN? WHAT DO I MEAN?!
GAIL, WE FOUND A DINOSAUR! I MEAN, IT'S DEAD... BUT STILL!
EVERY NEWSPAPER IN THE WORLD WILL WANT TO INTERVIEW US. WE'LL BE FAMOUS!
FAMOUS?
FAMOUS! AND EVERYONE KNOWS FAMOUS PEOPLE ARE ALL RICH! WE'LL BE SET UP FOR LIFE!
JUST THINK ABOUT IT!
THINK ABOUT WHAT WE COULD DO WITH ALL THE PILES OF CASH THEY'RE GOING TO GIVE US...

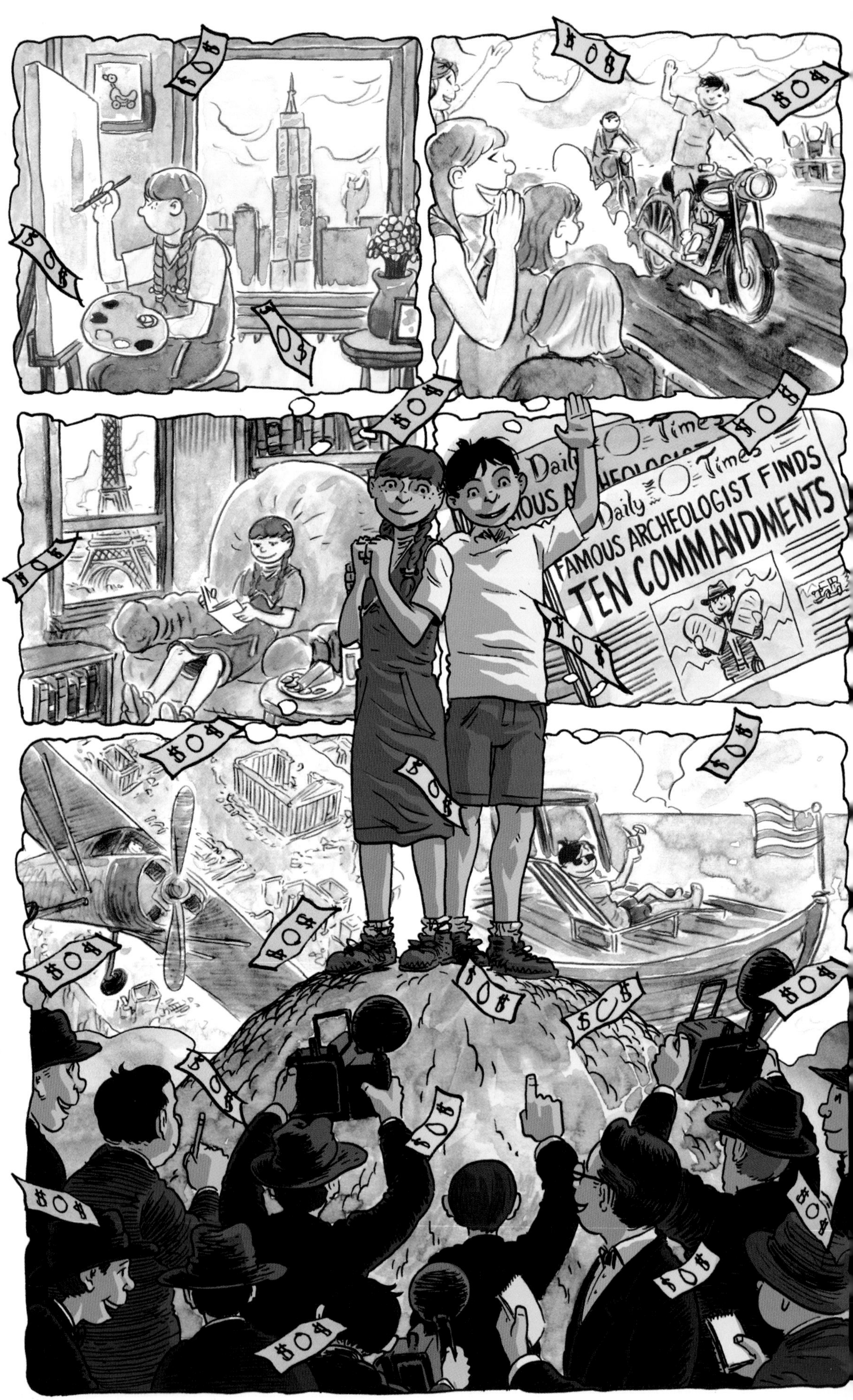
Daily Times
FAMOUS ARCHEOLOGIST FINDS
TEN COMMANDMENTS

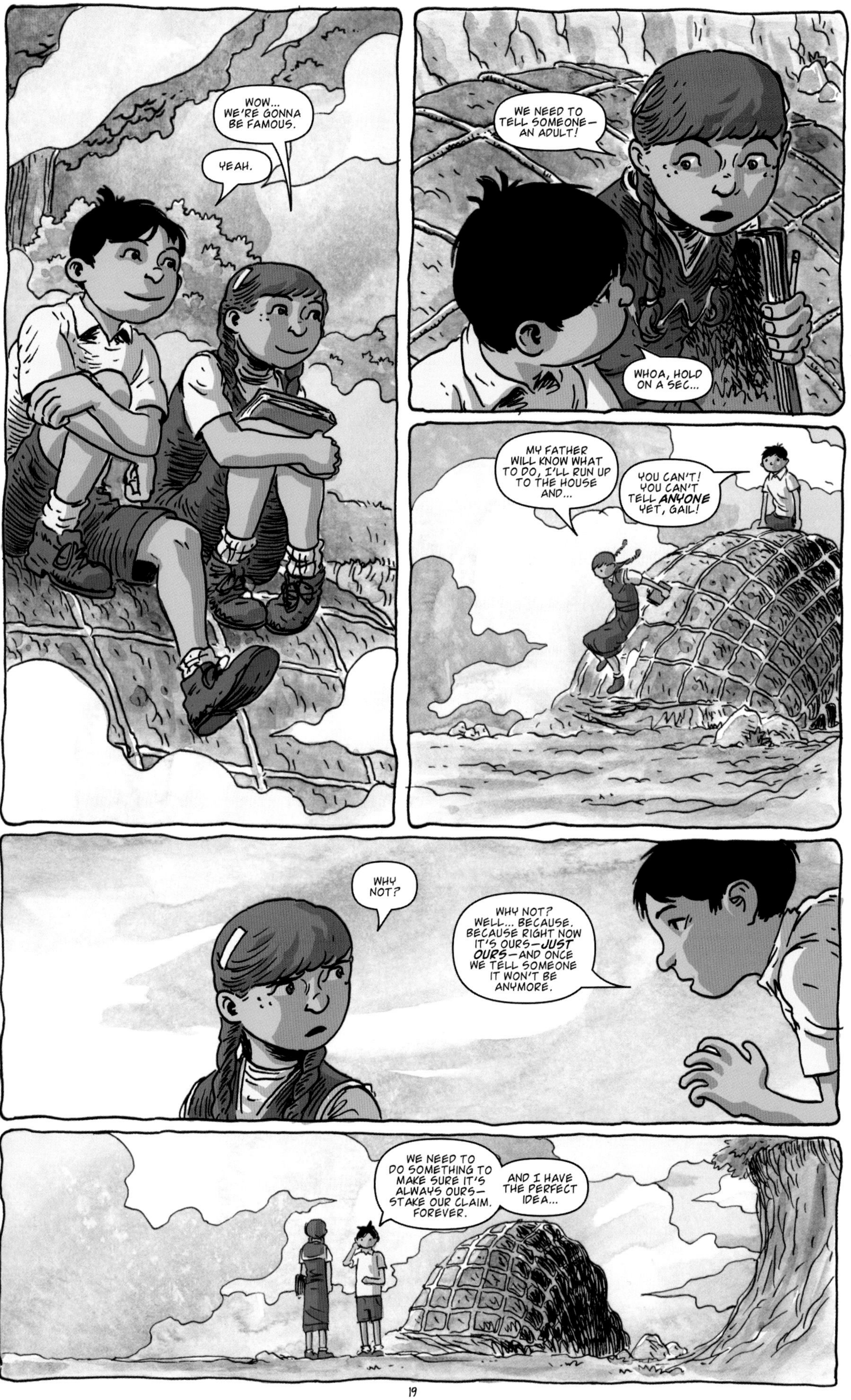
WOW... WE'RE GONNA BE FAMOUS.
YEAH.
WE NEED TO TELL SOMEONE— AN ADULT!
WHOA, HOLD ON A SEC...
MY FATHER WILL KNOW WHAT TO DO, I'LL RUN UP TO THE HOUSE AND...
YOU CAN'T! YOU CAN'T TELL **ANYONE** YET, GAIL!
WHY NOT?
WHY NOT? WELL... BECAUSE. BECAUSE RIGHT NOW IT'S OURS—***JUST OURS***—AND ONCE WE TELL SOMEONE IT WON'T BE ANYMORE.
WE NEED TO DO SOMETHING TO MAKE SURE IT'S ALWAYS OURS— STAKE OUR CLAIM. FOREVER.
AND I HAVE THE PERFECT IDEA...

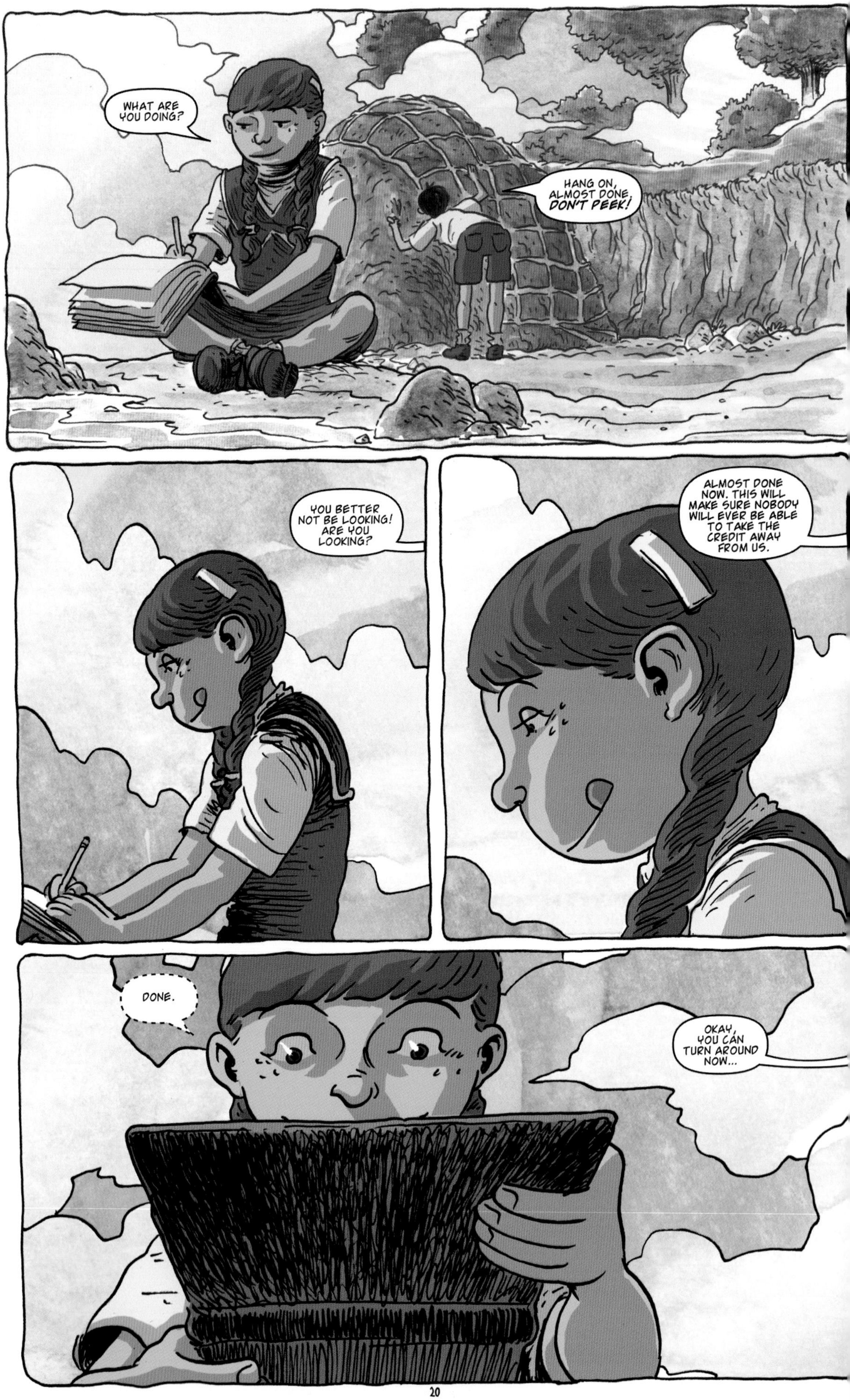
WHAT ARE YOU DOING?
HANG ON, ALMOST DONE. DON'T PEEK!
YOU BETTER NOT BE LOOKING! ARE YOU LOOKING?
ALMOST DONE NOW. THIS WILL MAKE SURE NOBODY WILL EVER BE ABLE TO TAKE THE CREDIT AWAY FROM US.
DONE.
OKAY, YOU CAN TURN AROUND NOW...

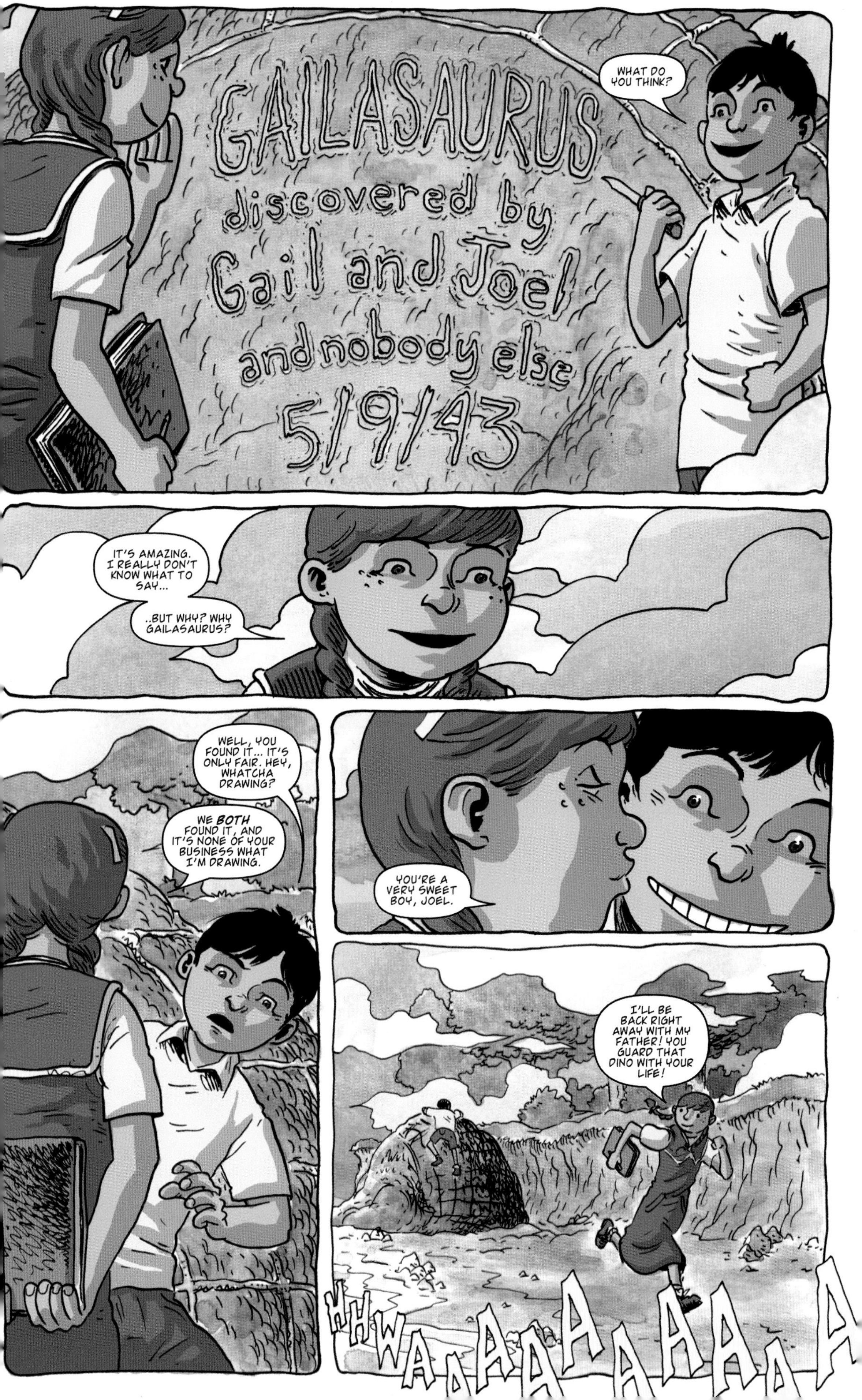
GAILASAURUS
discovered by
Gail and Joel
and nobody else
5/9/43
WHAT DO YOU THINK?
IT'S AMAZING. I REALLY DON'T KNOW WHAT TO SAY...
..BUT WHY? WHY GAILASAURUS?
WELL, YOU FOUND IT... IT'S ONLY FAIR. HEY, WHATCHA DRAWING?
WE BOTH FOUND IT, AND IT'S NONE OF YOUR BUSINESS WHAT I'M DRAWING.
YOU'RE A VERY SWEET BOY, JOEL.
I'LL BE BACK RIGHT AWAY WITH MY FATHER! YOU GUARD THAT DINO WITH YOUR LIFE!
HHWAAAAAAAAAAA

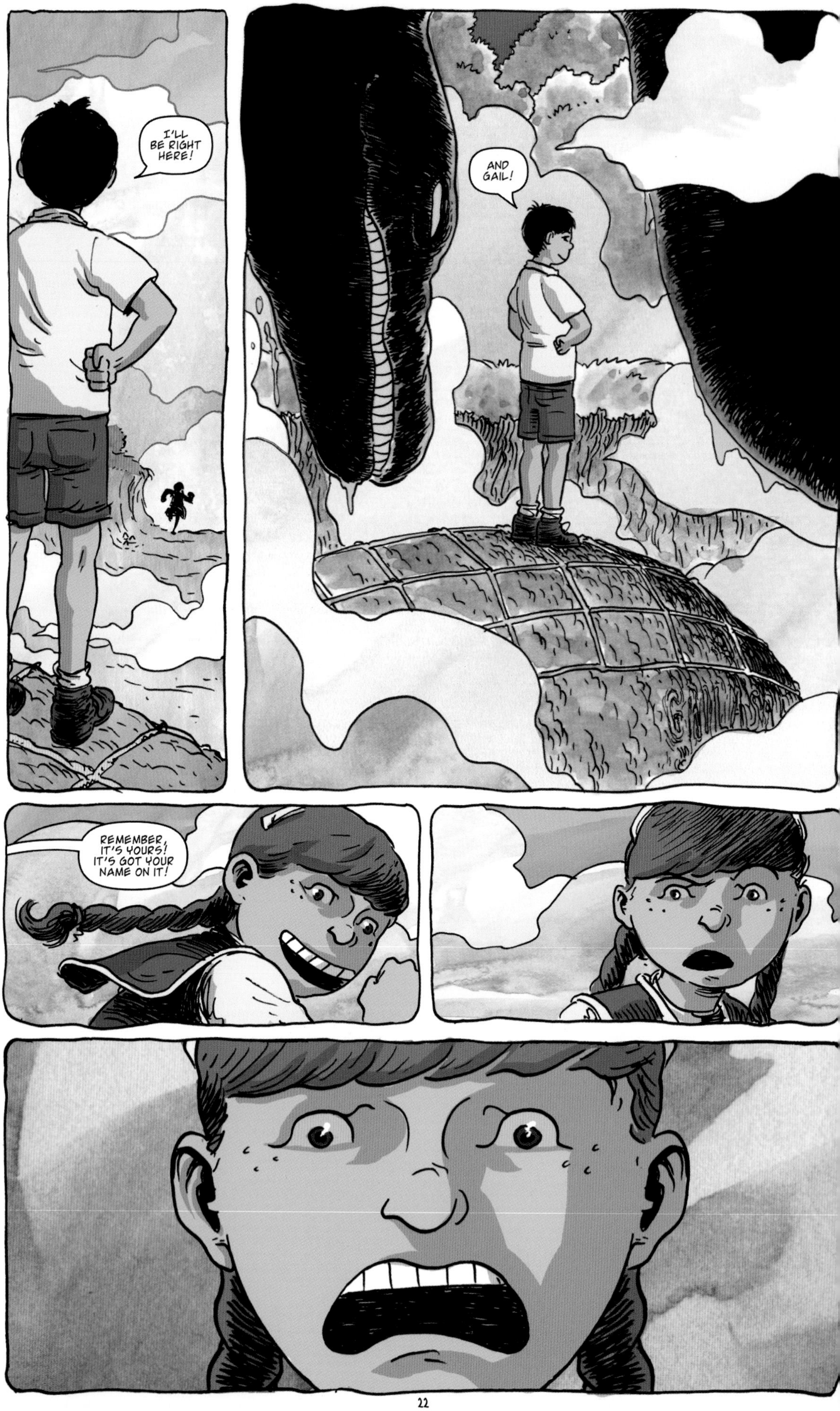
I'LL BE RIGHT HERE!
AND GAIL!
REMEMBER, IT'S YOURS! IT'S GOT YOUR NAME ON IT!

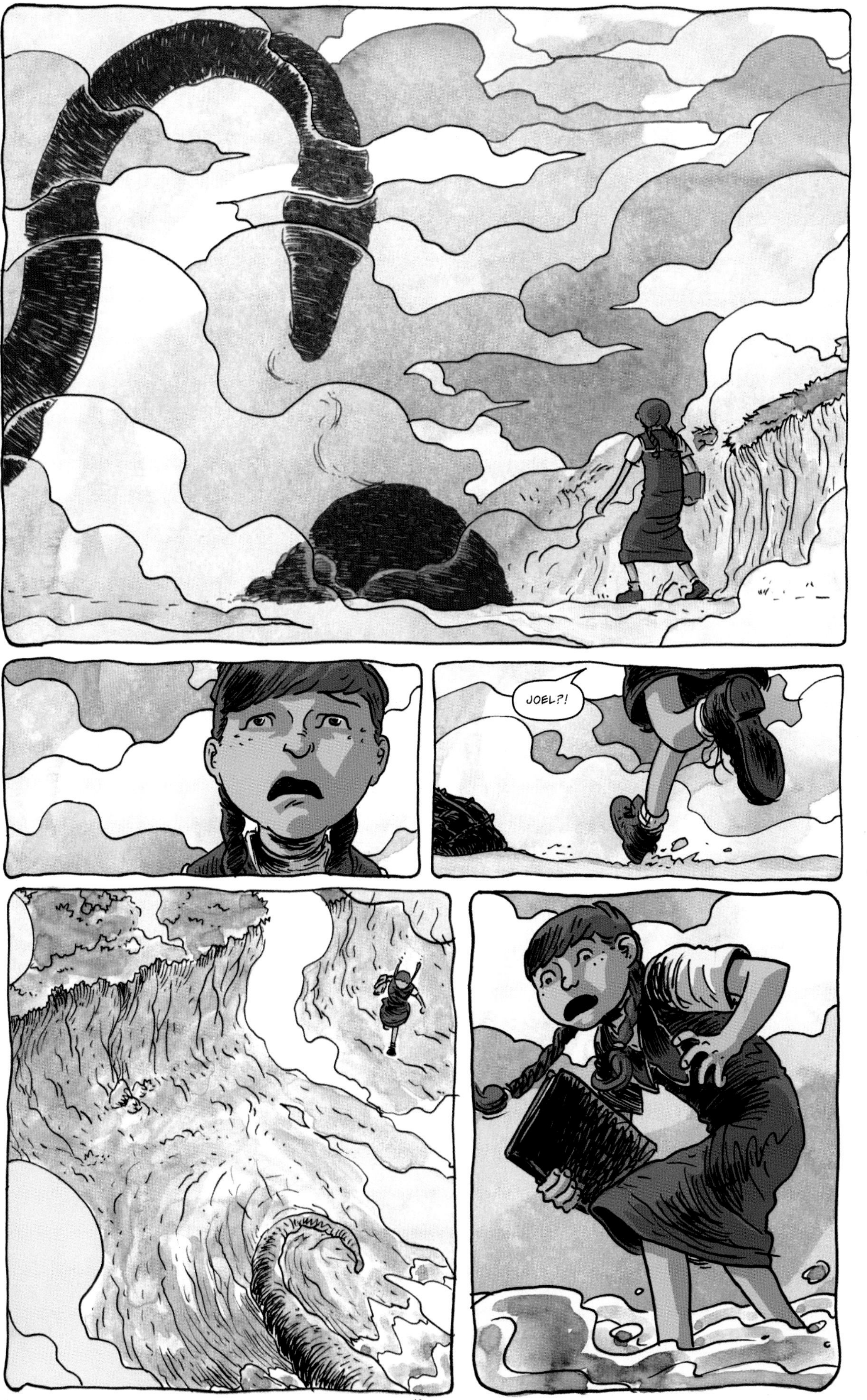
JOEL?!

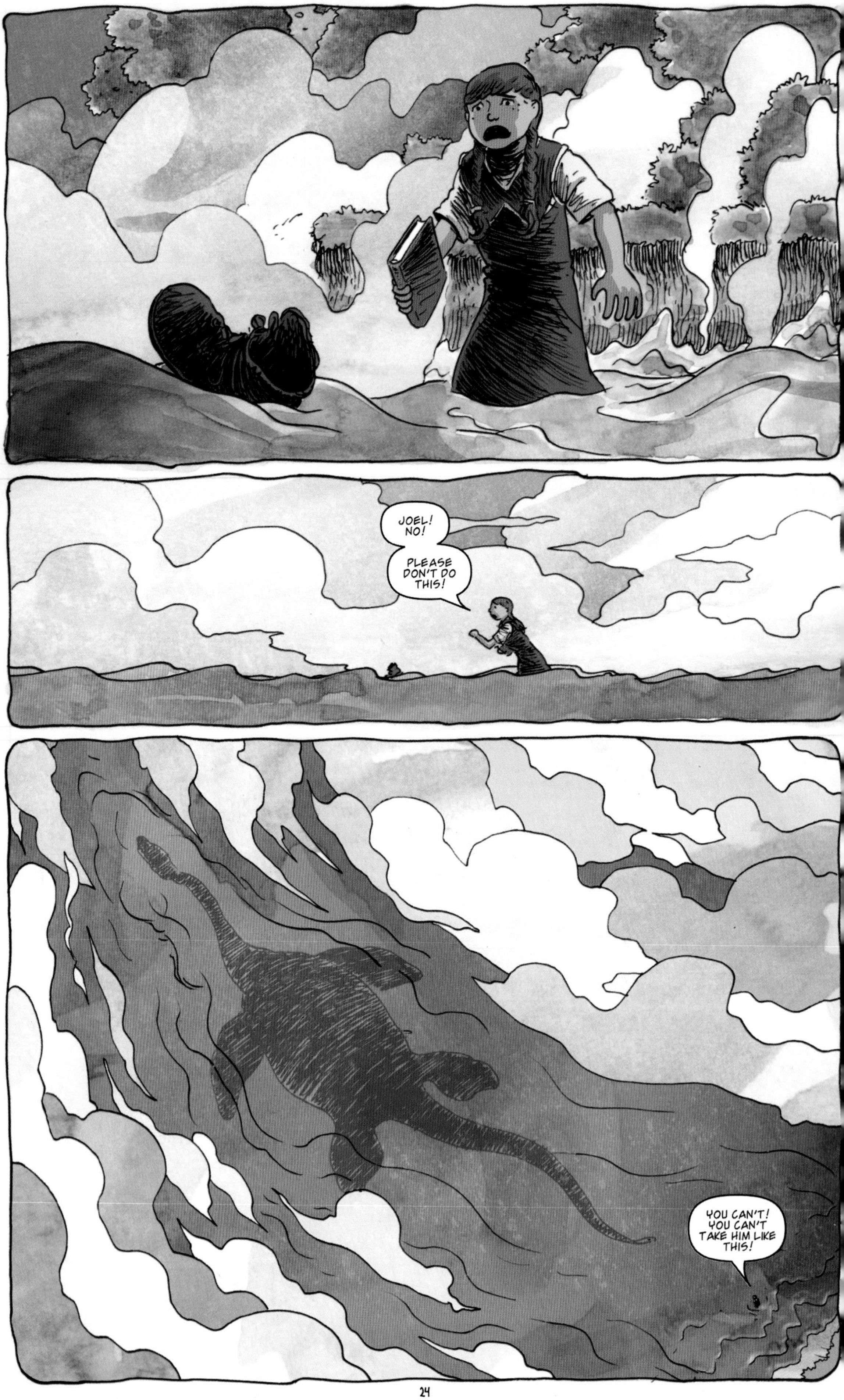
JOEL! NO!
PLEASE DON'T DO THIS!
YOU CAN'T! YOU CAN'T TAKE HIM LIKE THIS!

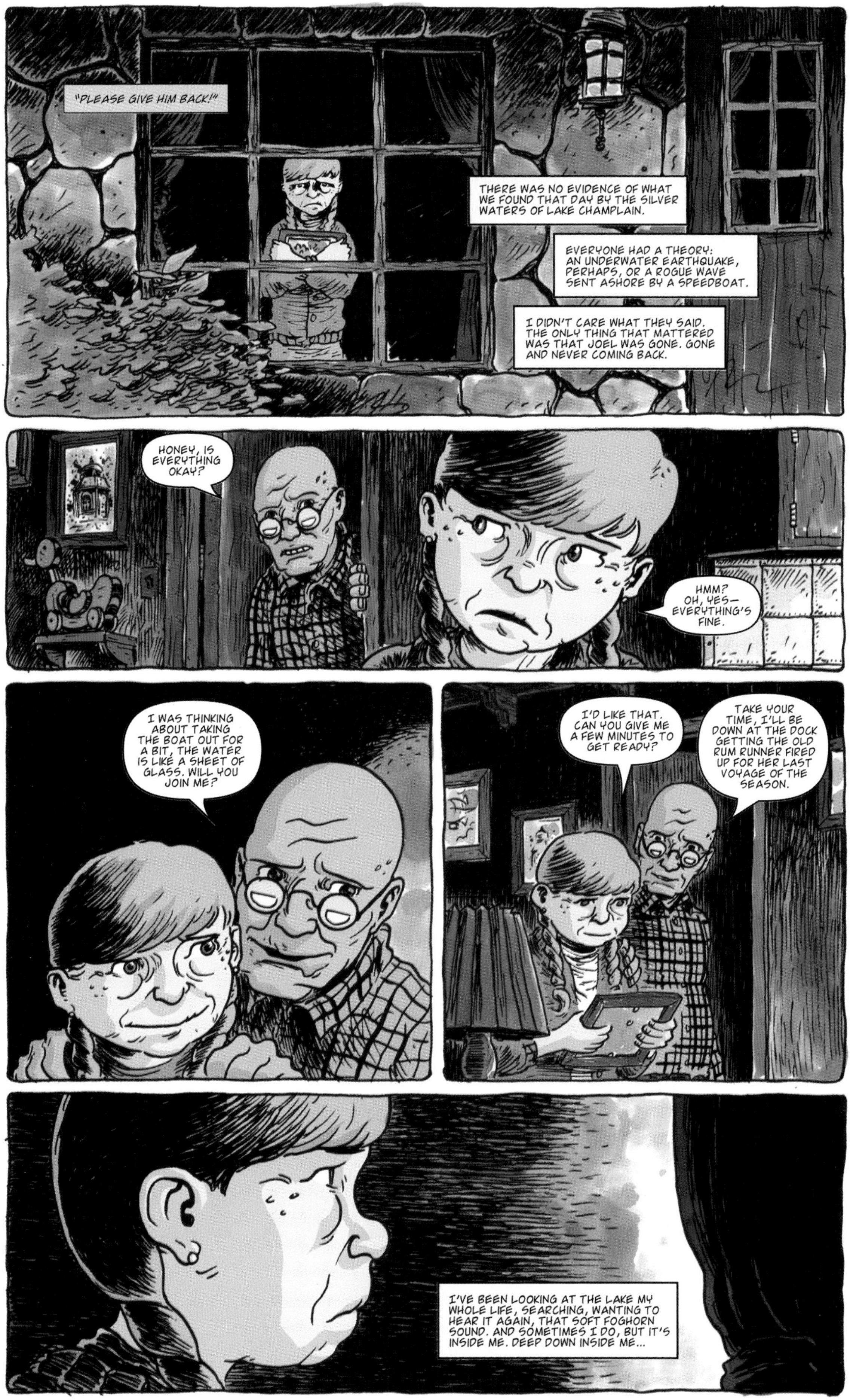
"PLEASE GIVE HIM BACK!"
THERE WAS NO EVIDENCE OF WHAT WE FOUND THAT DAY BY THE SILVER WATERS OF LAKE CHAMPLAIN.
EVERYONE HAD A THEORY: AN UNDERWATER EARTHQUAKE, PERHAPS, OR A ROGUE WAVE SENT ASHORE BY A SPEEDBOAT.
I DIDN'T CARE WHAT THEY SAID. THE ONLY THING THAT MATTERED WAS THAT JOEL WAS GONE. GONE AND NEVER COMING BACK.
HONEY, IS EVERYTHING OKAY?
HMM? OH, YES— EVERYTHING'S FINE.
I WAS THINKING ABOUT TAKING THE BOAT OUT FOR A BIT, THE WATER IS LIKE A SHEET OF GLASS. WILL YOU JOIN ME?
I'D LIKE THAT. CAN YOU GIVE ME A FEW MINUTES TO GET READY?
TAKE YOUR TIME, I'LL BE DOWN AT THE DOCK GETTING THE OLD RUM RUNNER FIRED UP FOR HER LAST VOYAGE OF THE SEASON.
I'VE BEEN LOOKING AT THE LAKE MY WHOLE LIFE, SEARCHING, WANTING TO HEAR IT AGAIN, THAT SOFT FOGHORN SOUND. AND SOMETIMES I DO, BUT IT'S INSIDE ME. DEEP DOWN INSIDE ME...

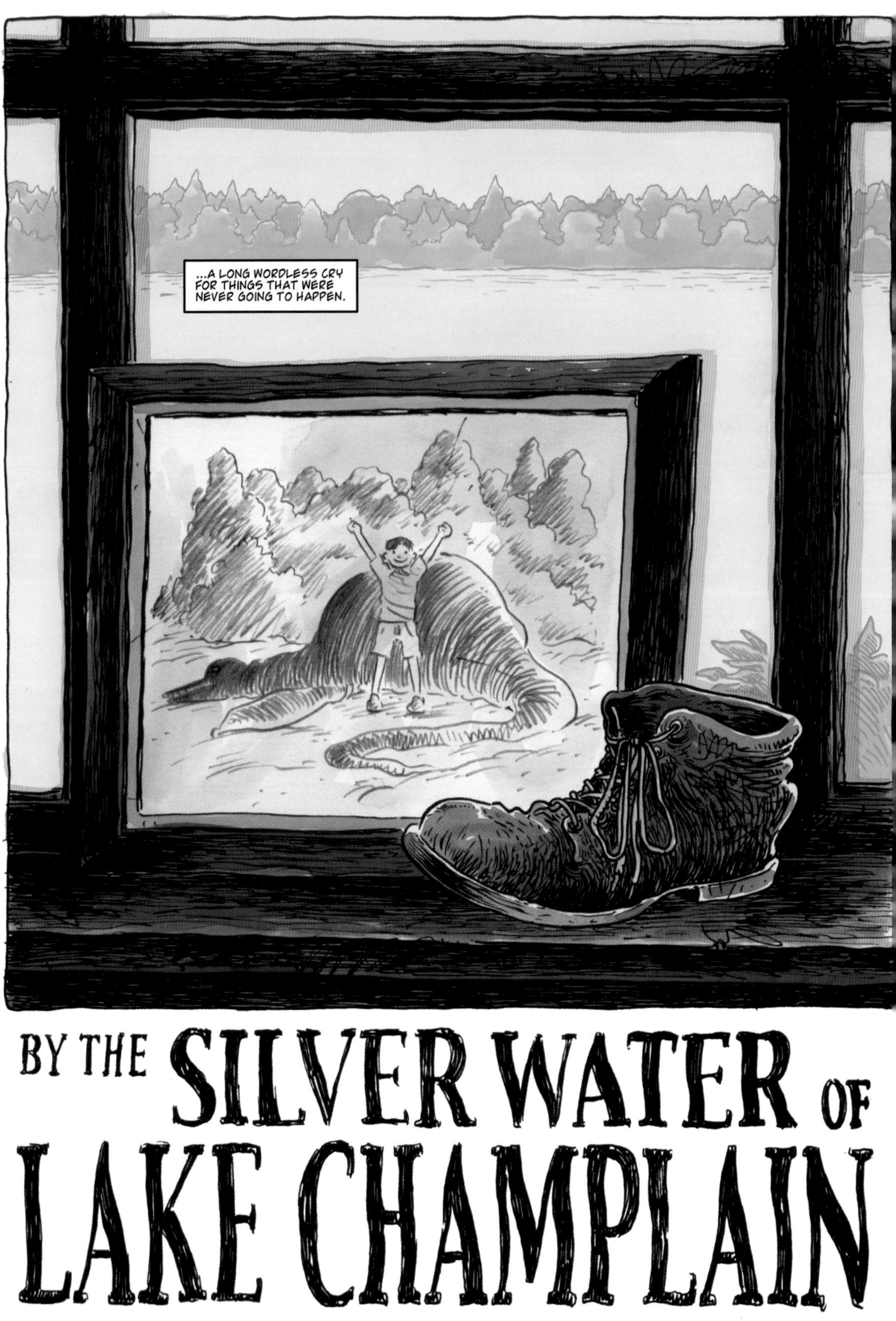
...A LONG WORDLESS CRY FOR THINGS THAT WERE NEVER GOING TO HAPPEN.

BY THE SILVER WATER OF LAKE CHAMPLAIN

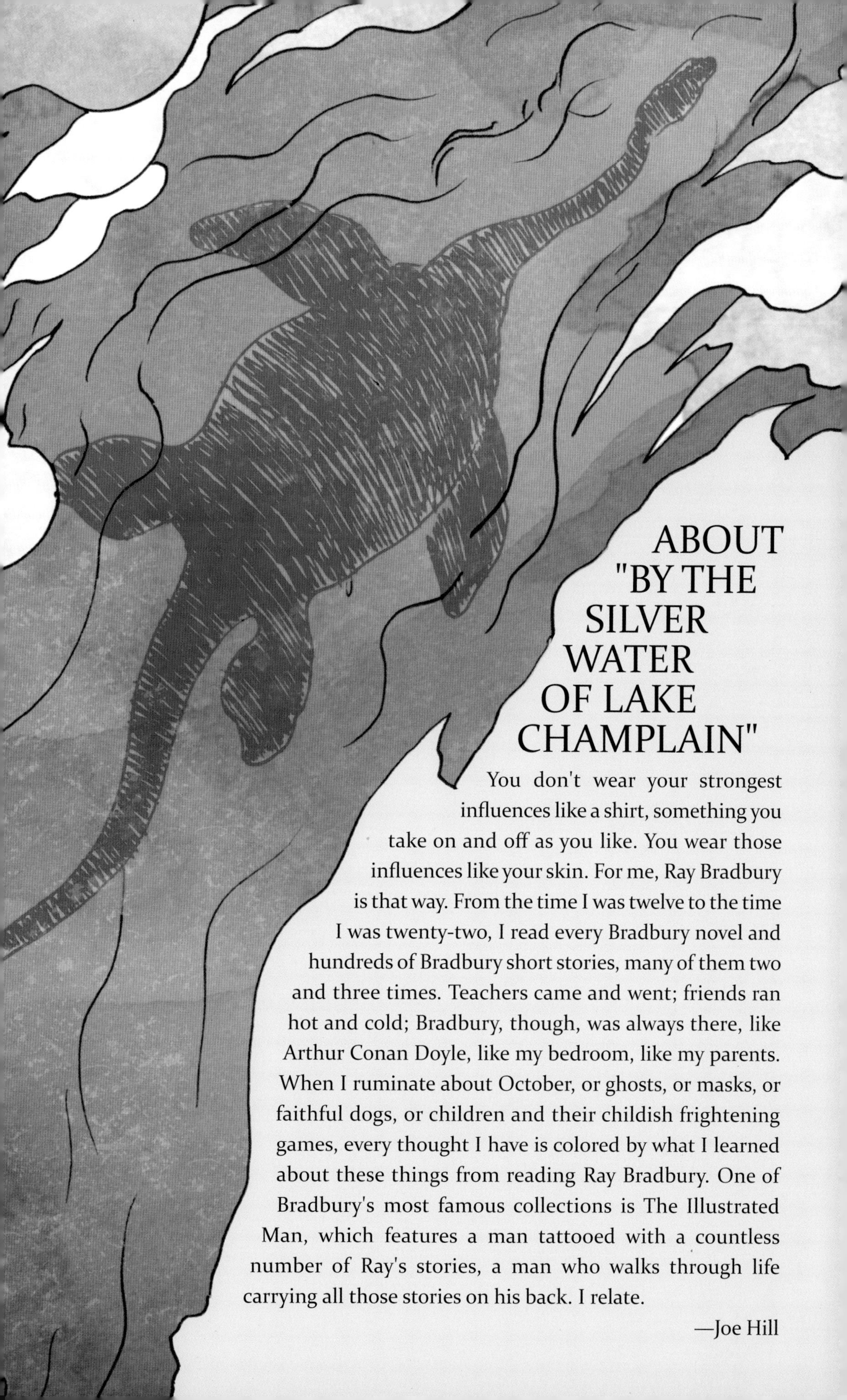

ABOUT "BY THE SILVER WATER OF LAKE CHAMPLAIN"

You don't wear your strongest influences like a shirt, something you take on and off as you like. You wear those influences like your skin. For me, Ray Bradbury is that way. From the time I was twelve to the time I was twenty-two, I read every Bradbury novel and hundreds of Bradbury short stories, many of them two and three times. Teachers came and went; friends ran hot and cold; Bradbury, though, was always there, like Arthur Conan Doyle, like my bedroom, like my parents. When I ruminate about October, or ghosts, or masks, or faithful dogs, or children and their childish frightening games, every thought I have is colored by what I learned about these things from reading Ray Bradbury. One of Bradbury's most famous collections is The Illustrated Man, which features a man tattooed with a countless number of Ray's stories, a man who walks through life carrying all those stories on his back. I relate.

—Joe Hill

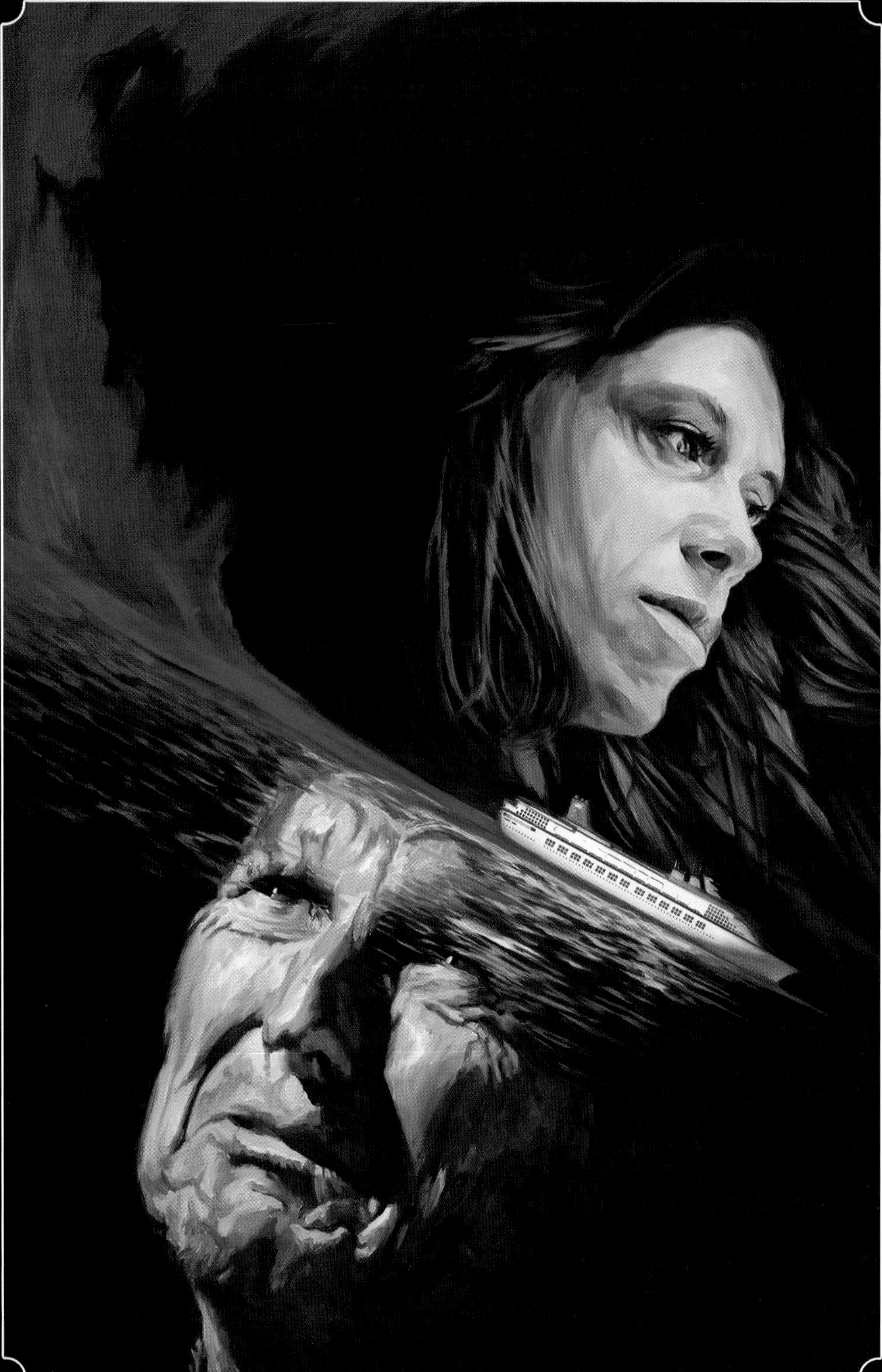

art by SHANE PIERCE

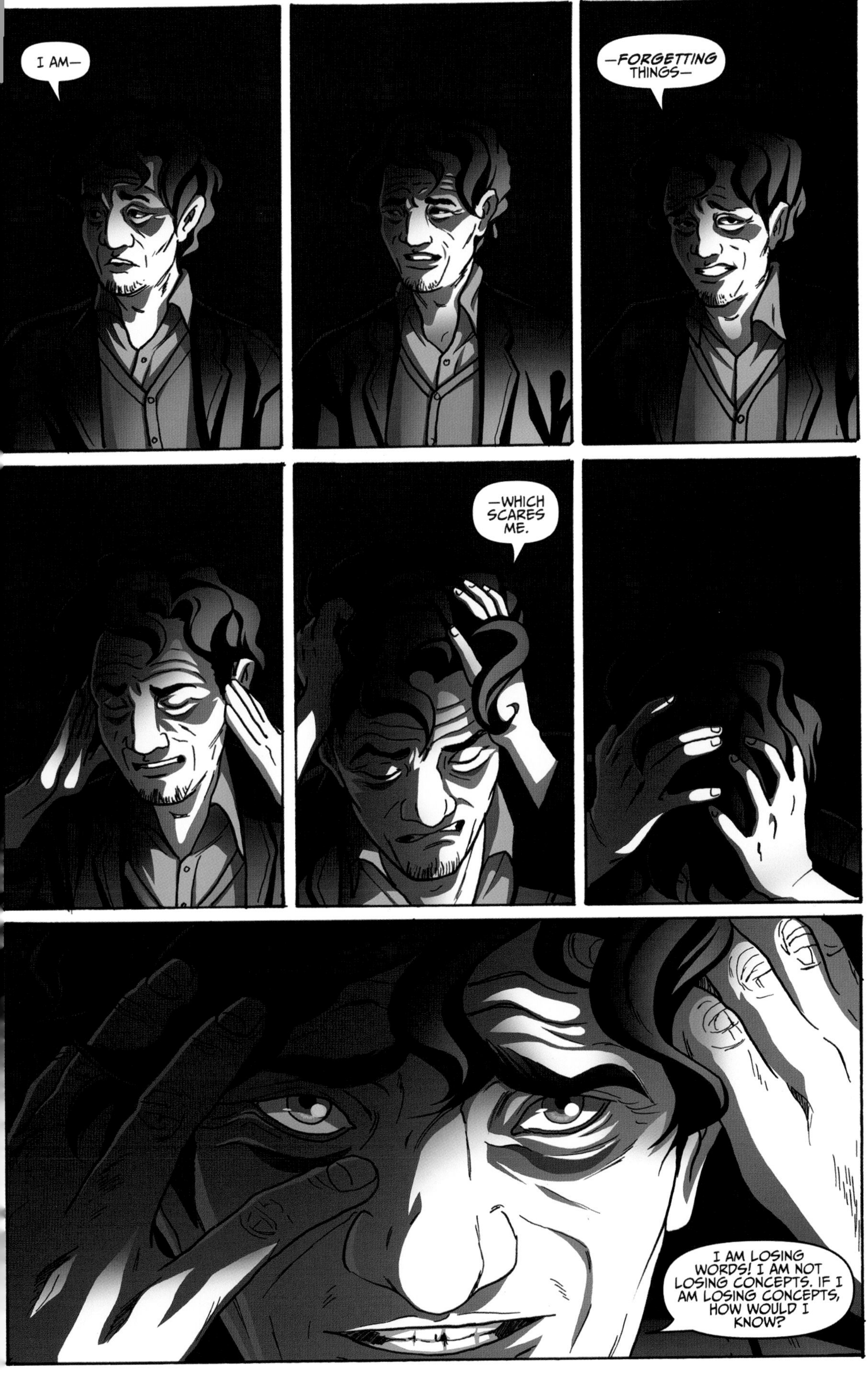

I AM—
—FORGETTING THINGS—
—WHICH SCARES ME.
I AM LOSING WORDS! I AM NOT LOSING CONCEPTS. IF I AM LOSING CONCEPTS, HOW WOULD I KNOW?

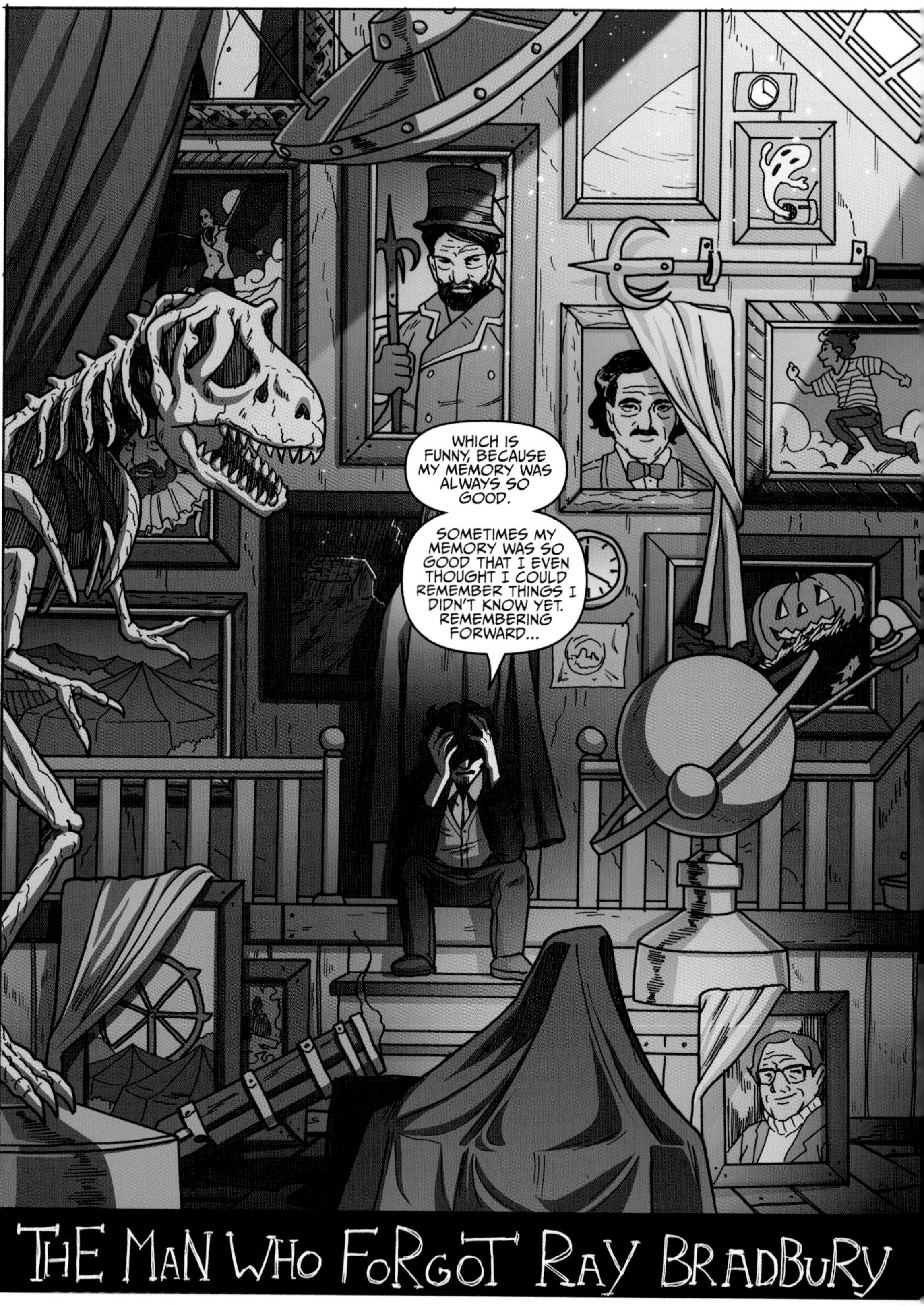
WHICH IS FUNNY, BECAUSE MY MEMORY WAS ALWAYS SO GOOD.
SOMETIMES MY MEMORY WAS SO GOOD THAT I EVEN THOUGHT I COULD REMEMBER THINGS I DIDN'T KNOW YET. REMEMBERING FORWARD...

THE MAN WHO FORGOT RAY BRADBURY

STORY BY NEIL GAIMAN
ADAPTATION/SCRIPT BY MORT CASTLE · ART BY MARIA FRÖHLICH
COLORED BY GABRIELLE NILSSON · LETTERED BY ROBBIE ROBBINS
EDITED BY CARLOS GUZMAN

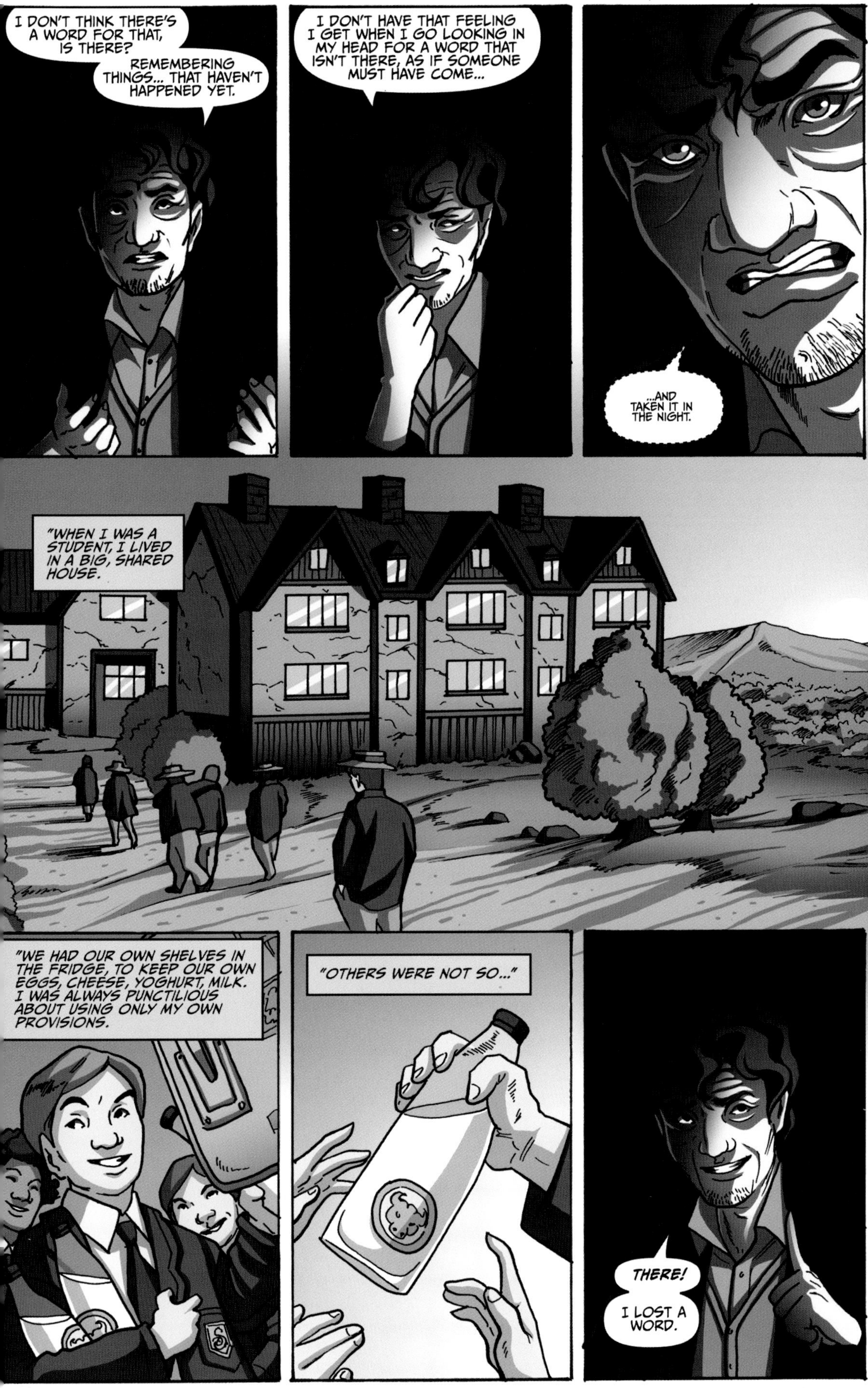
I DON'T THINK THERE'S A WORD FOR THAT, IS THERE?
REMEMBERING THINGS... THAT HAVEN'T HAPPENED YET.
I DON'T HAVE THAT FEELING I GET WHEN I GO LOOKING IN MY HEAD FOR A WORD THAT ISN'T THERE, AS IF SOMEONE MUST HAVE COME...
...AND TAKEN IT IN THE NIGHT.
"WHEN I WAS A STUDENT, I LIVED IN A BIG, SHARED HOUSE.
"WE HAD OUR OWN SHELVES IN THE FRIDGE, TO KEEP OUR OWN EGGS, CHEESE, YOGHURT, MILK. I WAS ALWAYS PUNCTILIOUS ABOUT USING ONLY MY OWN PROVISIONS.
"OTHERS WERE NOT SO..."
THERE!
I LOST A WORD.

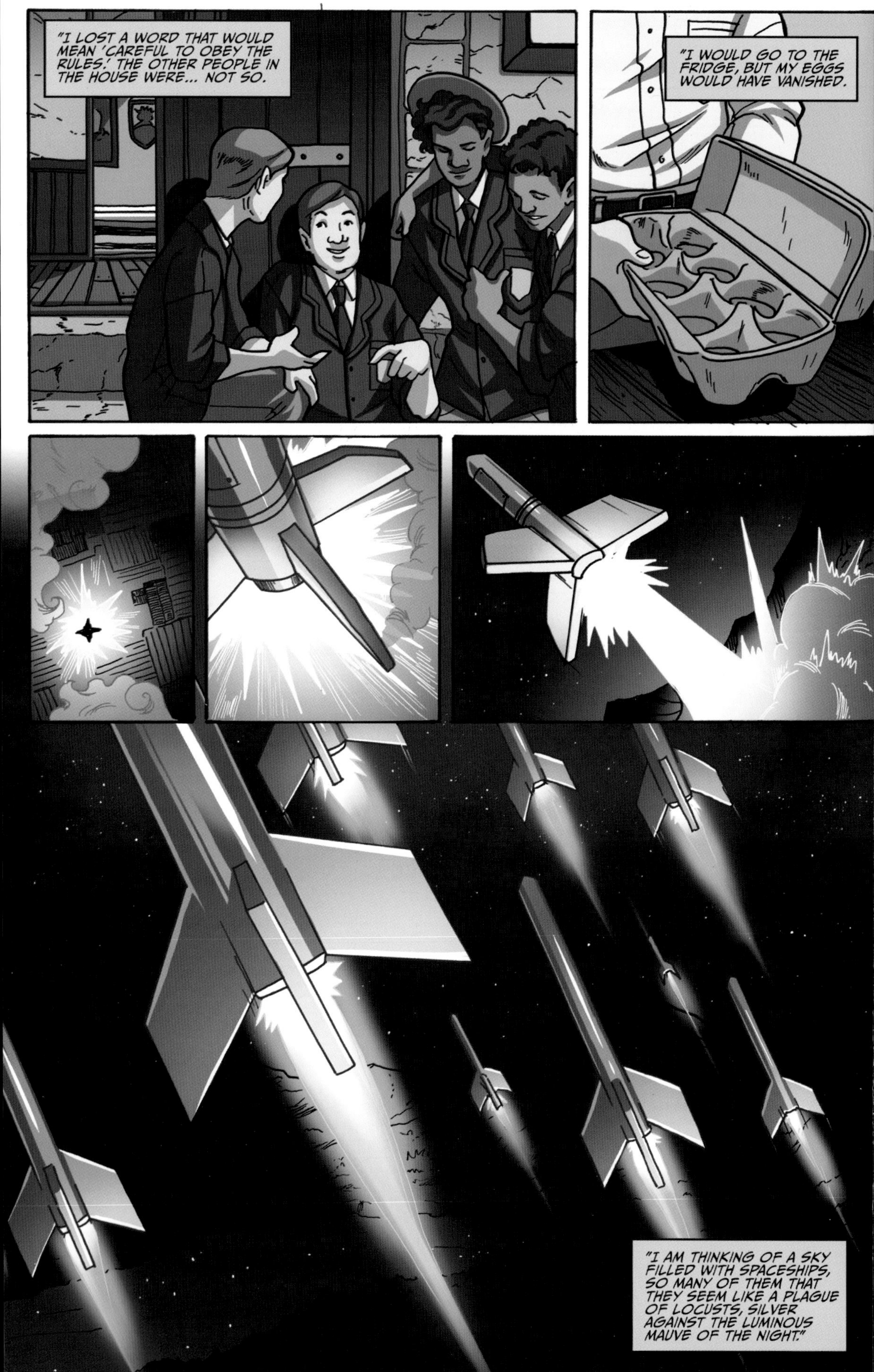
"I LOST A WORD THAT WOULD MEAN 'CAREFUL TO OBEY THE RULES.' THE OTHER PEOPLE IN THE HOUSE WERE... NOT SO.
"I WOULD GO TO THE FRIDGE, BUT MY EGGS WOULD HAVE VANISHED.
"I AM THINKING OF A SKY FILLED WITH SPACESHIPS, SO MANY OF THEM THAT THEY SEEM LIKE A PLAGUE OF LOCUSTS, SILVER AGAINST THE LUMINOUS MAUVE OF THE NIGHT."

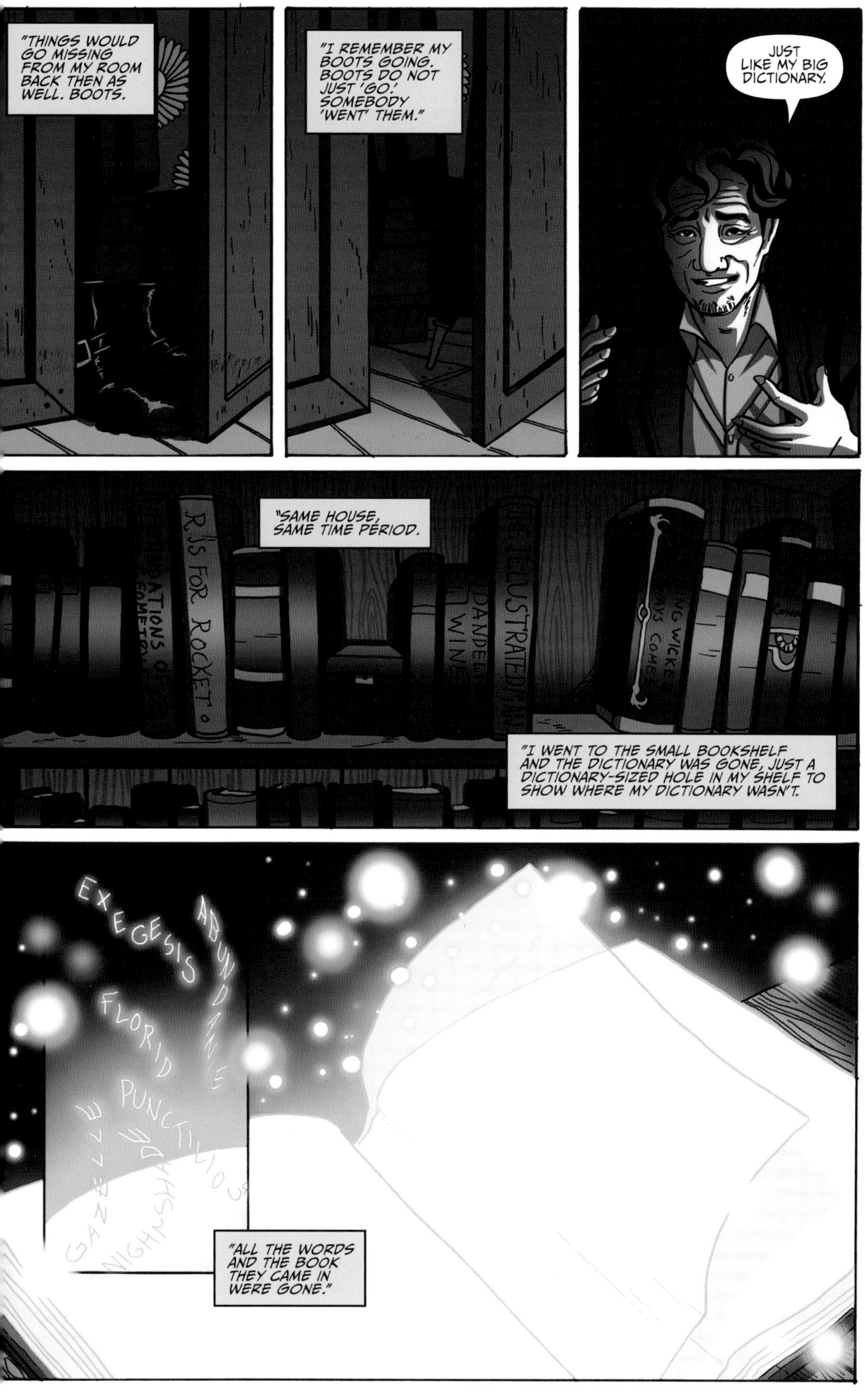
"THINGS WOULD GO MISSING FROM MY ROOM BACK THEN AS WELL. BOOTS.
"I REMEMBER MY BOOTS GOING. BOOTS DO NOT JUST 'GO.' SOMEBODY 'WENT' THEM."
JUST LIKE MY BIG DICTIONARY.
"SAME HOUSE, SAME TIME PERIOD.
R IS FOR ROCKET
"I WENT TO THE SMALL BOOKSHELF AND THE DICTIONARY WAS GONE, JUST A DICTIONARY-SIZED HOLE IN MY SHELF TO SHOW WHERE MY DICTIONARY WASN'T.
EXEGESIS
ABUNDANCE
FLORID
PUNCTILIOUS
"ALL THE WORDS AND THE BOOK THEY CAME IN WERE GONE."

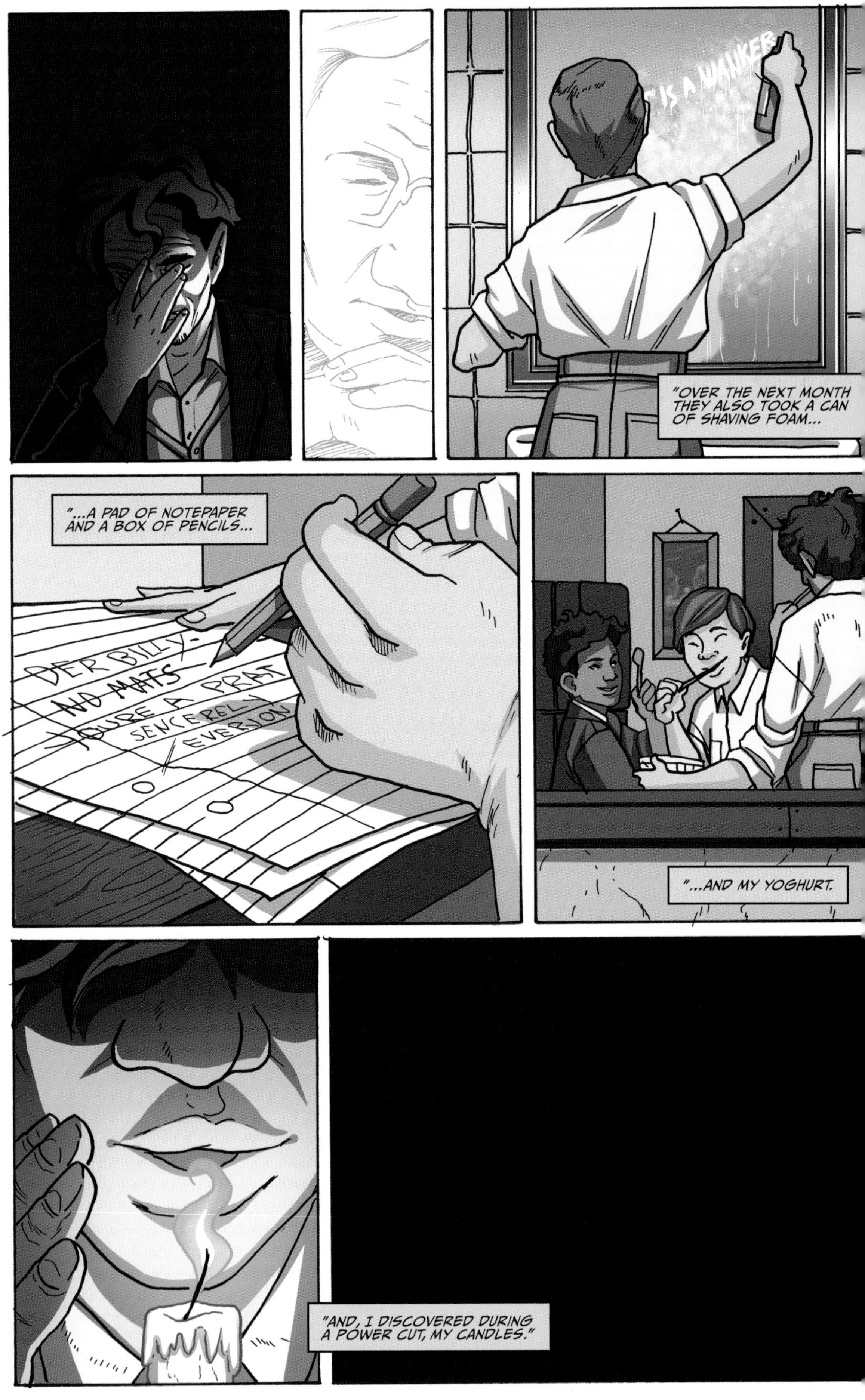
IS A WANKER
"OVER THE NEXT MONTH THEY ALSO TOOK A CAN OF SHAVING FOAM...
"...A PAD OF NOTEPAPER AND A BOX OF PENCILS...
DER BILLY-
NO MATS
YOURE A PRAT
SENCERELY
EVERYON
"...AND MY YOGHURT.
"AND, I DISCOVERED DURING A POWER CUT, MY CANDLES."

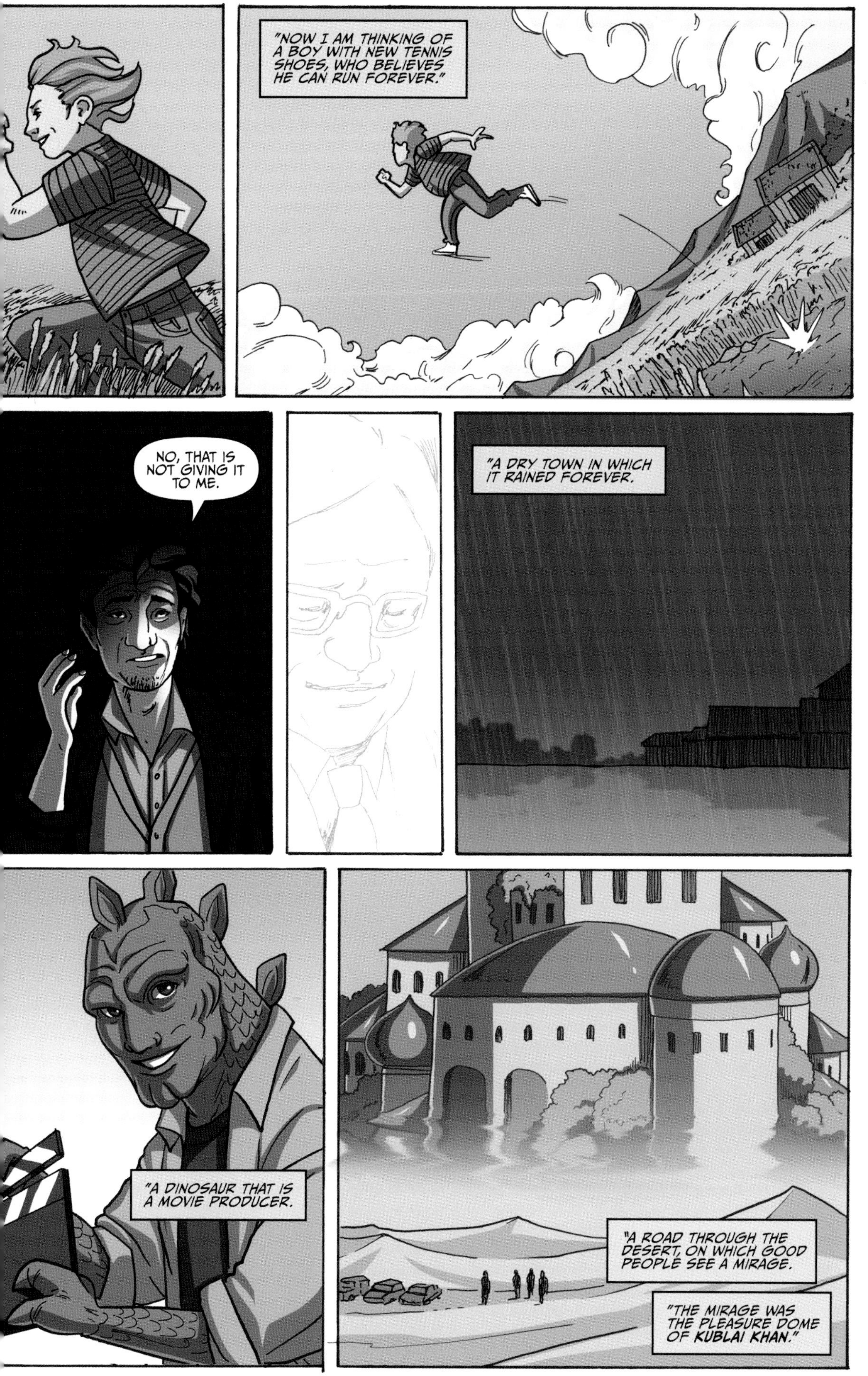
"NOW I AM THINKING OF A BOY WITH NEW TENNIS SHOES, WHO BELIEVES HE CAN RUN FOREVER."
NO, THAT IS NOT GIVING IT TO ME.
"A DRY TOWN IN WHICH IT RAINED FOREVER.
"A DINOSAUR THAT IS A MOVIE PRODUCER.
"A ROAD THROUGH THE DESERT, ON WHICH GOOD PEOPLE SEE A MIRAGE.
"THE MIRAGE WAS THE PLEASURE DOME OF KUBLAI KHAN."

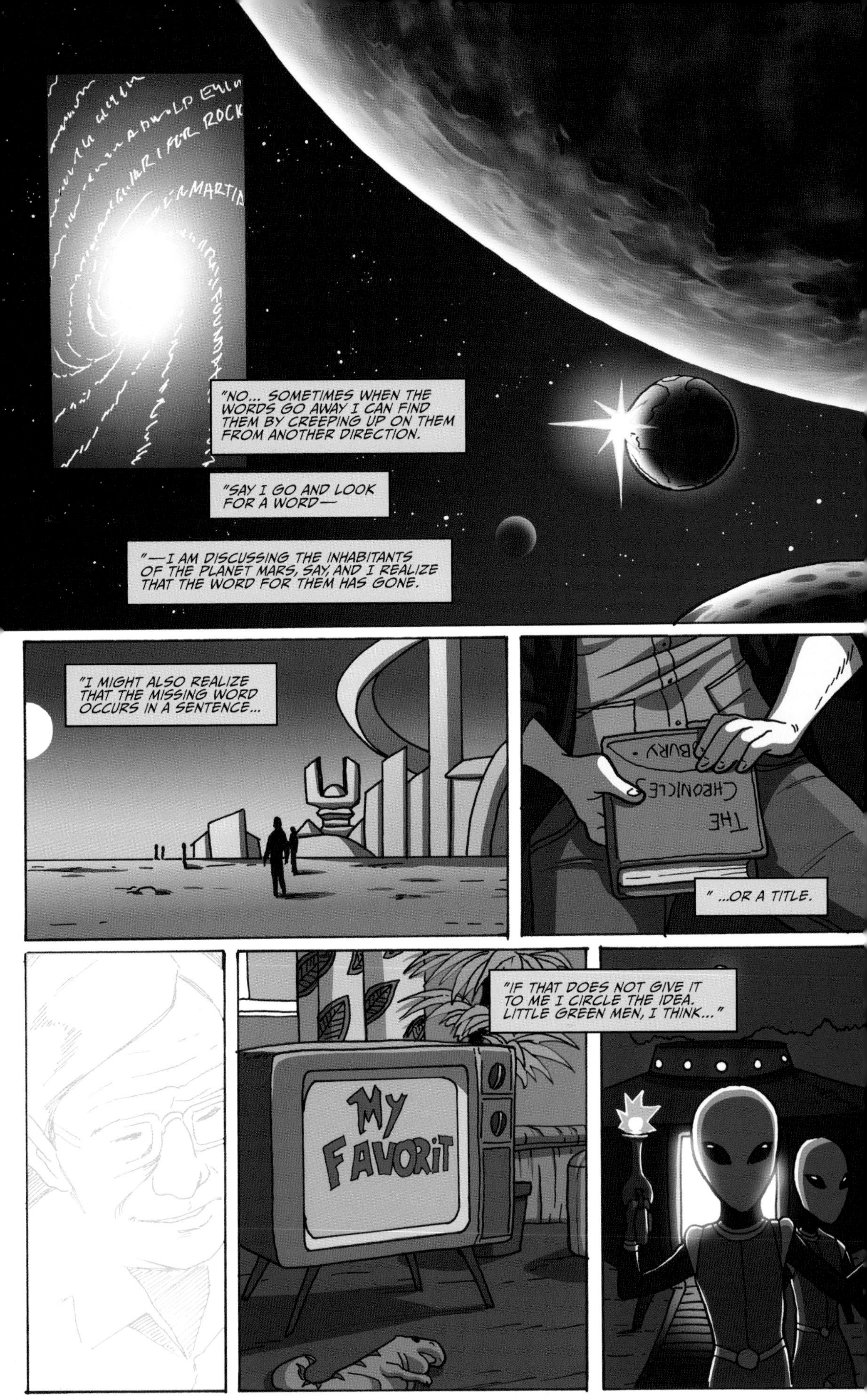
"NO... SOMETIMES WHEN THE WORDS GO AWAY I CAN FIND THEM BY CREEPING UP ON THEM FROM ANOTHER DIRECTION.
"SAY I GO AND LOOK FOR A WORD—
"—I AM DISCUSSING THE INHABITANTS OF THE PLANET MARS, SAY, AND I REALIZE THAT THE WORD FOR THEM HAS GONE.
"I MIGHT ALSO REALIZE THAT THE MISSING WORD OCCURS IN A SENTENCE...
" ...OR A TITLE.
My FAVORiT
"IF THAT DOES NOT GIVE IT TO ME I CIRCLE THE IDEA. LITTLE GREEN MEN, I THINK..."

"OR TALL, DARK-SKINNED, GENTLE..."

DARK THEY WERE AND GOLDEN-EYED...

"—AND SUDDENLY THE WORD MARTIANS IS WAITING FOR ME—

"—LIKE A FRIEND OR A LOVER AT THE END OF A LONG DAY.

"I LEFT THAT HOUSE WHEN MY RADIO WENT. IT WAS TOO WEARYING, THE SLOW DISAPPEARANCE OF THE THINGS I HAD THOUGHT SO SAFELY MINE, ITEM BY ITEM—

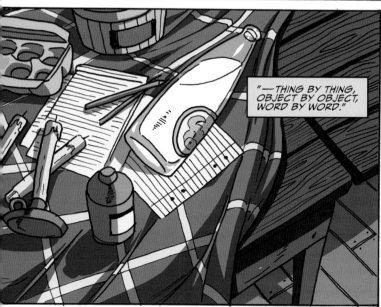

"—THING BY THING, OBJECT BY OBJECT, WORD BY WORD."

WHEN I WAS TWELVE, I WAS TOLD A STORY BY AN OLD MAN THAT I HAVE NEVER FORGOTTEN.

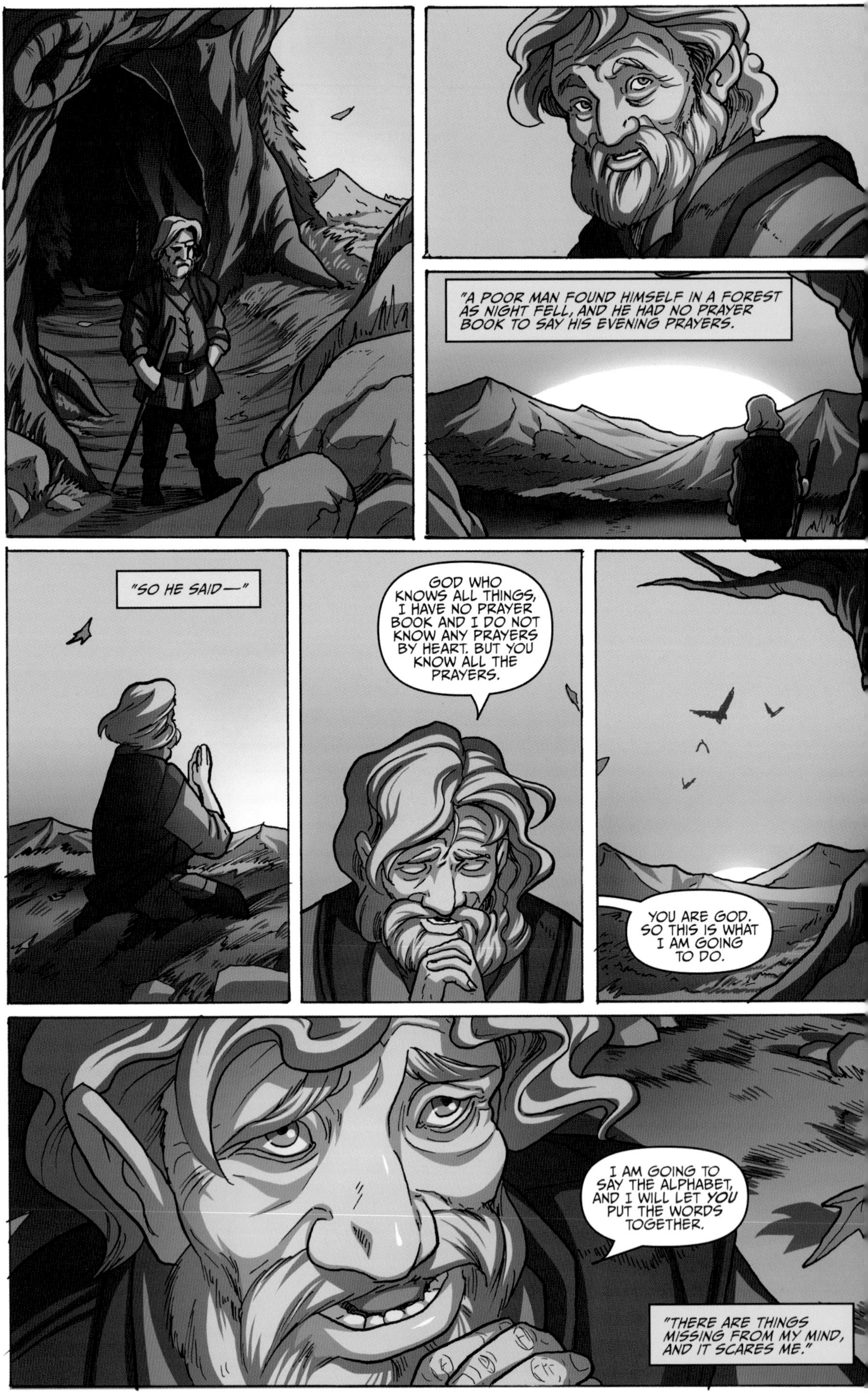
"A POOR MAN FOUND HIMSELF IN A FOREST AS NIGHT FELL, AND HE HAD NO PRAYER BOOK TO SAY HIS EVENING PRAYERS.
"SO HE SAID—"
GOD WHO KNOWS ALL THINGS, I HAVE NO PRAYER BOOK AND I DO NOT KNOW ANY PRAYERS BY HEART. BUT YOU KNOW ALL THE PRAYERS.
YOU ARE GOD. SO THIS IS WHAT I AM GOING TO DO.
I AM GOING TO SAY THE ALPHABET, AND I WILL LET *YOU* PUT THE WORDS TOGETHER.
"THERE ARE THINGS MISSING FROM MY MIND, AND IT SCARES ME."

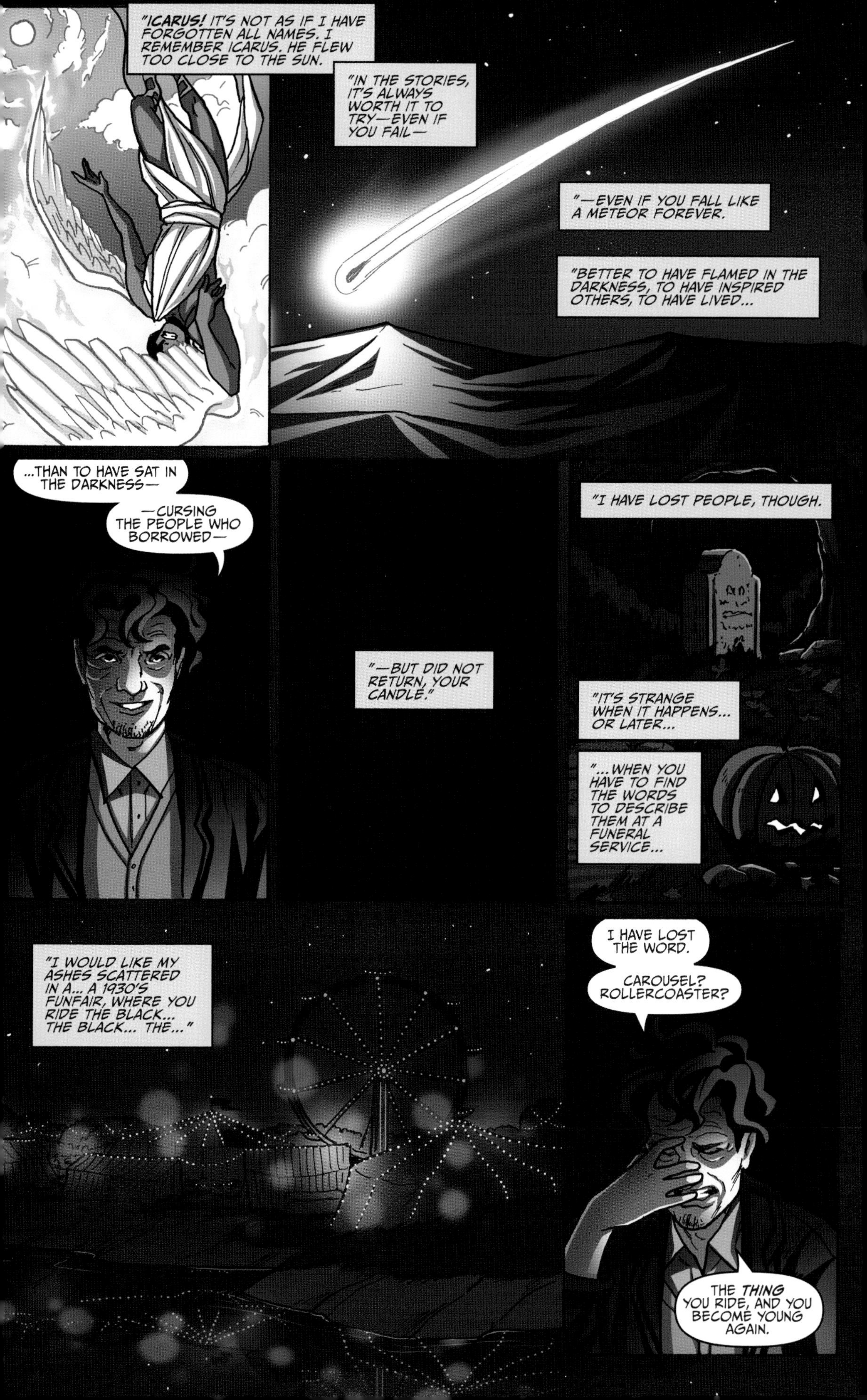
"ICARUS! IT'S NOT AS IF I HAVE FORGOTTEN ALL NAMES. I REMEMBER ICARUS. HE FLEW TOO CLOSE TO THE SUN.
"IN THE STORIES, IT'S ALWAYS WORTH IT TO TRY—EVEN IF YOU FAIL—
"—EVEN IF YOU FALL LIKE A METEOR FOREVER.
"BETTER TO HAVE FLAMED IN THE DARKNESS, TO HAVE INSPIRED OTHERS, TO HAVE LIVED...
...THAN TO HAVE SAT IN THE DARKNESS—
—CURSING THE PEOPLE WHO BORROWED—
"—BUT DID NOT RETURN, YOUR CANDLE."
"I HAVE LOST PEOPLE, THOUGH.
"IT'S STRANGE WHEN IT HAPPENS... OR LATER...
"...WHEN YOU HAVE TO FIND THE WORDS TO DESCRIBE THEM AT A FUNERAL SERVICE...
"I WOULD LIKE MY ASHES SCATTERED IN A... A 1930'S FUNFAIR, WHERE YOU RIDE THE BLACK... THE BLACK... THE..."
I HAVE LOST THE WORD.
CAROUSEL? ROLLERCOASTER?
THE THING YOU RIDE, AND YOU BECOME YOUNG AGAIN.

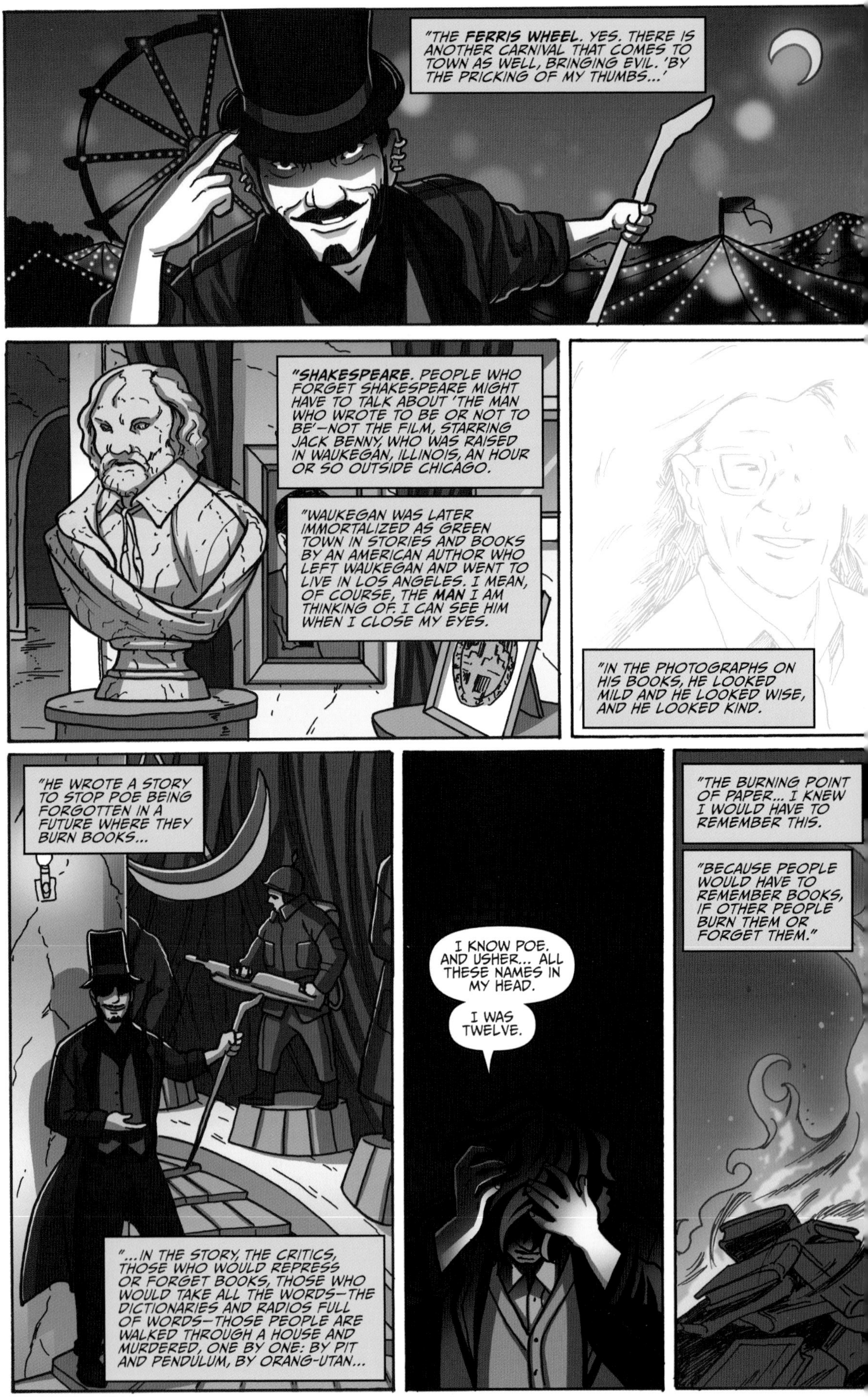
"THE FERRIS WHEEL. YES. THERE IS ANOTHER CARNIVAL THAT COMES TO TOWN AS WELL, BRINGING EVIL. 'BY THE PRICKING OF MY THUMBS...'
"SHAKESPEARE. PEOPLE WHO FORGET SHAKESPEARE MIGHT HAVE TO TALK ABOUT 'THE MAN WHO WROTE TO BE OR NOT TO BE'—NOT THE FILM, STARRING JACK BENNY, WHO WAS RAISED IN WAUKEGAN, ILLINOIS, AN HOUR OR SO OUTSIDE CHICAGO.
"WAUKEGAN WAS LATER IMMORTALIZED AS GREEN TOWN IN STORIES AND BOOKS BY AN AMERICAN AUTHOR WHO LEFT WAUKEGAN AND WENT TO LIVE IN LOS ANGELES. I MEAN, OF COURSE, THE MAN I AM THINKING OF. I CAN SEE HIM WHEN I CLOSE MY EYES.
"IN THE PHOTOGRAPHS ON HIS BOOKS, HE LOOKED MILD AND HE LOOKED WISE, AND HE LOOKED KIND.
"HE WROTE A STORY TO STOP POE BEING FORGOTTEN IN A FUTURE WHERE THEY BURN BOOKS...
"...IN THE STORY, THE CRITICS, THOSE WHO WOULD REPRESS OR FORGET BOOKS, THOSE WHO WOULD TAKE ALL THE WORDS—THE DICTIONARIES AND RADIOS FULL OF WORDS—THOSE PEOPLE ARE WALKED THROUGH A HOUSE AND MURDERED, ONE BY ONE: BY PIT AND PENDULUM, BY ORANG-UTAN...
I KNOW POE. AND USHER... ALL THESE NAMES IN MY HEAD.
I WAS TWELVE.
"THE BURNING POINT OF PAPER... I KNEW I WOULD HAVE TO REMEMBER THIS.
"BECAUSE PEOPLE WOULD HAVE TO REMEMBER BOOKS, IF OTHER PEOPLE BURN THEM OR FORGET THEM."

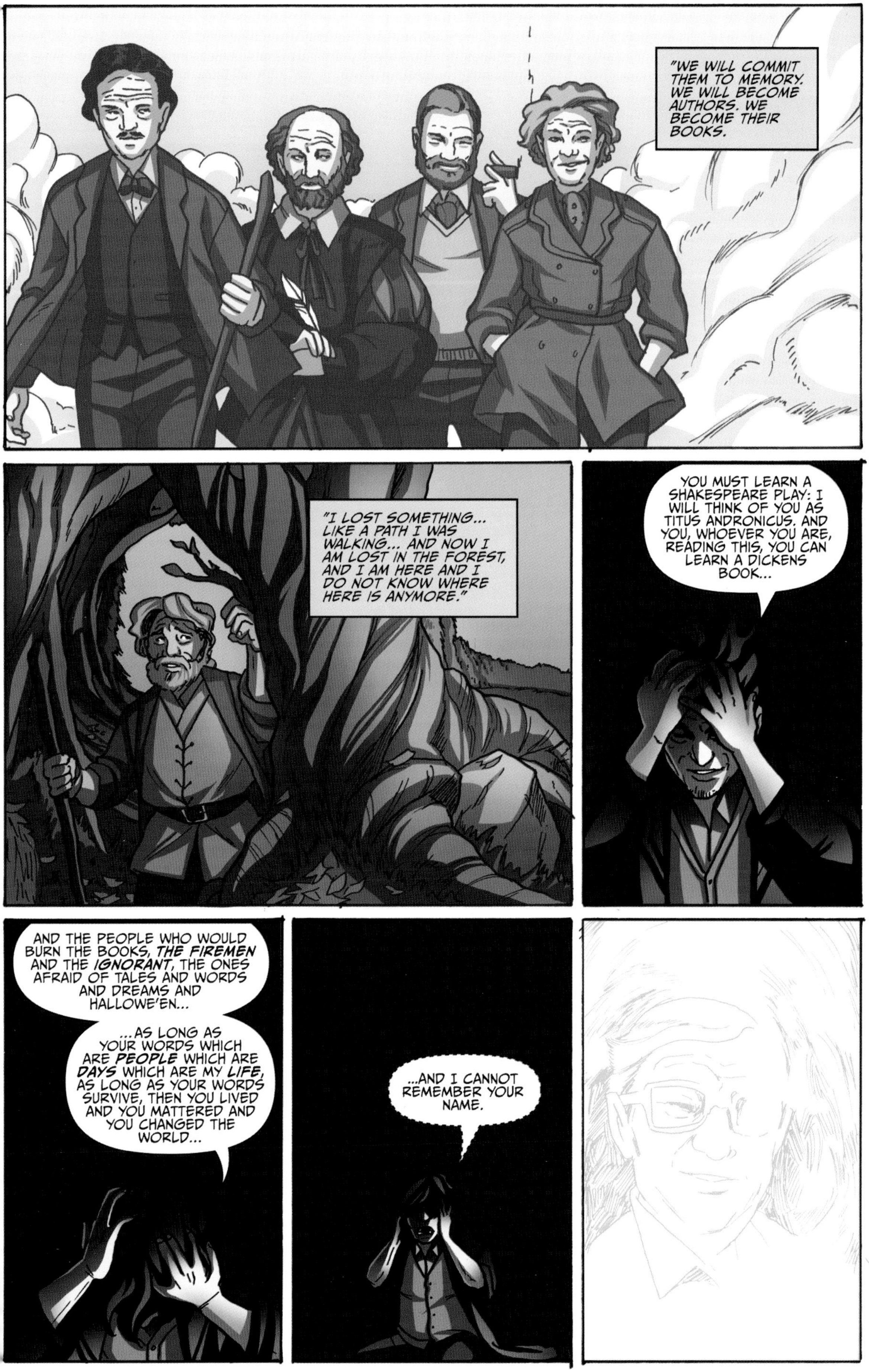
"WE WILL COMMIT THEM TO MEMORY. WE WILL BECOME AUTHORS. WE BECOME THEIR BOOKS.
"I LOST SOMETHING... LIKE A PATH I WAS WALKING... AND NOW I AM LOST IN THE FOREST, AND I AM HERE AND I DO NOT KNOW WHERE HERE IS ANYMORE."
YOU MUST LEARN A SHAKESPEARE PLAY: I WILL THINK OF YOU AS TITUS ANDRONICUS. AND YOU, WHOEVER YOU ARE, READING THIS, YOU CAN LEARN A DICKENS BOOK...
AND THE PEOPLE WHO WOULD BURN THE BOOKS, THE FIREMEN AND THE IGNORANT, THE ONES AFRAID OF TALES AND WORDS AND DREAMS AND HALLOWE'EN...
...AS LONG AS YOUR WORDS WHICH ARE PEOPLE WHICH ARE DAYS WHICH ARE MY LIFE, AS LONG AS YOUR WORDS SURVIVE, THEN YOU LIVED AND YOU MATTERED AND YOU CHANGED THE WORLD...
...AND I CANNOT REMEMBER YOUR NAME.

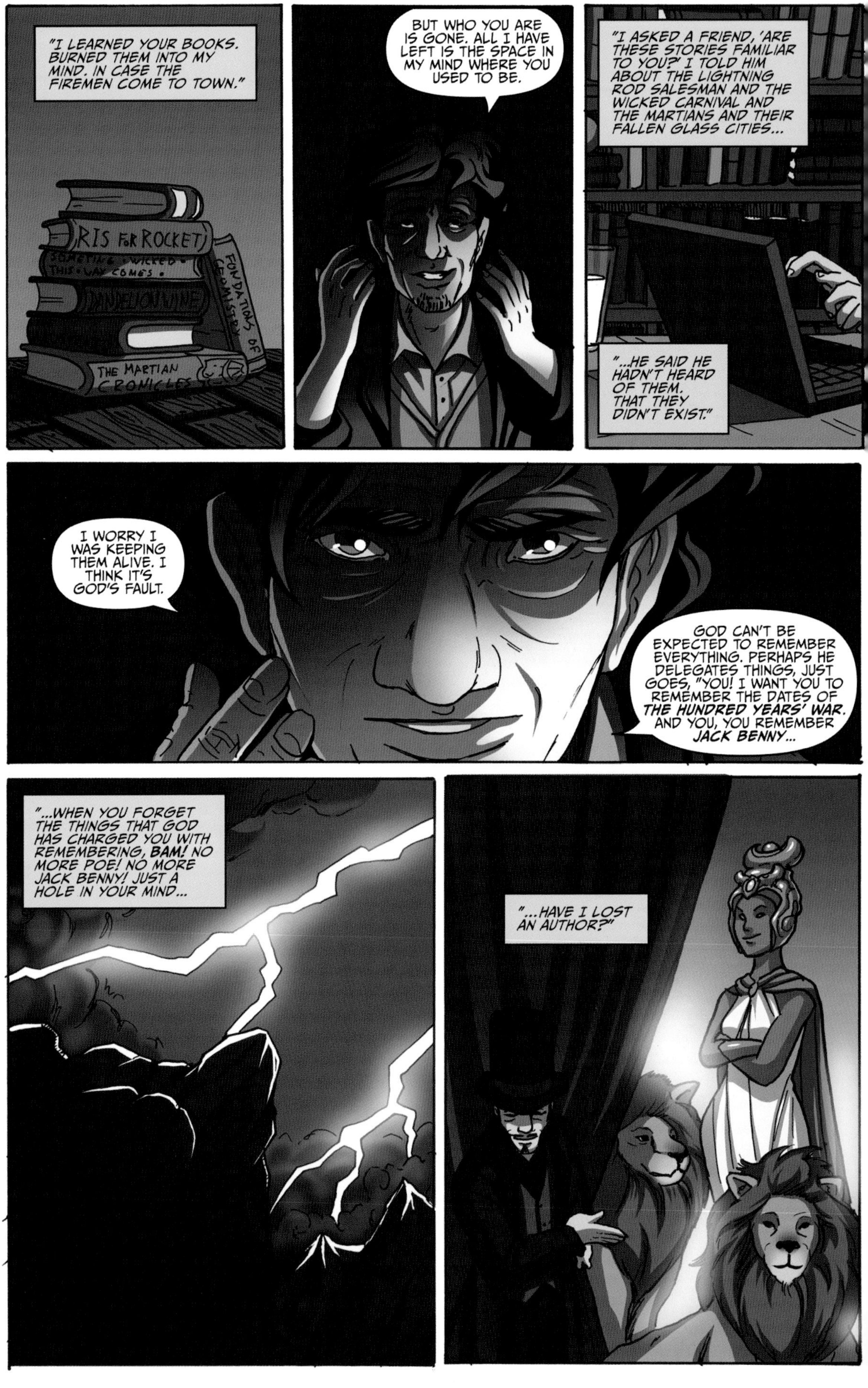
"I LEARNED YOUR BOOKS. BURNED THEM INTO MY MIND. IN CASE THE FIREMEN COME TO TOWN."
R IS FOR ROCKET
DANDELION WINE
FOUNDATIONS OF GEOMISTRY
THE MARTIAN CRONICLES
BUT WHO YOU ARE IS GONE. ALL I HAVE LEFT IS THE SPACE IN MY MIND WHERE YOU USED TO BE.
"I ASKED A FRIEND, 'ARE THESE STORIES FAMILIAR TO YOU?' I TOLD HIM ABOUT THE LIGHTNING ROD SALESMAN AND THE WICKED CARNIVAL AND THE MARTIANS AND THEIR FALLEN GLASS CITIES...
"...HE SAID HE HADN'T HEARD OF THEM. THAT THEY DIDN'T EXIST."
I WORRY I WAS KEEPING THEM ALIVE. I THINK IT'S GOD'S FAULT.
GOD CAN'T BE EXPECTED TO REMEMBER EVERYTHING. PERHAPS HE DELEGATES THINGS, JUST GOES, "YOU! I WANT YOU TO REMEMBER THE DATES OF THE HUNDRED YEARS' WAR. AND YOU, YOU REMEMBER JACK BENNY...
"...WHEN YOU FORGET THE THINGS THAT GOD HAS CHARGED YOU WITH REMEMBERING, BAM! NO MORE POE! NO MORE JACK BENNY! JUST A HOLE IN YOUR MIND...
"...HAVE I LOST AN AUTHOR?"

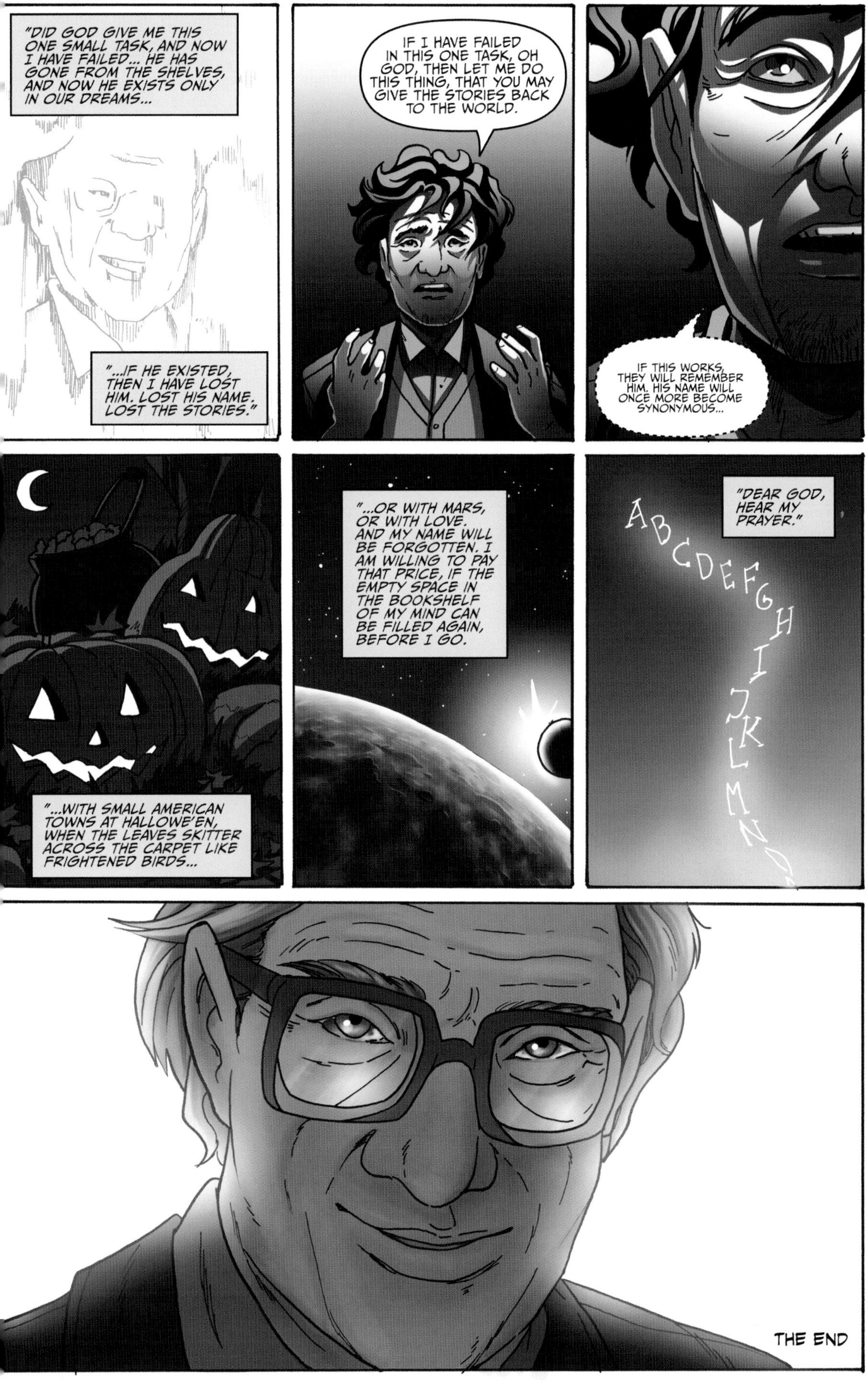
"DID GOD GIVE ME THIS ONE SMALL TASK, AND NOW I HAVE FAILED... HE HAS GONE FROM THE SHELVES, AND NOW HE EXISTS ONLY IN OUR DREAMS...
"...IF HE EXISTED, THEN I HAVE LOST HIM. LOST HIS NAME. LOST THE STORIES."
IF I HAVE FAILED IN THIS ONE TASK, OH GOD, THEN LET ME DO THIS THING, THAT YOU MAY GIVE THE STORIES BACK TO THE WORLD.
IF THIS WORKS, THEY WILL REMEMBER HIM. HIS NAME WILL ONCE MORE BECOME SYNONYMOUS...
"...WITH SMALL AMERICAN TOWNS AT HALLOWE'EN, WHEN THE LEAVES SKITTER ACROSS THE CARPET LIKE FRIGHTENED BIRDS...
"...OR WITH MARS, OR WITH LOVE. AND MY NAME WILL BE FORGOTTEN. I AM WILLING TO PAY THAT PRICE, IF THE EMPTY SPACE IN THE BOOKSHELF OF MY MIND CAN BE FILLED AGAIN, BEFORE I GO.
"DEAR GOD, HEAR MY PRAYER."
ABCDEFGHIJKLMN
THE END

ABOUT "THE MAN WHO FORGOT RAY BRADBURY"

I wanted to write about Ray Bradbury. I wanted to write about him in the way that he wrote about Poe in Usher II—a way that drove me to Poe.

I was going to read something in an intimate theatre space, very late at night, during the Edinburgh Fringe Festival. My wife, Amanda, and I were hosting a midnight show of songs and readings. I promised myself that I would finish it in time to read it to forty people seated on sofas and on cushions on the floor in a tiny, beautiful room that normally contained the Belt Up Theatre Company's intimate plays.

Very well, it would be a monologue, if I was going to read it.

The inspiration came from forgetting a friend of mine. He died a decade ago. And I went to look in my head for his name, and it was gone. I knew everything else about him—the periodicals he had written for, his favorite brand of bourbon. I could have recited every conversation he and I had ever had, told you what we talked about. I could remember the names of the books he had written.

But his name was gone. And it scared me. I waited for his name to return, promised myself I wouldn't Google it, would just wait and remember. But nothing came. It was as if there was a hole in the universe the size of my friend. I would walk home at night trying to think of his name, running through names in alphabetical order. "Al? No. Bob? No. Charles? Chris? Not them..."

And I thought, What if it were an author? What if it was everything he'd done? What if everyone else had forgotten him, too?

I wrote the story by hand. I finished it five minutes before we had to leave the house to go to the theatre. I was a mass of nerves—I'd never read something to an audience straight out of the pen.

When I read it, I finished it with a recital of the whole alphabet.

Then I typed it out, and sent it to Ray for his ninety-first birthday.

I was there at his seventieth birthday, in the Natural History Museum in London.

It was, like everything else about the man and his work, unforgettable.

—Neil Gaiman

Backwards in Seville by Audrey Niffenegger

ILLUSTRATED BY
EDDIE CAMPBELL

Helene stood at the front railing on the upper deck in the dark, watching as the ship maneuvered at a funny angle too close to a low bridge. A few people stood near her, all watching quietly as the crew worked on the deck below them. The band was playing Ellington at the other end of the ship; couples would be dancing neatly, persistently. In the cabins below most of the passengers were asleep.

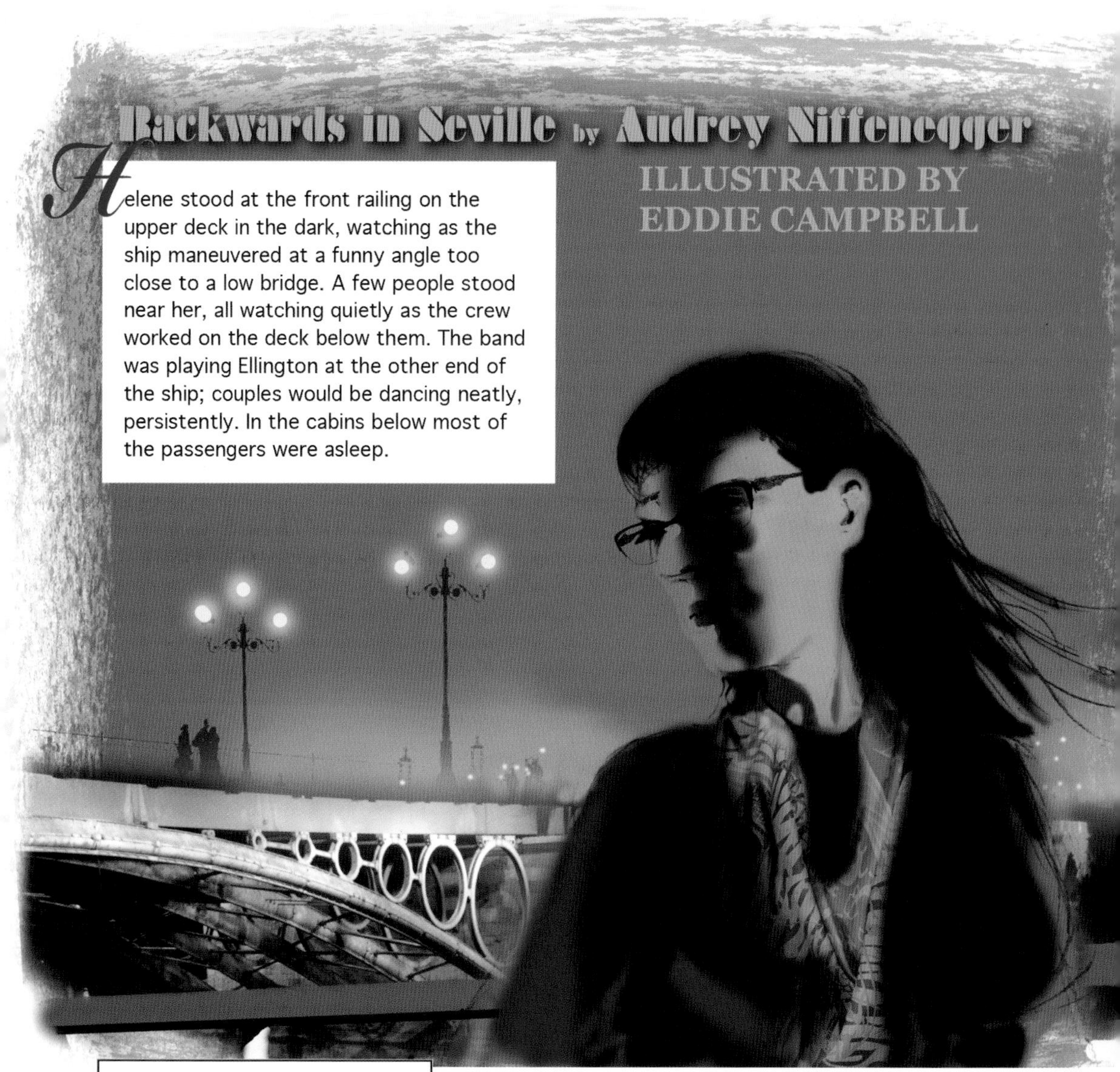

Helene's father, Lewis, had been sleeping when she left their cabin. In sleep he frightened her. *Let him wake up tomorrow,* she prayed every night, though she was not religious. *Don't take him from me yet.*

The Persephone wasn't very large for a cruise ship. There were three hundred passengers and one hundred and fifty crew members. Helene had never been on a cruise before and had braced herself for bingo, sea sickness and enforced camaraderie, though her father kept assuring her it wasn't that kind of cruise.

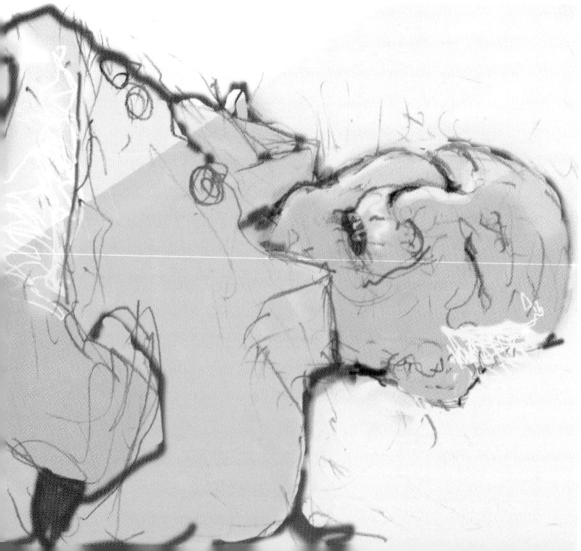

"It's low-key, mostly excursions to churches and lectures on Matisse. You've never been to Rome or Barcelona, you'll love it. The Mediterranean is very calm in June. Don't worry so much, Sweet Pea."

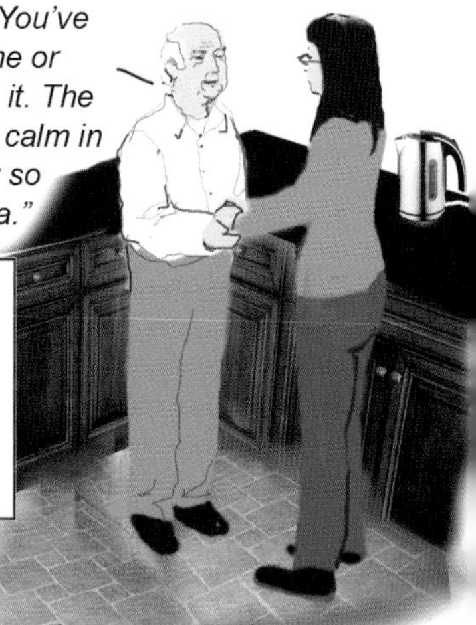

She had nodded and smiled. Of course she would love it; he wanted her to love it.

The ship moved backwards and then sideways, away from the port and the bridge. They were in a canal, they had been docked in Seville for two days.

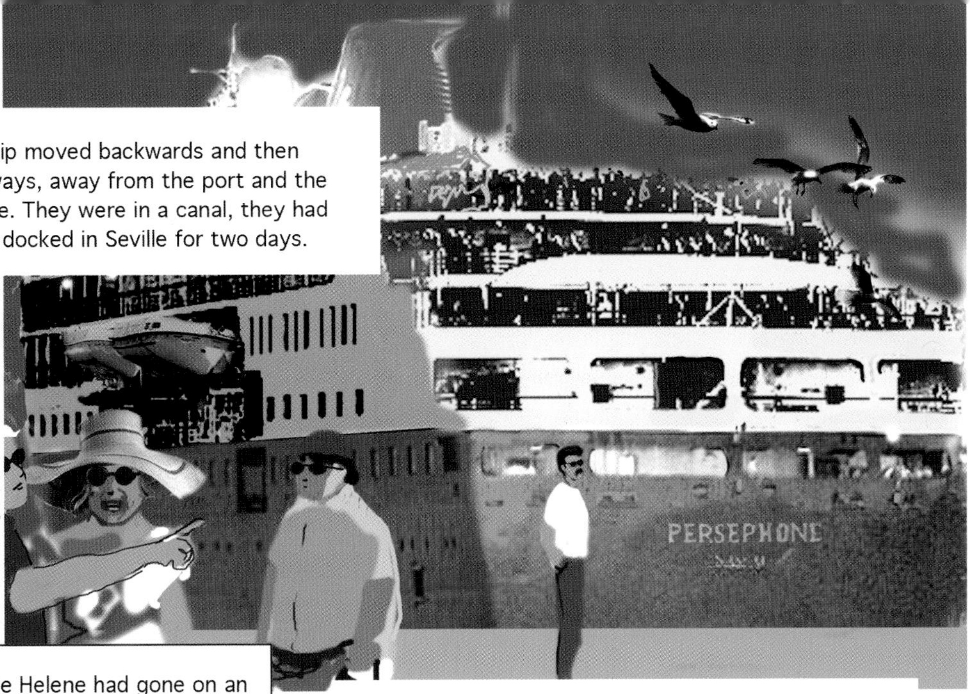
PERSEPHONE

In Seville Helene had gone on an excursion to a convent, a very sad convent run by an order called the Poor Clares.

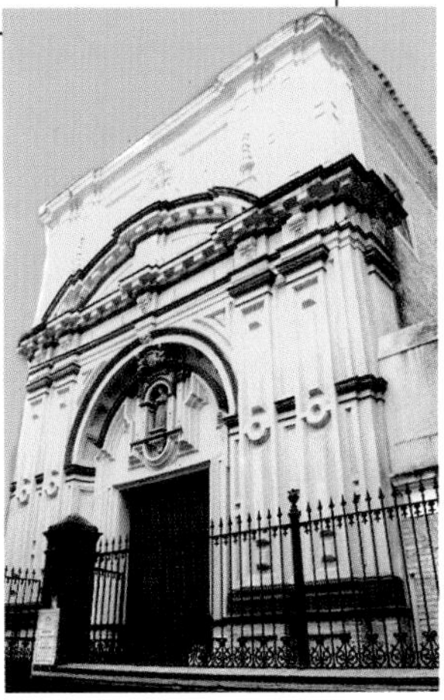

All the nuns were from Africa and had been cloistered until recently, but then the Poor Clares had become too poor and now they sold baked goods and let tourists come inside for a few euros each.

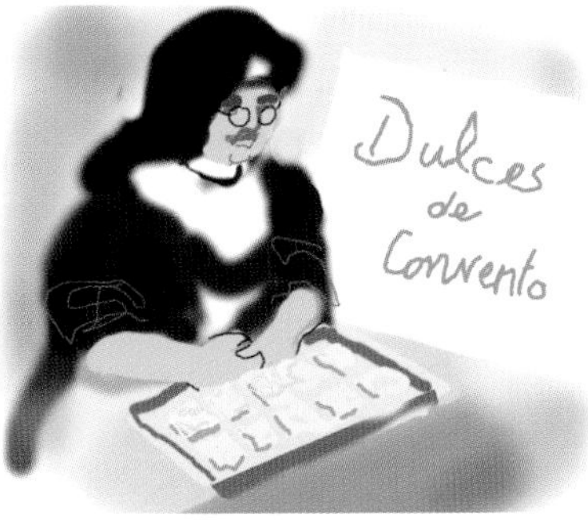
Dulces
de
Convento

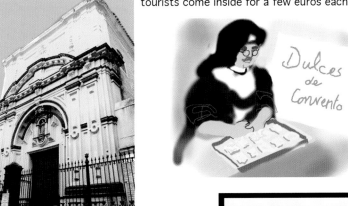

Helene felt bad for them. She thought of the Sistine Chapel and St. Peter's, which had been her first excursion.

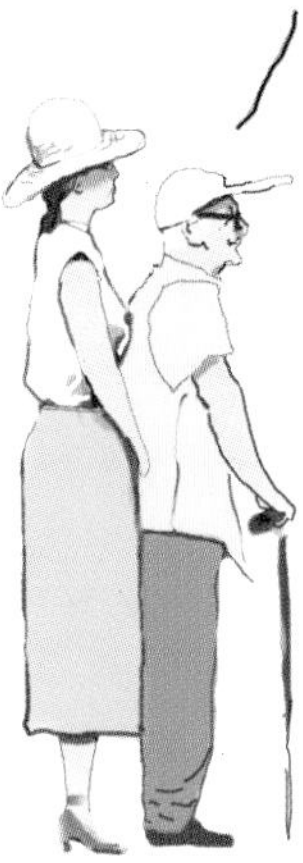
You'd think they could redistribute the wealth a little.
Don't imagine nuns are too high on the food chain.

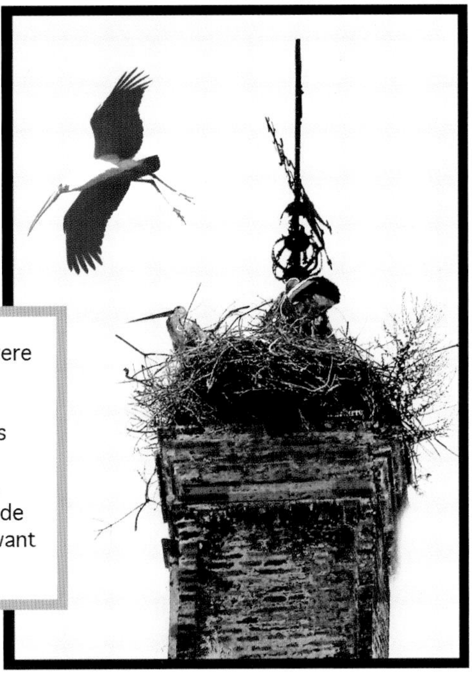

Storks were nesting in the chimneys of the convent. They made Helene want to cry.

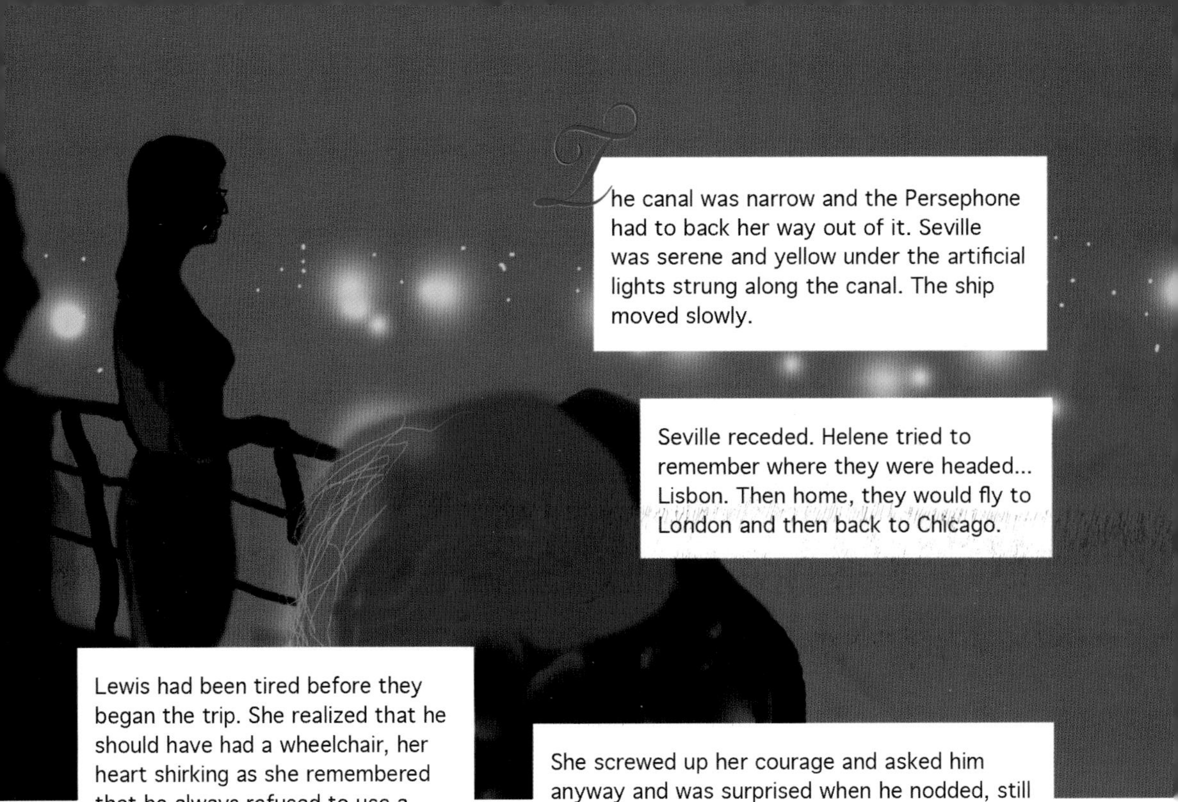

The canal was narrow and the Persephone had to back her way out of it. Seville was serene and yellow under the artificial lights strung along the canal. The ship moved slowly.

Seville receded. Helene tried to remember where they were headed... Lisbon. Then home, they would fly to London and then back to Chicago.

Lewis had been tired before they began the trip. She realized that he should have had a wheelchair, her heart shirking as she remembered that he always refused to use a wheelchair.

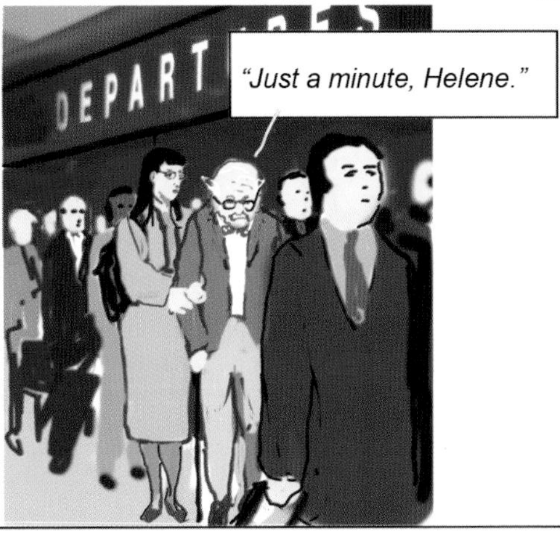
DEPART
"Just a minute, Helene."

She screwed up her courage and asked him anyway and was surprised when he nodded, still breathing heavily. Helene didn't travel much but Lewis always had. It was all familiar to him.

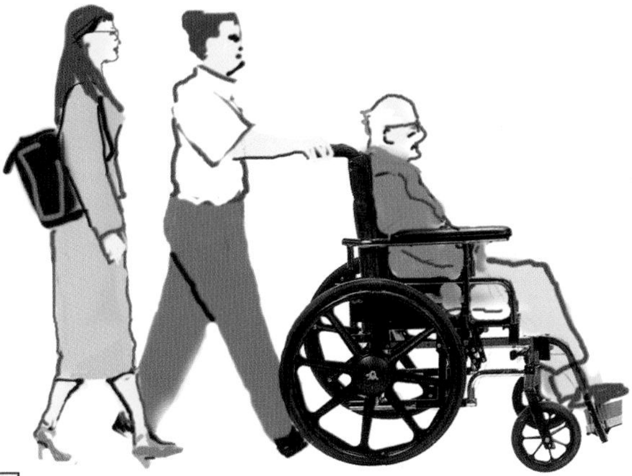

She watched her father sit, and finally admitted to herself that he was terribly old. *When did this happen? He was always fine and now...* Her mother had died in February. It was her mother's place Helene occupied here on the ship. She slept in the narrow bed her mother should have slept in, ate the bland food her mother would have eaten.

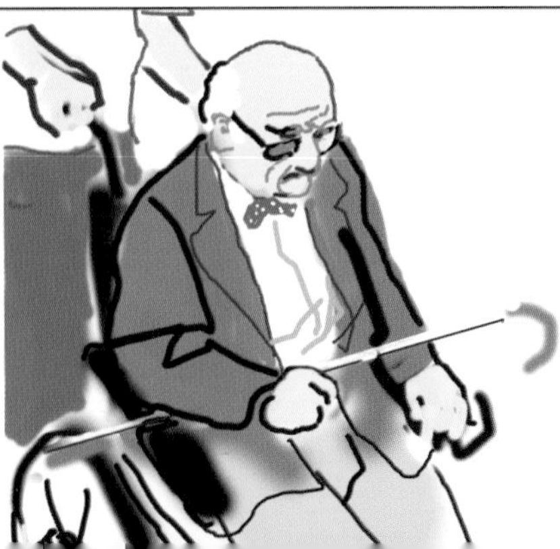

Lewis accepted Nora's absence with grace; he might say, "Your mother would have liked that," or "Your mother always did this," but he never made Helene feel that he would have preferred his wife's company to hers.

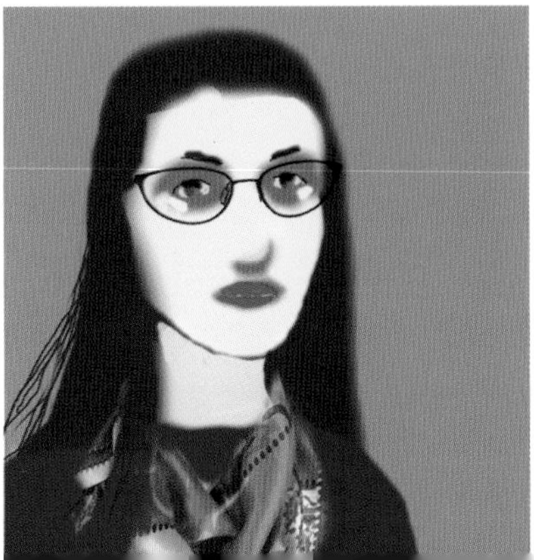

When Helene was small she had stolen her mother's lipstick and gone down to breakfast with scarlet lips. Her parents had smiled at each other and pretended not to notice as she left lip prints on her juice glass. It was like that.

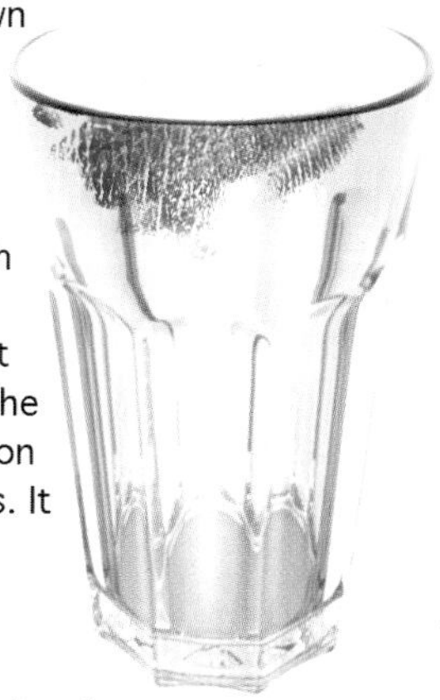

Helene was forty-five years old, by far the youngest passenger on the ship. The other passengers at the rail were all in pairs. They were white-haired and bent but exceedingly compatible, each husband inclining toward his wife when she spoke quietly into his ear, all of them dressed for dinner with care, all leaning on the rail for support with a glass of wine or a cocktail clutched in one hand.

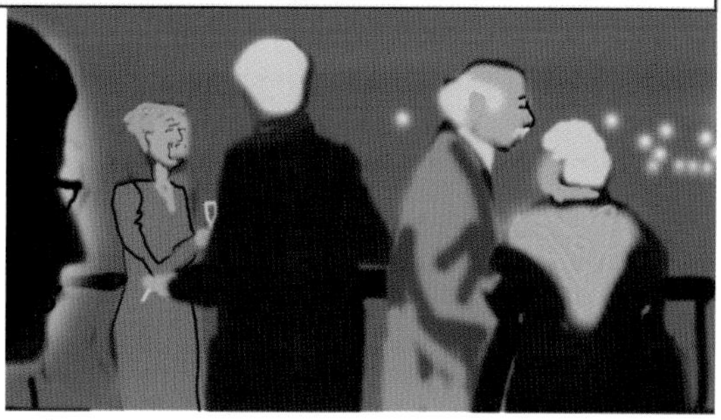

Helene thought of Evan. *Is that what we would have looked like in forty years?*

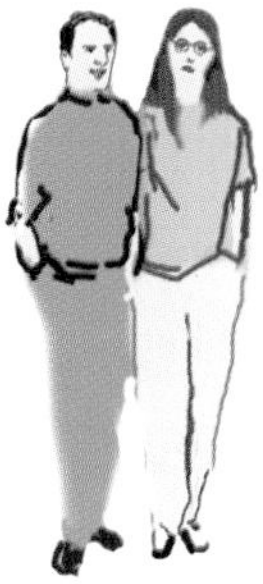

She had met Evan when she was twenty-eight and he was thirty-six. He'd always seemed on the verge of marrying her; she was patient.

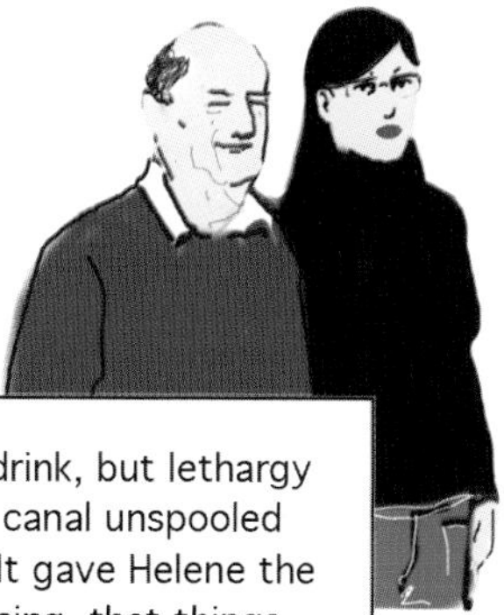

When he broke up with her fourteen years later and married a girl half her age she understood that she'd been gullible and that he was a jerk, but oh well and so she had lapsed into a quiet permanent rage.

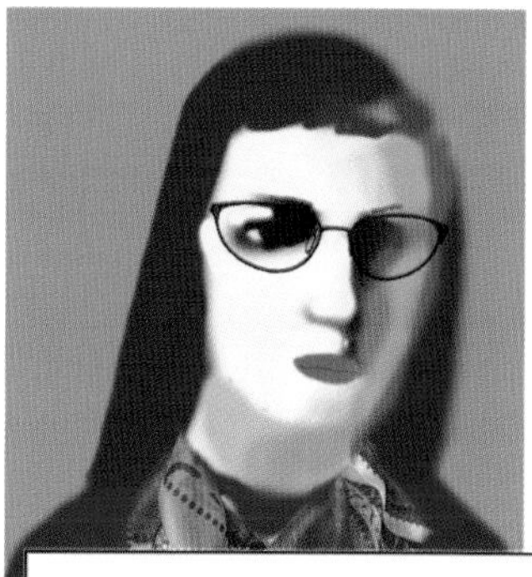

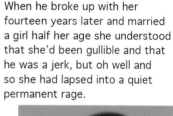

It would be nice to have a drink, but lethargy kept her at the railing. The canal unspooled backward around the ship. It gave Helene the feeling that time was reversing, that things might be undone. *Daddy wouldn't be old, Mom wouldn't have died, Evan would come back and we'd have kids, it would all be different, I would change everything. I would change.*

Trees and houses came from behind her, little boats began to appear in the water as the canal widened. Soon they would turn the ship and sail forwards. Everything flowed away into the distance and the darkness.

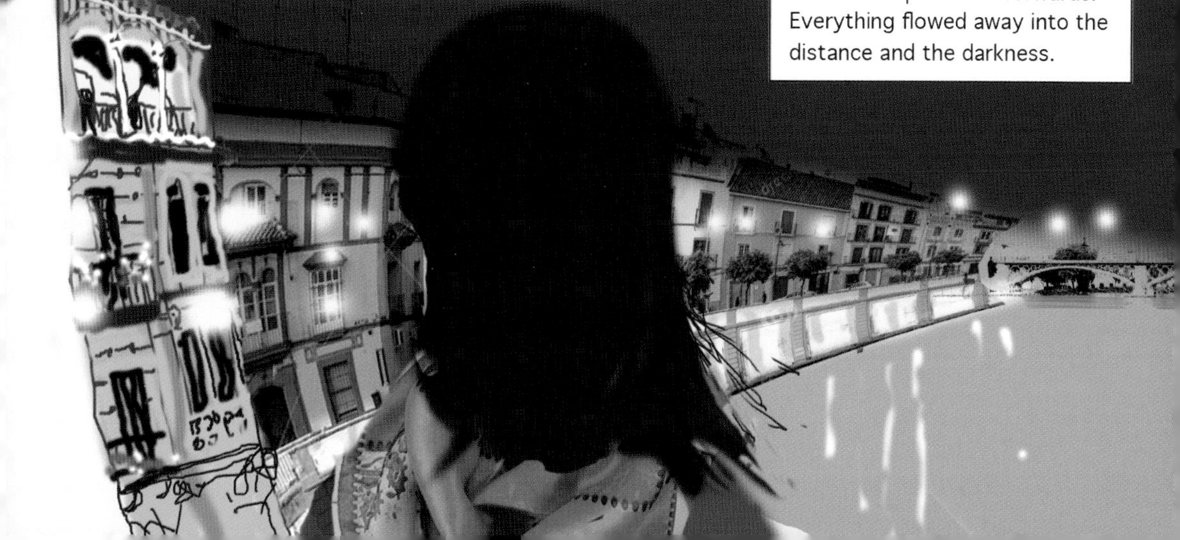

One of the women at the rail dropped her cane and her husband bent painfully and retrieved it for her. *How he cares for her,* Helene thought. *No one takes care of me, it's always me taking care of somebody.* When she was a child she had been very timid, scared of strangers, thunder, the poodle next door, escalators, anything new or loud, anything that moved, pretty much. Her mother had kept her close, kissed her on the tip of her ear, whispered encouragement. Her father had brought her funny presents,

a tiny silk umbrella from Paris,

a tin of green tea from Kyoto.

It's okay, Sweet Pea, I've got your back. Now go get 'em."

I wasted my life.

She imagined the Poor Clares, tucked into their neat beds in their cloister, secure in the night, in belief. How good it must be to believe. Lewis and Nora were indifferent to religion. When Helene was nine she had asked about God. Lewis had taken her to synagogue and Nora had taken her to church, once each, and they had asked very carefully if she wanted to go back and she'd said no thank you, sensing their lack of enthusiasm.

Now Helene wondered what her father believed, now when he was so close to death, when death had already claimed her mother. *He was never afraid.* He'd watched the couples dancing tonight with a smile.

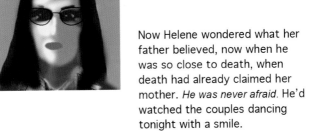

Want to?

Your heart!

Not me, you—you go on.

She shook her head and continued to sit by him.

Helene looked over the railing. The water was down there somewhere, she could hear it churning. The first day they were on the ship there had been a muster of all the passengers. They had been instructed in how to use their life jackets and where to gather if the alarm sounded. They had been told never to even think of diving off the ship; it was a long way down, you could break your neck, you could drown. Sharks could eat you. You might never be found.

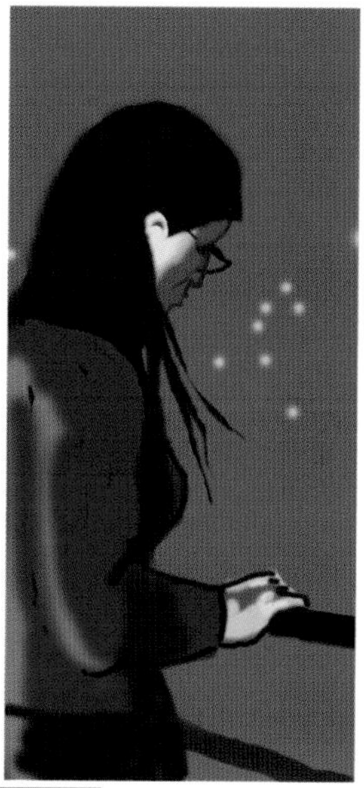

I wish I could give the rest of it to him, Helene thought. *Daddy would know what to do with another half a life. To me it's just a burden.*
Helene closed her eyes and tried to pray. She opened her eyes and felt foolish.

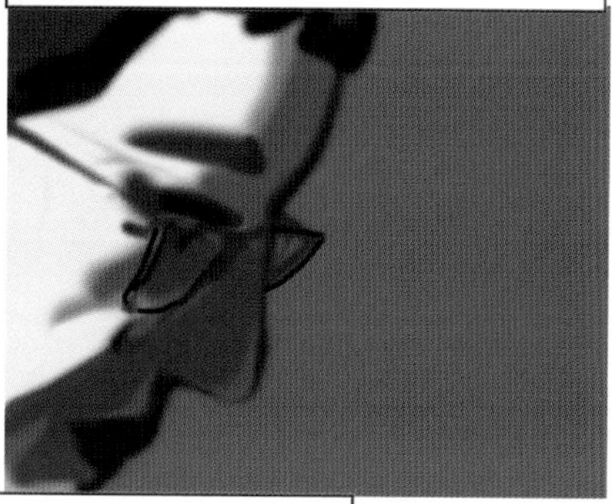

The ship began to turn. The world revolved around Helene and she saw the way ahead, they were about to pass under an enormous bridge.

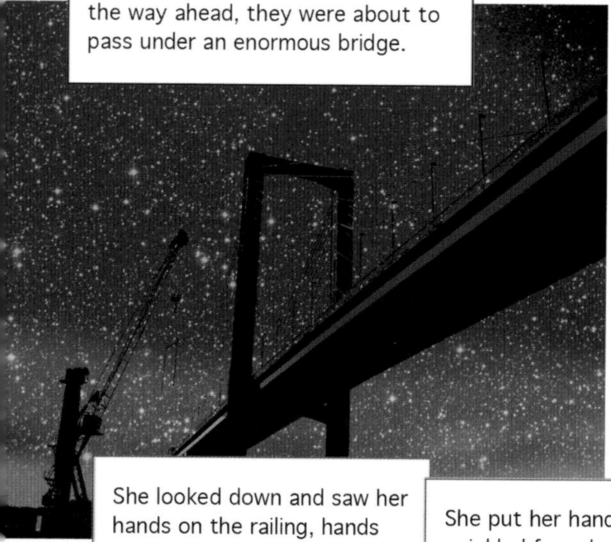

She tilted her head back to see the silhouette of the underside of the bridge, menacing and close in the dark. She felt dizzy.

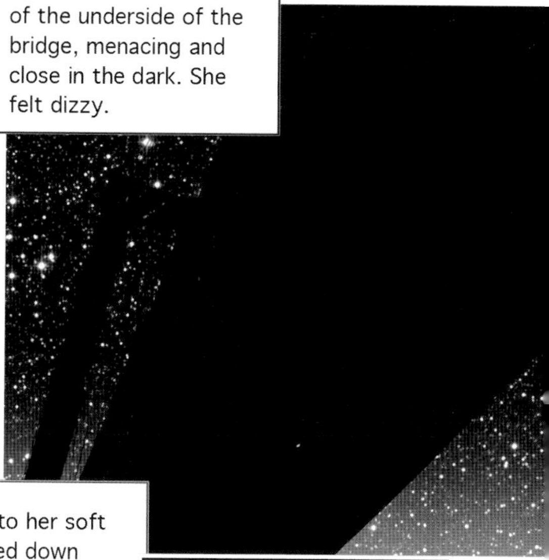

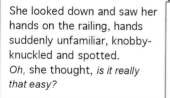

She looked down and saw her hands on the railing, hands suddenly unfamiliar, knobby-knuckled and spotted.
Oh, she thought, *is it really that easy?*

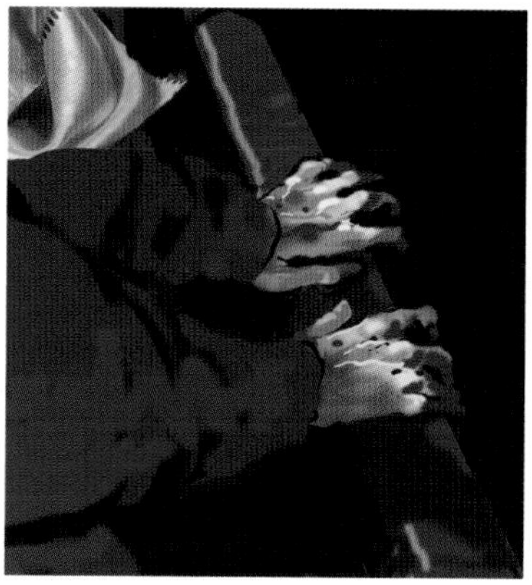

She put her hands to her soft wrinkled face, looked down at her now-loose clothing.
Her heart pounded, her vision blurred. Aches and pains beset her. The sounds of the world were suddenly muted. The ship sailed on as before.

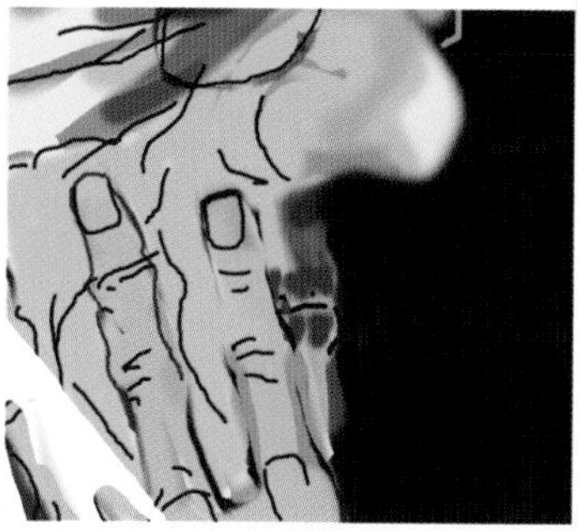

Helene began to creep along the railing, back to the cabin, joyously certain of what she would find there.

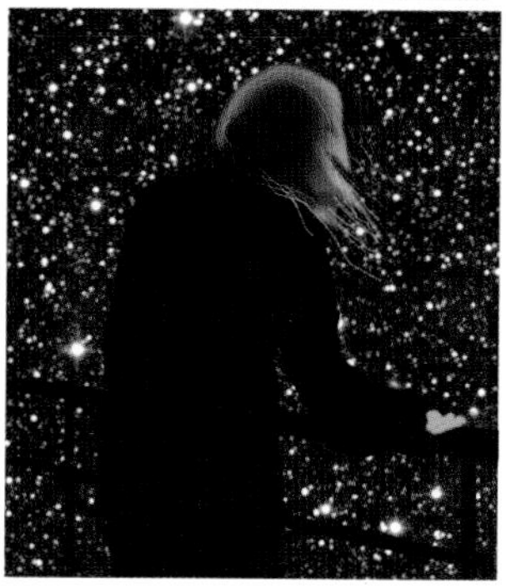

ABOUT "BACKWARDS IN SEVILLE"

In June 2011, I accompanied a friend on a Mediterranean cruise. The ship was small (for a cruise ship) and most of the other passengers were older British people, many of them regulars who came every year and knew one another. My friend had been on many such cruises. She had taken them with her husband and after he died she had been accompanied by various friends. We sat with different people at meals, and when our dining companions discovered I was a writer they always asked, "Are you going to write about this cruise?" "No, no," I said. "I'm just here to hang out with my friend."

Before I got onto the ship I had already decided to write in response to Ray Bradbury's "The Playground," which has always seemed to me equally horrifying and touching, a perfect evocation of the terrors of parenting and childhood. So as I wandered the ship's decks watching the other passengers, I was thinking about impossible gifts, and it was a very small mental flip to imagine a grown child trading places with her elderly parent, instead of a parent taking the place of his child.

So I did end up writing about the cruise after all, and if any of my fellow passengers read this, I hope you will pardon my impudence. It was too perfect to resist.

—Audrey Niffenegger

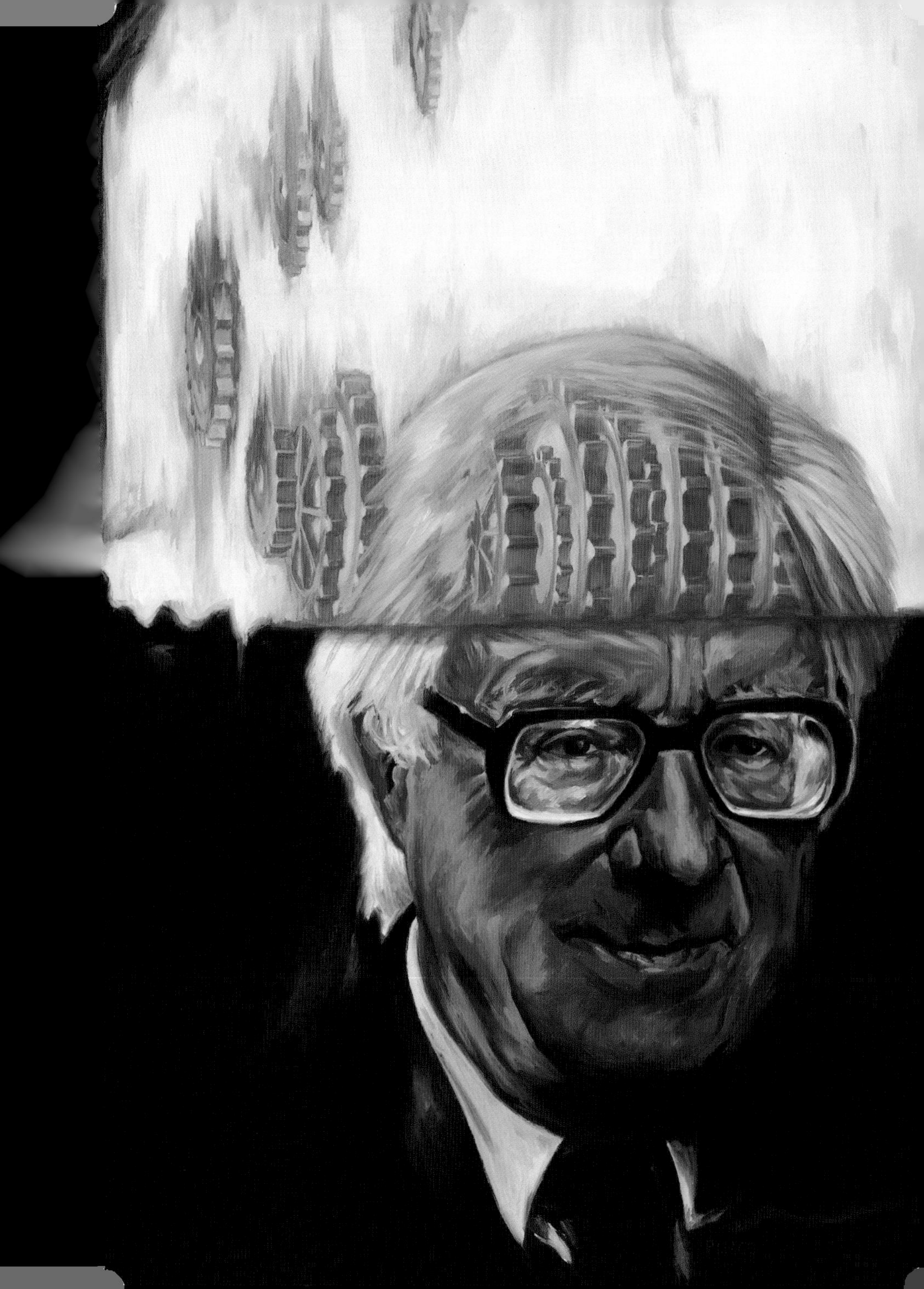

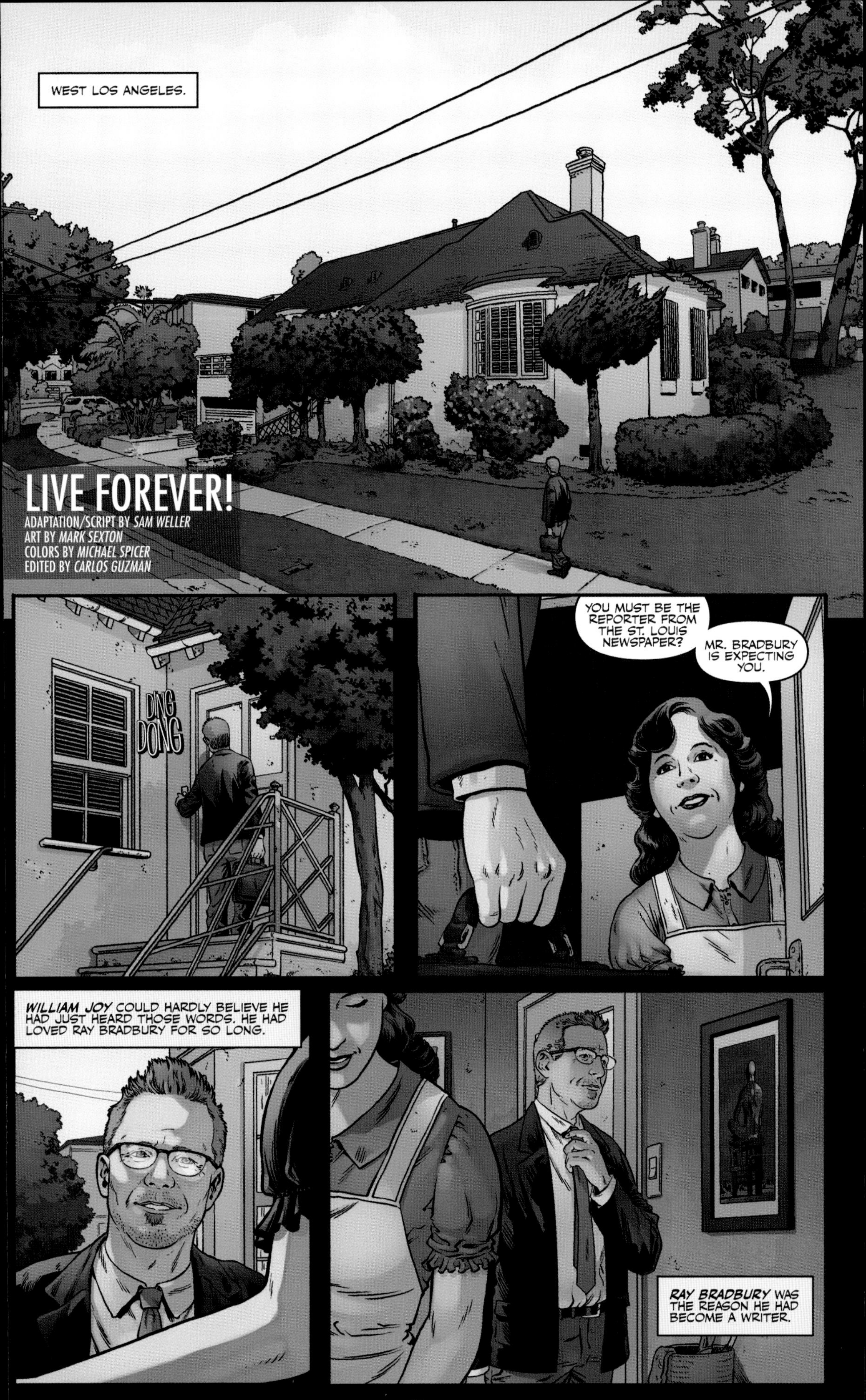
WEST LOS ANGELES.
LIVE FOREVER!
ADAPTATION/SCRIPT BY SAM WELLER
ART BY MARK SEXTON
COLORS BY MICHAEL SPICER
EDITED BY CARLOS GUZMAN
DING DONG
YOU MUST BE THE REPORTER FROM THE ST. LOUIS NEWSPAPER?
MR. BRADBURY IS EXPECTING YOU.
WILLIAM JOY COULD HARDLY BELIEVE HE HAD JUST HEARD THOSE WORDS. HE HAD LOVED RAY BRADBURY FOR SO LONG.
RAY BRADBURY WAS THE REASON HE HAD BECOME A WRITER.

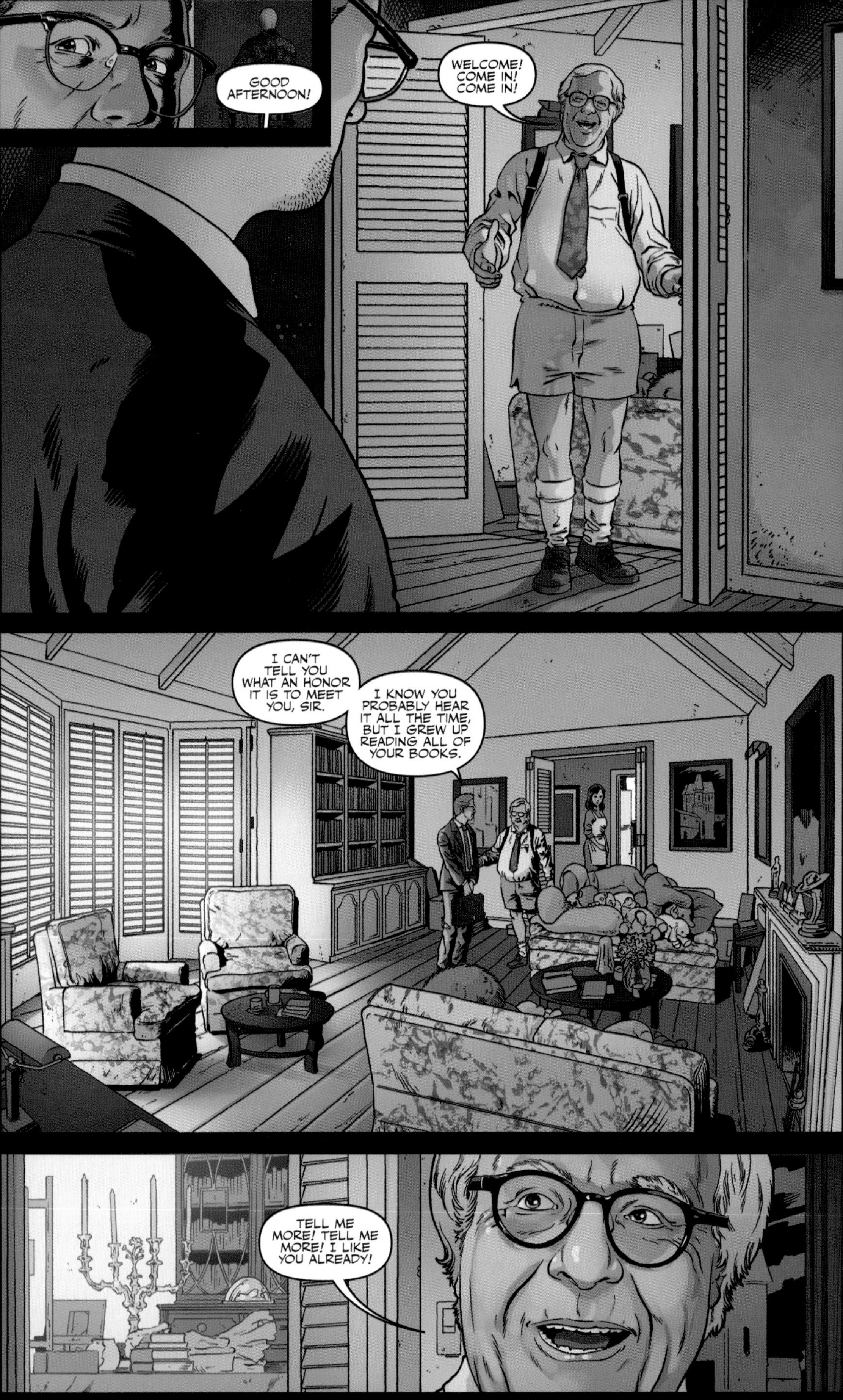
GOOD AFTERNOON!
WELCOME! COME IN! COME IN!
I CAN'T TELL YOU WHAT AN HONOR IT IS TO MEET YOU, SIR.
I KNOW YOU PROBABLY HEAR IT ALL THE TIME, BUT I GREW UP READING ALL OF YOUR BOOKS.
TELL ME MORE! TELL ME MORE! I LIKE YOU ALREADY!

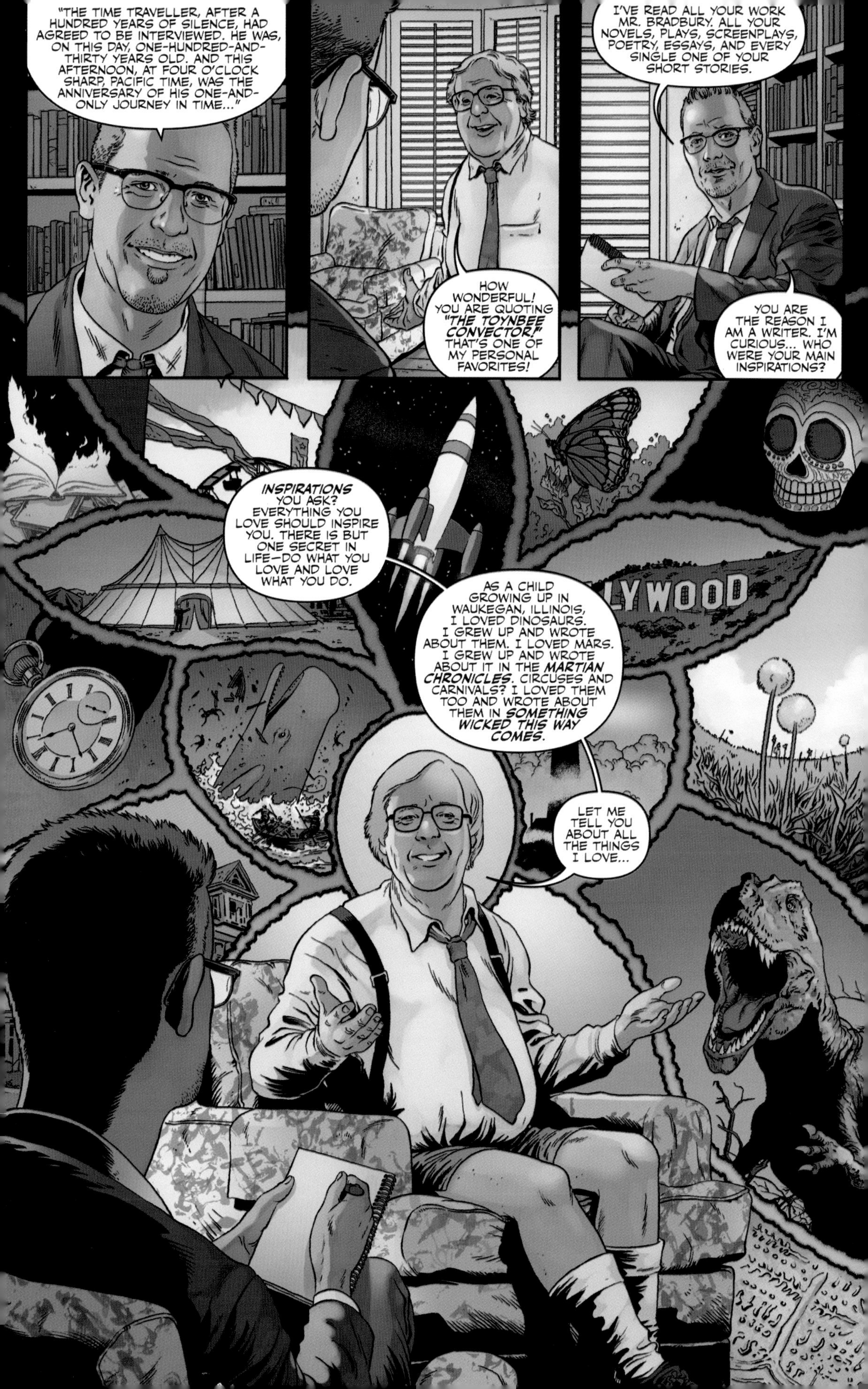
"THE TIME TRAVELLER, AFTER A HUNDRED YEARS OF SILENCE, HAD AGREED TO BE INTERVIEWED. HE WAS, ON THIS DAY, ONE-HUNDRED-AND-THIRTY YEARS OLD. AND THIS AFTERNOON, AT FOUR O'CLOCK SHARP, PACIFIC TIME, WAS THE ANNIVERSARY OF HIS ONE-AND-ONLY JOURNEY IN TIME..."
HOW WONDERFUL! YOU ARE QUOTING *"THE TOYNBEE CONVECTOR!"* THAT'S ONE OF MY PERSONAL FAVORITES!
I'VE READ ALL YOUR WORK MR. BRADBURY. ALL YOUR NOVELS, PLAYS, SCREENPLAYS, POETRY, ESSAYS, AND EVERY SINGLE ONE OF YOUR SHORT STORIES.
YOU ARE THE REASON I AM A WRITER. I'M CURIOUS... WHO WERE YOUR MAIN INSPIRATIONS?
INSPIRATIONS YOU ASK? EVERYTHING YOU LOVE SHOULD INSPIRE YOU. THERE IS BUT ONE SECRET IN LIFE—DO WHAT YOU LOVE AND LOVE WHAT YOU DO.
AS A CHILD GROWING UP IN WAUKEGAN, ILLINOIS, I LOVED DINOSAURS. I GREW UP AND WROTE ABOUT THEM. I LOVED MARS. I GREW UP AND WROTE ABOUT IT IN THE *MARTIAN CHRONICLES*. CIRCUSES AND CARNIVALS? I LOVED THEM TOO AND WROTE ABOUT THEM IN *SOMETHING WICKED THIS WAY COMES*.
LET ME TELL YOU ABOUT ALL THE THINGS I LOVE...
LLYWOOD

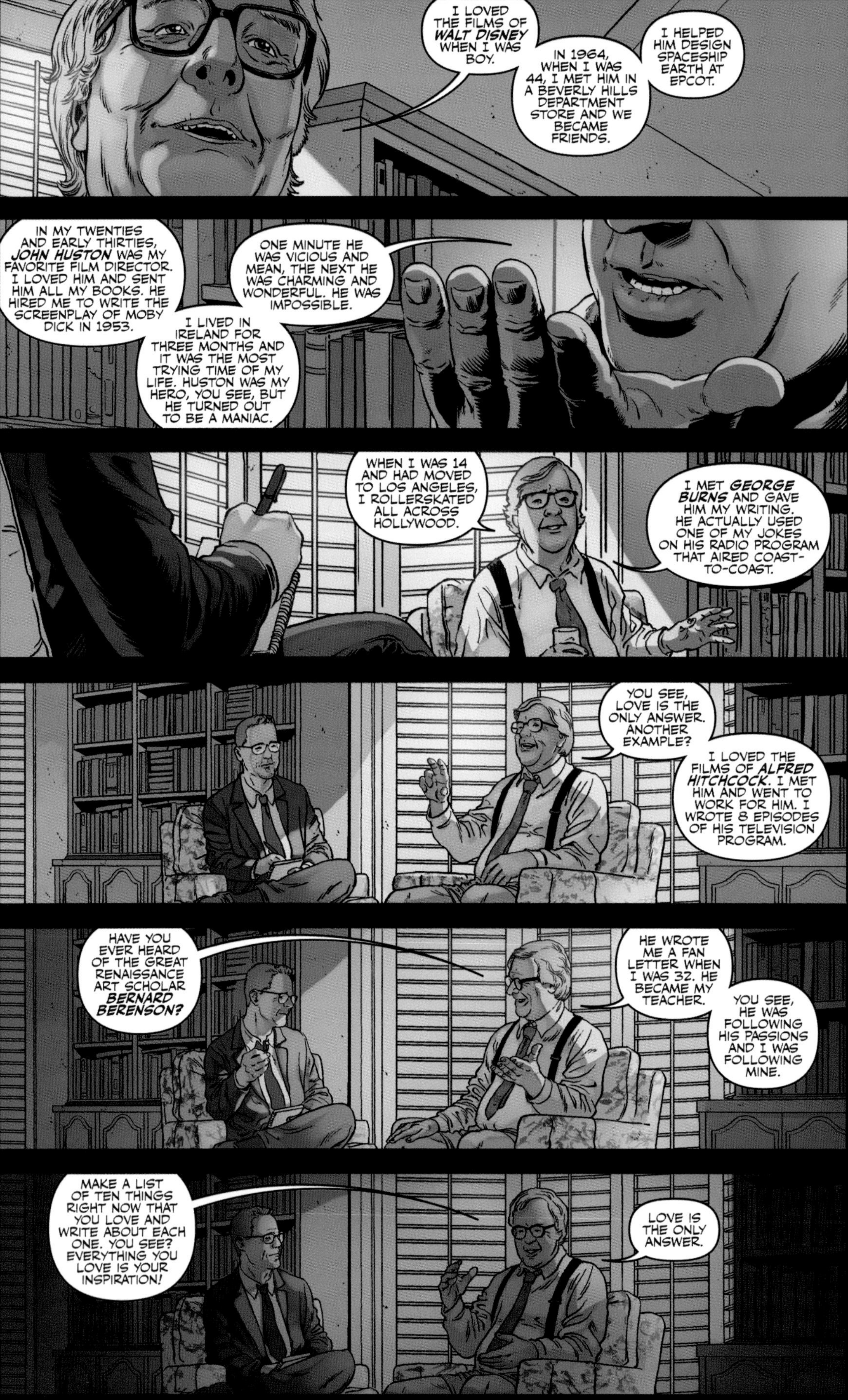

I LOVED THE FILMS OF WALT DISNEY WHEN I WAS BOY.
IN 1964, WHEN I WAS 44, I MET HIM IN A BEVERLY HILLS DEPARTMENT STORE AND WE BECAME FRIENDS.
I HELPED HIM DESIGN SPACESHIP EARTH AT EPCOT.
IN MY TWENTIES AND EARLY THIRTIES, JOHN HUSTON WAS MY FAVORITE FILM DIRECTOR. I LOVED HIM AND SENT HIM ALL MY BOOKS. HE HIRED ME TO WRITE THE SCREENPLAY OF MOBY DICK IN 1953.
I LIVED IN IRELAND FOR THREE MONTHS AND IT WAS THE MOST TRYING TIME OF MY LIFE. HUSTON WAS MY HERO, YOU SEE, BUT HE TURNED OUT TO BE A MANIAC.
ONE MINUTE HE WAS VICIOUS AND MEAN, THE NEXT HE WAS CHARMING AND WONDERFUL. HE WAS IMPOSSIBLE.
WHEN I WAS 14 AND HAD MOVED TO LOS ANGELES, I ROLLERSKATED ALL ACROSS HOLLYWOOD.
I MET GEORGE BURNS AND GAVE HIM MY WRITING. HE ACTUALLY USED ONE OF MY JOKES ON HIS RADIO PROGRAM THAT AIRED COAST-TO-COAST.
YOU SEE, LOVE IS THE ONLY ANSWER. ANOTHER EXAMPLE?
I LOVED THE FILMS OF ALFRED HITCHCOCK. I MET HIM AND WENT TO WORK FOR HIM. I WROTE 8 EPISODES OF HIS TELEVISION PROGRAM.
HAVE YOU EVER HEARD OF THE GREAT RENAISSANCE ART SCHOLAR BERNARD BERENSON?
HE WROTE ME A FAN LETTER WHEN I WAS 32. HE BECAME MY TEACHER.
YOU SEE, HE WAS FOLLOWING HIS PASSIONS AND I WAS FOLLOWING MINE.
MAKE A LIST OF TEN THINGS RIGHT NOW THAT YOU LOVE AND WRITE ABOUT EACH ONE. YOU SEE? EVERYTHING YOU LOVE IS YOUR INSPIRATION!
LOVE IS THE ONLY ANSWER.

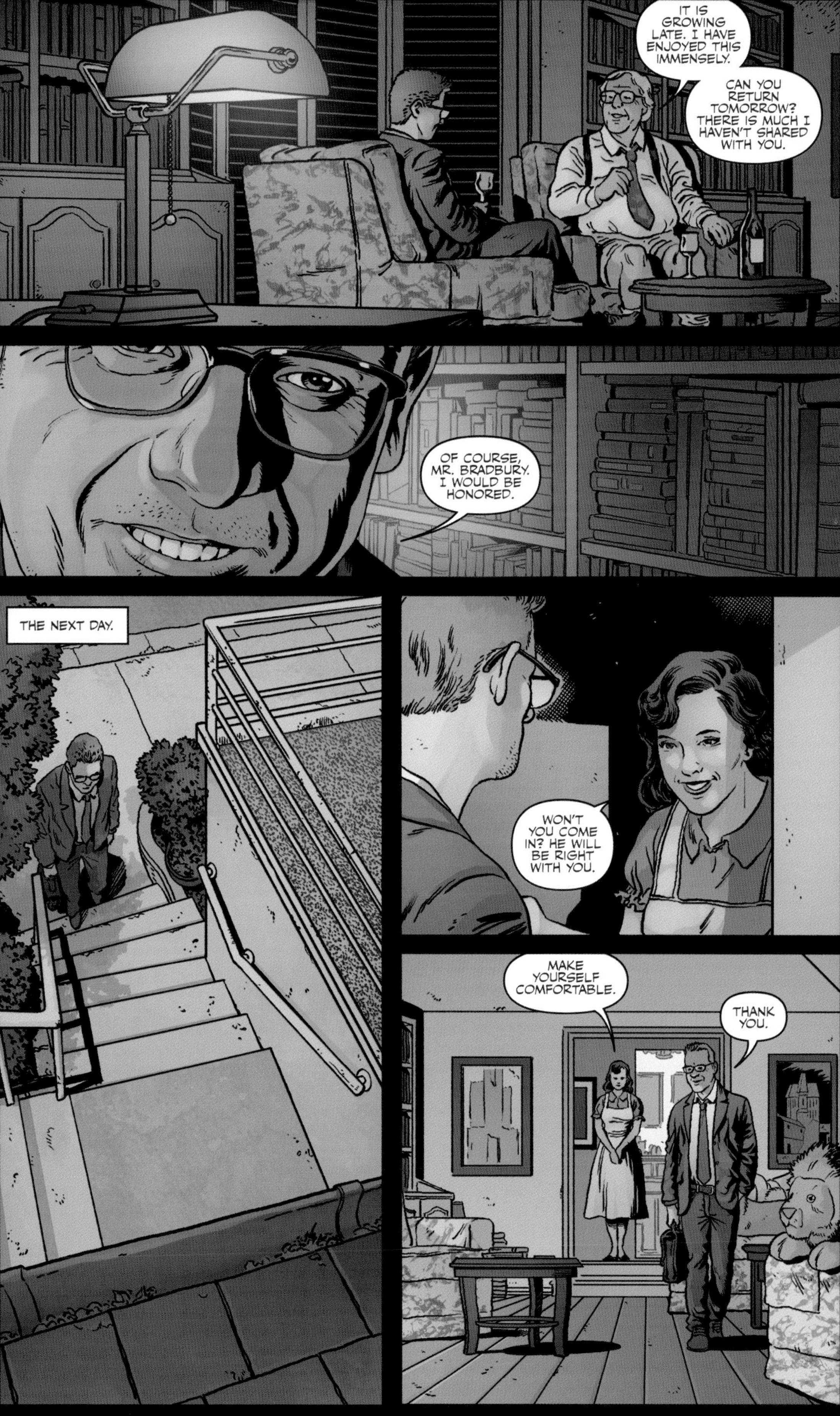

IT IS GROWING LATE. I HAVE ENJOYED THIS IMMENSELY.
CAN YOU RETURN TOMORROW? THERE IS MUCH I HAVEN'T SHARED WITH YOU.
OF COURSE, MR. BRADBURY. I WOULD BE HONORED.
THE NEXT DAY.
WON'T YOU COME IN? HE WILL BE RIGHT WITH YOU.
MAKE YOURSELF COMFORTABLE.
THANK YOU.

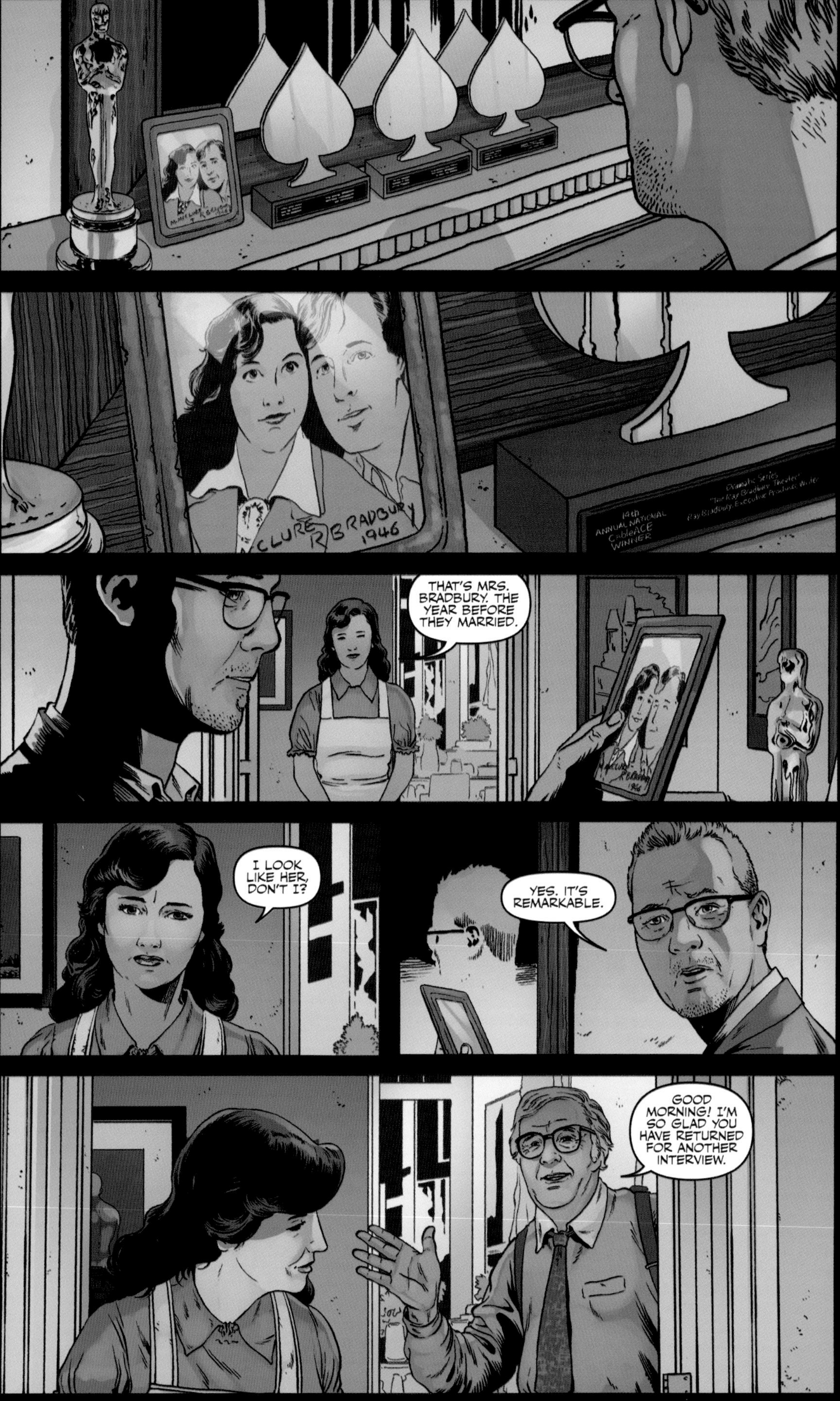
CLURE R BRADBURY 1946
14th ANNUAL NATIONAL CableACE WINNER
THAT'S MRS. BRADBURY. THE YEAR BEFORE THEY MARRIED.
I LOOK LIKE HER, DON'T I?
YES. IT'S REMARKABLE.
GOOD MORNING! I'M SO GLAD YOU HAVE RETURNED FOR ANOTHER INTERVIEW.

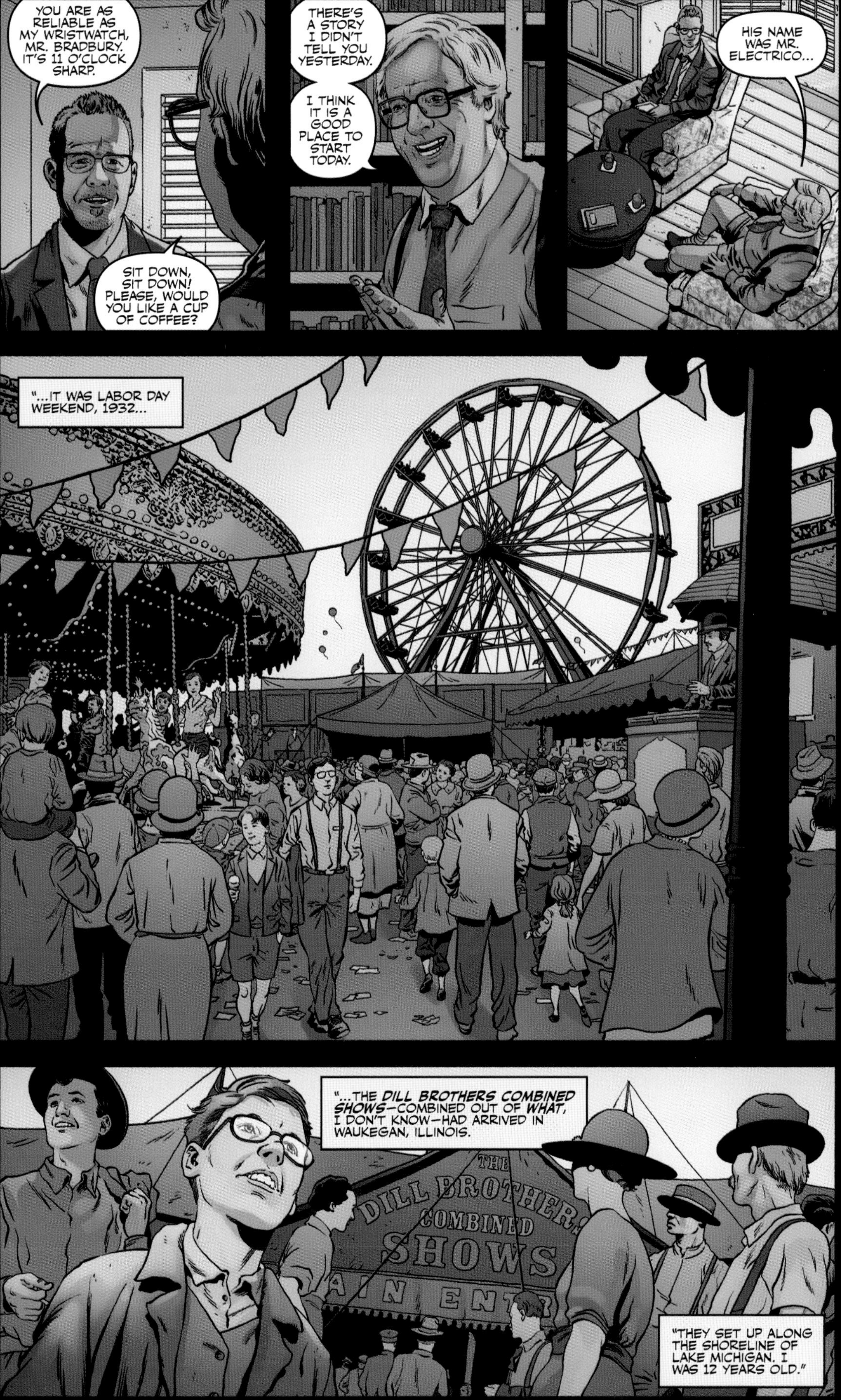
YOU ARE AS RELIABLE AS MY WRISTWATCH, MR. BRADBURY. IT'S 11 O'CLOCK SHARP.
SIT DOWN, SIT DOWN! PLEASE, WOULD YOU LIKE A CUP OF COFFEE?
THERE'S A STORY I DIDN'T TELL YOU YESTERDAY.
I THINK IT IS A GOOD PLACE TO START TODAY.
HIS NAME WAS MR. ELECTRICO...
"...IT WAS LABOR DAY WEEKEND, 1932...
"...THE *DILL BROTHERS COMBINED SHOWS*—COMBINED OUT OF *WHAT*, I DON'T KNOW—HAD ARRIVED IN WAUKEGAN, ILLINOIS.
THE DILL BROTHERS COMBINED SHOWS
"THEY SET UP ALONG THE SHORELINE OF LAKE MICHIGAN. I WAS 12 YEARS OLD."

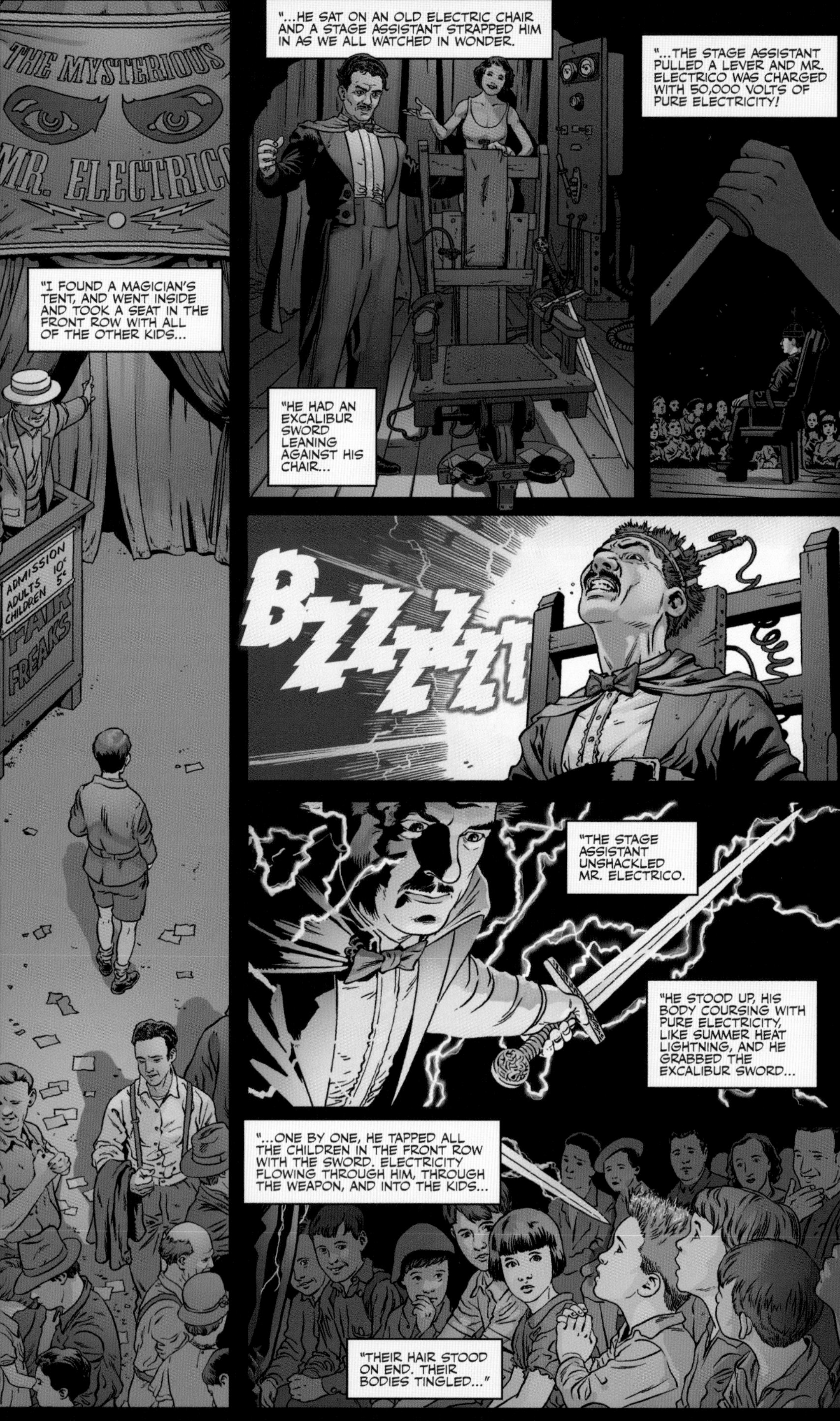
THE MYSTERIOUS
MR. ELECTRICO
"I FOUND A MAGICIAN'S TENT, AND WENT INSIDE AND TOOK A SEAT IN THE FRONT ROW WITH ALL OF THE OTHER KIDS...
ADMISSION ADULTS 10¢ CHILDREN 5¢
FREAKS
"...HE SAT ON AN OLD ELECTRIC CHAIR AND A STAGE ASSISTANT STRAPPED HIM IN AS WE ALL WATCHED IN WONDER.
"HE HAD AN EXCALIBUR SWORD LEANING AGAINST HIS CHAIR...
"...THE STAGE ASSISTANT PULLED A LEVER AND MR. ELECTRICO WAS CHARGED WITH 50,000 VOLTS OF PURE ELECTRICITY!
BZZZZZZT
"THE STAGE ASSISTANT UNSHACKLED MR. ELECTRICO.
"HE STOOD UP, HIS BODY COURSING WITH PURE ELECTRICITY, LIKE SUMMER HEAT LIGHTNING, AND HE GRABBED THE EXCALIBUR SWORD...
"...ONE BY ONE, HE TAPPED ALL THE CHILDREN IN THE FRONT ROW WITH THE SWORD. ELECTRICITY FLOWING THROUGH HIM, THROUGH THE WEAPON, AND INTO THE KIDS...
"THEIR HAIR STOOD ON END. THEIR BODIES TINGLED..."

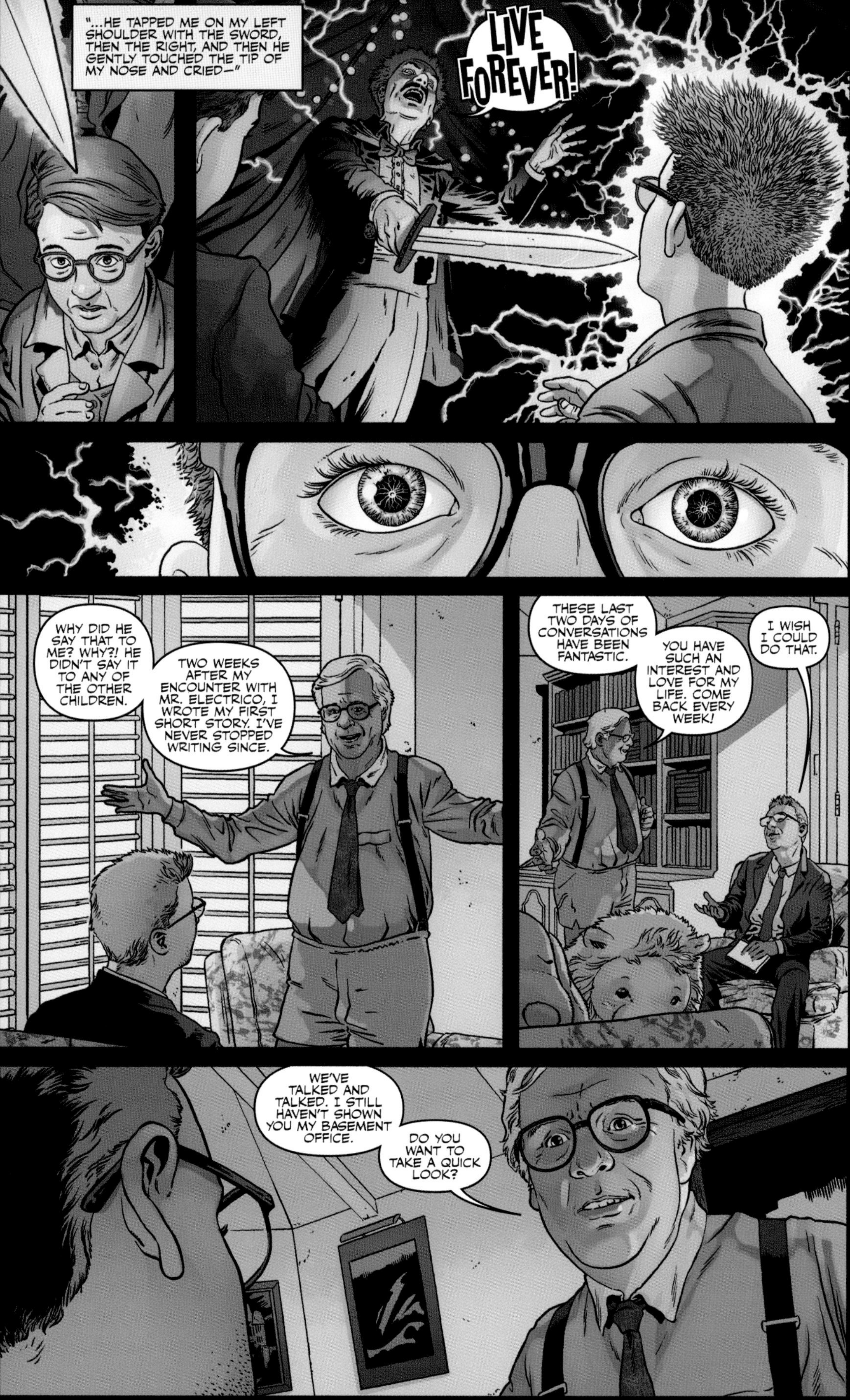
"...HE TAPPED ME ON MY LEFT SHOULDER WITH THE SWORD, THEN THE RIGHT, AND THEN HE GENTLY TOUCHED THE TIP OF MY NOSE AND CRIED—"
LIVE FOREVER!
WHY DID HE SAY THAT TO ME? WHY?! HE DIDN'T SAY IT TO ANY OF THE OTHER CHILDREN.
TWO WEEKS AFTER MY ENCOUNTER WITH MR. ELECTRICO, I WROTE MY FIRST SHORT STORY. I'VE NEVER STOPPED WRITING SINCE.
THESE LAST TWO DAYS OF CONVERSATIONS HAVE BEEN FANTASTIC.
YOU HAVE SUCH AN INTEREST AND LOVE FOR MY LIFE. COME BACK EVERY WEEK!
I WISH I COULD DO THAT.
WE'VE TALKED AND TALKED. I STILL HAVEN'T SHOWN YOU MY BASEMENT OFFICE.
DO YOU WANT TO TAKE A QUICK LOOK?

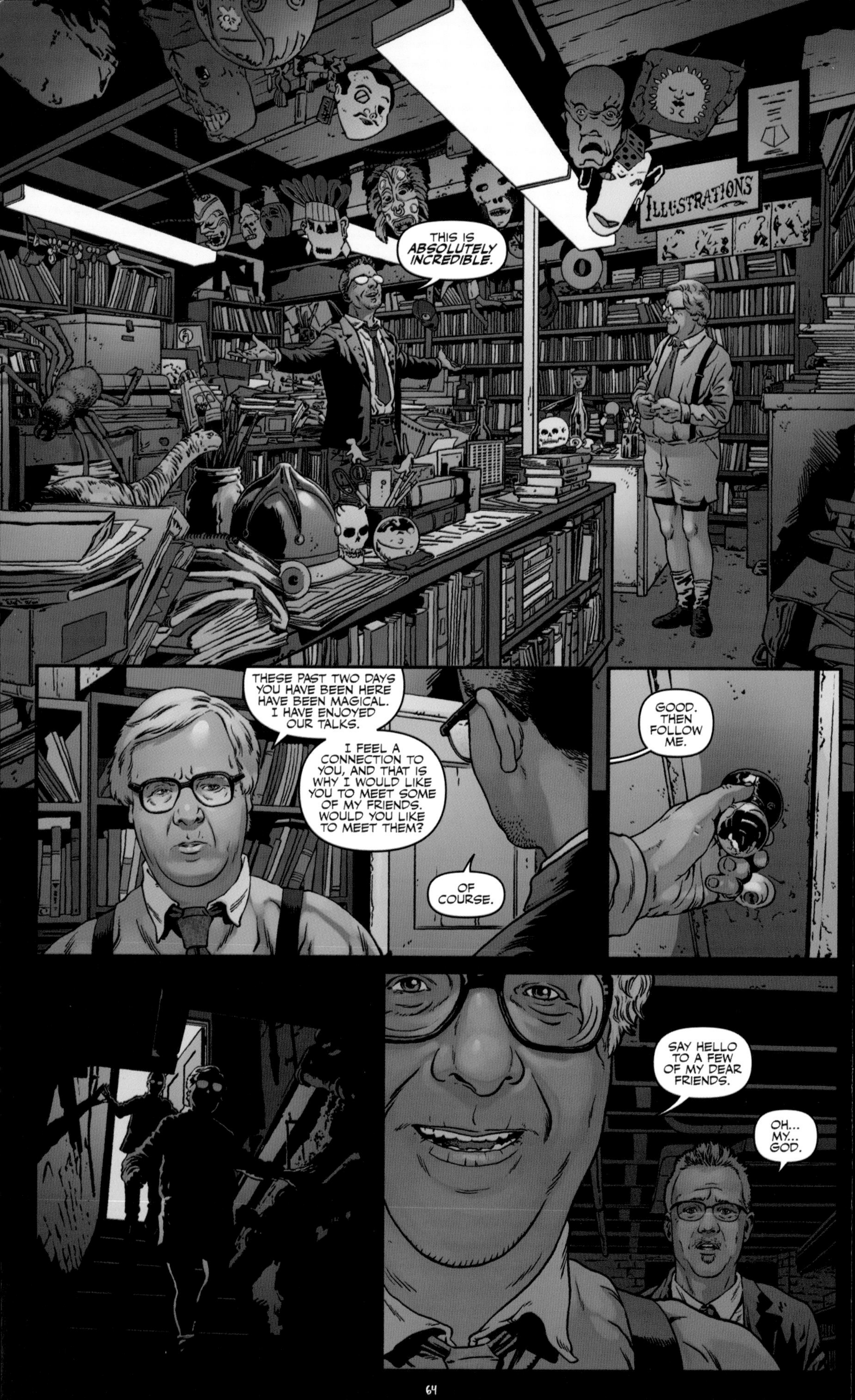
ILLUSTRATIONS
THIS IS ABSOLUTELY INCREDIBLE.
THESE PAST TWO DAYS YOU HAVE BEEN HERE HAVE BEEN MAGICAL. I HAVE ENJOYED OUR TALKS.
I FEEL A CONNECTION TO YOU, AND THAT IS WHY I WOULD LIKE YOU TO MEET SOME OF MY FRIENDS. WOULD YOU LIKE TO MEET THEM?
OF COURSE.
GOOD. THEN FOLLOW ME.
SAY HELLO TO A FEW OF MY DEAR FRIENDS.
OH... MY... GOD.

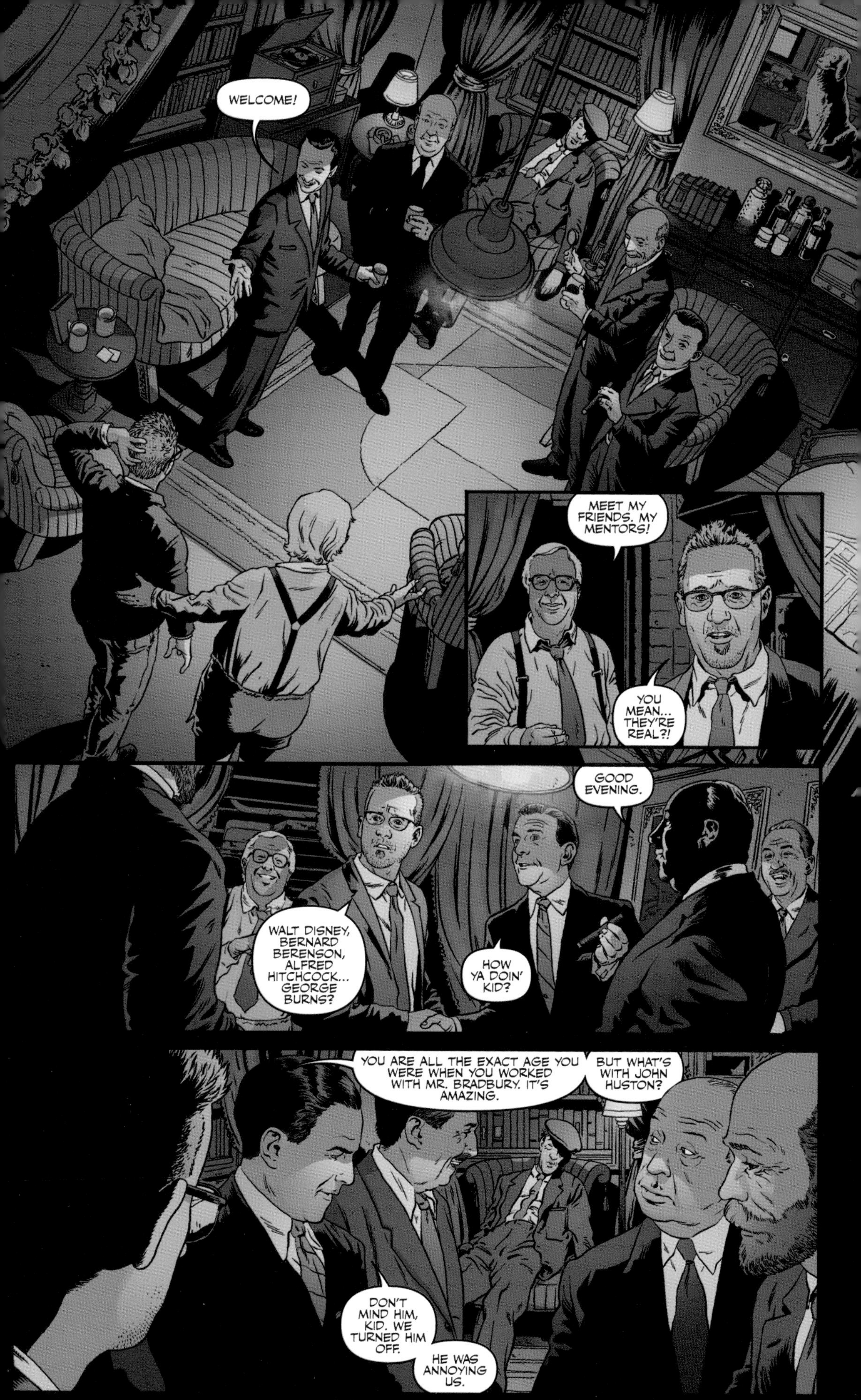
WELCOME!
MEET MY FRIENDS. MY MENTORS!
YOU MEAN... THEY'RE REAL?!
GOOD EVENING.
WALT DISNEY, BERNARD BERENSON, ALFRED HITCHCOCK... GEORGE BURNS?
HOW YA DOIN' KID?
YOU ARE ALL THE EXACT AGE YOU WERE WHEN YOU WORKED WITH MR. BRADBURY. IT'S AMAZING.
BUT WHAT'S WITH JOHN HUSTON?
DON'T MIND HIM, KID. WE TURNED HIM OFF.
HE WAS ANNOYING US.

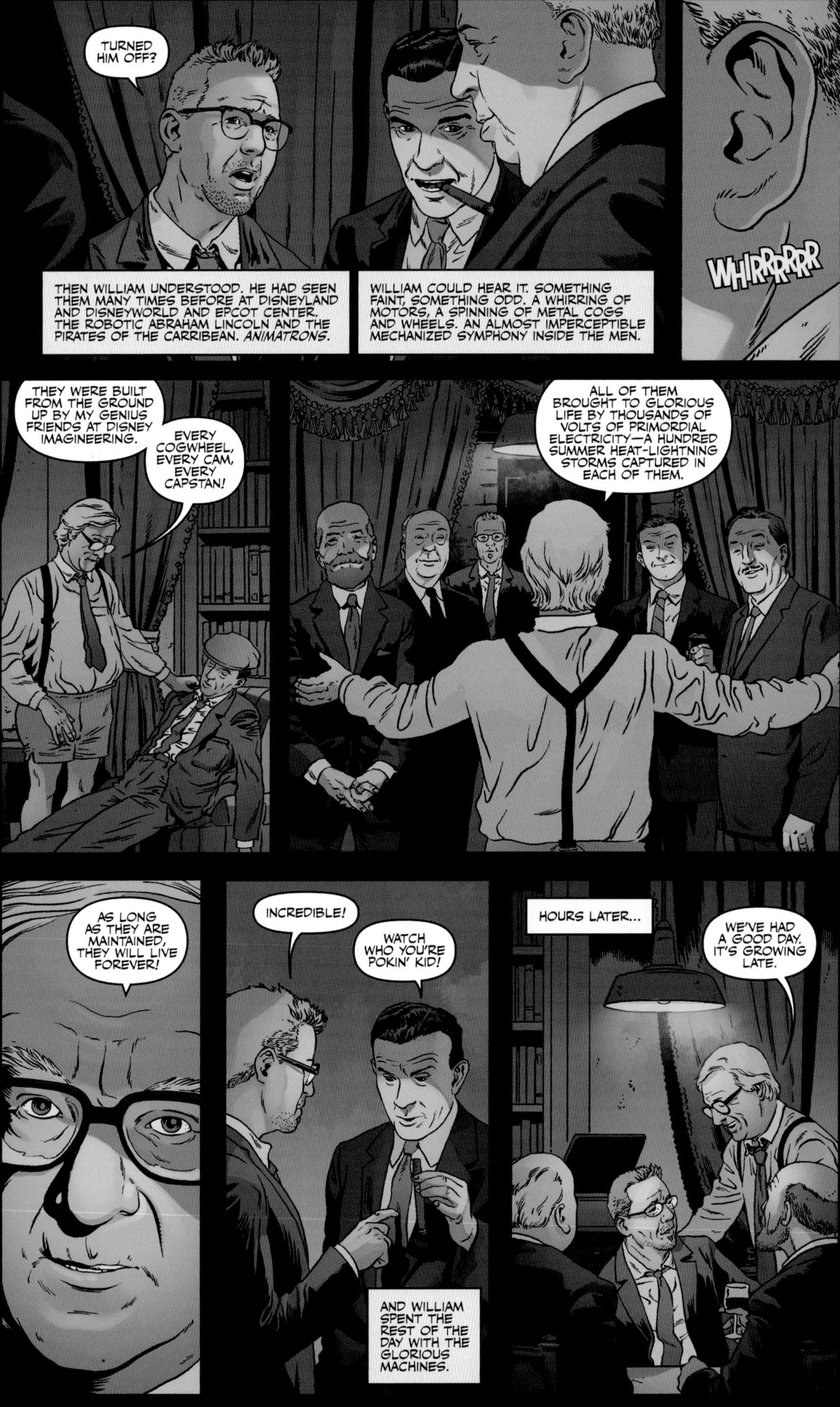
TURNED HIM OFF?
THEN WILLIAM UNDERSTOOD. HE HAD SEEN THEM MANY TIMES BEFORE AT DISNEYLAND AND DISNEYWORLD AND EPCOT CENTER. THE ROBOTIC ABRAHAM LINCOLN AND THE PIRATES OF THE CARRIBEAN. *ANIMATRONS*.
WILLIAM COULD HEAR IT. SOMETHING FAINT, SOMETHING ODD. A WHIRRING OF MOTORS, A SPINNING OF METAL COGS AND WHEELS. AN ALMOST IMPERCEPTIBLE MECHANIZED SYMPHONY INSIDE THE MEN.
WHIRRRRRR
THEY WERE BUILT FROM THE GROUND UP BY MY GENIUS FRIENDS AT DISNEY IMAGINEERING.
EVERY COGWHEEL, EVERY CAM, EVERY CAPSTAN!
ALL OF THEM BROUGHT TO GLORIOUS LIFE BY THOUSANDS OF VOLTS OF PRIMORDIAL ELECTRICITY—A HUNDRED SUMMER HEAT-LIGHTNING STORMS CAPTURED IN EACH OF THEM.
AS LONG AS THEY ARE MAINTAINED, THEY WILL LIVE FOREVER!
INCREDIBLE!
WATCH WHO YOU'RE POKIN' KID!
AND WILLIAM SPENT THE REST OF THE DAY WITH THE GLORIOUS MACHINES.
HOURS LATER...
WE'VE HAD A GOOD DAY. IT'S GROWING LATE.

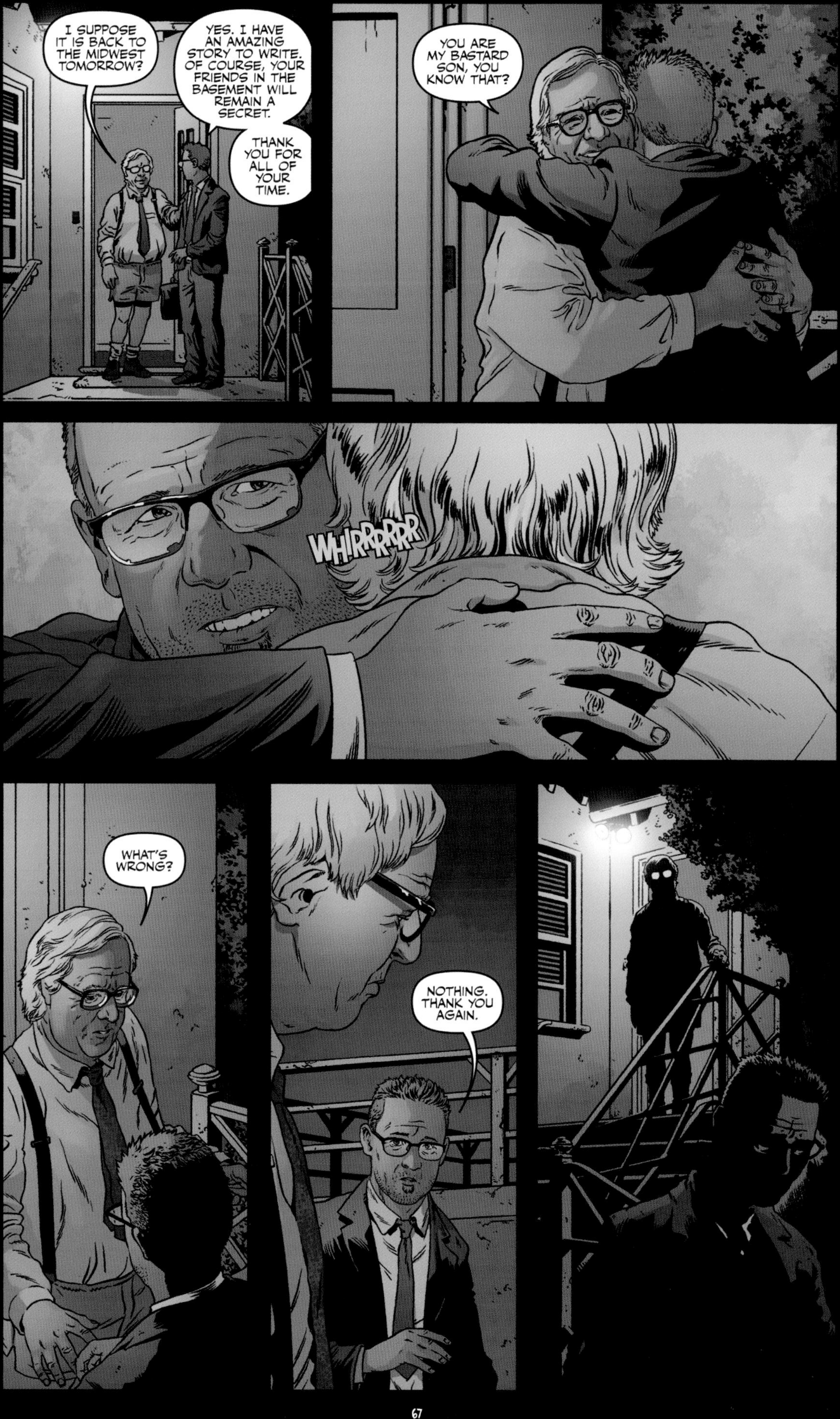
I SUPPOSE IT IS BACK TO THE MIDWEST TOMORROW?
YES. I HAVE AN AMAZING STORY TO WRITE. OF COURSE, YOUR FRIENDS IN THE BASEMENT WILL REMAIN A SECRET.
THANK YOU FOR ALL OF YOUR TIME.
YOU ARE MY BASTARD SON, YOU KNOW THAT?
WHIRRRRRR
WHAT'S WRONG?
NOTHING. THANK YOU AGAIN.

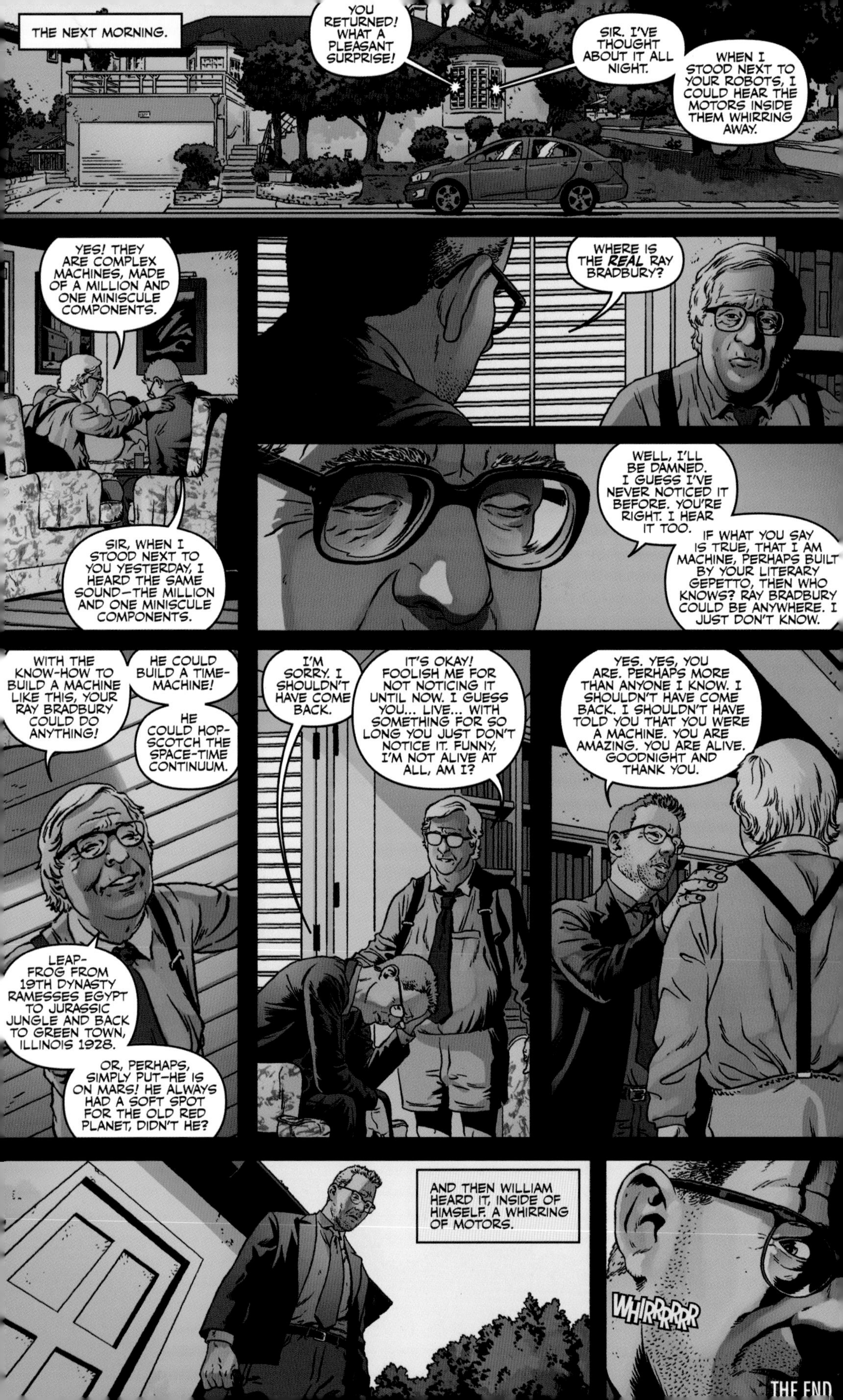
THE NEXT MORNING.
YOU RETURNED! WHAT A PLEASANT SURPRISE!
SIR. I'VE THOUGHT ABOUT IT ALL NIGHT.
WHEN I STOOD NEXT TO YOUR ROBOTS, I COULD HEAR THE MOTORS INSIDE THEM WHIRRING AWAY.
YES! THEY ARE COMPLEX MACHINES, MADE OF A MILLION AND ONE MINISCULE COMPONENTS.
SIR, WHEN I STOOD NEXT TO YOU YESTERDAY, I HEARD THE SAME SOUND—THE MILLION AND ONE MINISCULE COMPONENTS.
WHERE IS THE *REAL* RAY BRADBURY?
WELL, I'LL BE DAMNED. I GUESS I'VE NEVER NOTICED IT BEFORE. YOU'RE RIGHT. I HEAR IT TOO.
IF WHAT YOU SAY IS TRUE, THAT I AM MACHINE, PERHAPS BUILT BY YOUR LITERARY GEPETTO, THEN WHO KNOWS? RAY BRADBURY COULD BE ANYWHERE. I JUST DON'T KNOW.
WITH THE KNOW-HOW TO BUILD A MACHINE LIKE THIS, YOUR RAY BRADBURY COULD DO ANYTHING!
HE COULD BUILD A TIME-MACHINE!
HE COULD HOP-SCOTCH THE SPACE-TIME CONTINUUM.
LEAP-FROG FROM 19TH DYNASTY RAMESSES EGYPT TO JURASSIC JUNGLE AND BACK TO GREEN TOWN, ILLINOIS 1928.
OR, PERHAPS, SIMPLY PUT—HE IS ON MARS! HE ALWAYS HAD A SOFT SPOT FOR THE OLD RED PLANET, DIDN'T HE?
I'M SORRY. I SHOULDN'T HAVE COME BACK.
IT'S OKAY! FOOLISH ME FOR NOT NOTICING IT UNTIL NOW. I GUESS YOU... LIVE... WITH SOMETHING FOR SO LONG YOU JUST DON'T NOTICE IT. FUNNY, I'M NOT ALIVE AT ALL, AM I?
YES. YES, YOU ARE. PERHAPS MORE THAN ANYONE I KNOW. I SHOULDN'T HAVE COME BACK. I SHOULDN'T HAVE TOLD YOU THAT YOU WERE A MACHINE. YOU ARE AMAZING. YOU ARE ALIVE. GOODNIGHT AND THANK YOU.
AND THEN WILLIAM HEARD IT, INSIDE OF HIMSELF. A WHIRRING OF MOTORS.
WHIRRRRRR
THE END

Painting that inspired *Weariness*, "Nirvana" by **Hubert J. Daniel**

BY HARLAN ELLISON®

WEARINESS

"A painting is a sum of destructions."
—**Pablo Picasso** (1882-1973)

Very near the final thaw of the Universe, the last of them left behind, the last three of the most perfect beings who had ever existed, stood waiting for the transitional moment. The neap tide of all time. The eternal helix sang its silent song in stone; and the glow of What Was to Come had bruised itself to a ripe plumness.

The ostren fanned itself. Melancholia had shortened it, one entire set of faculties could do nothing but sigh. And it had grown uncommonly warm for her, in sight of the end.

The velv could not contain his trepidation, peering out around the perplexing curvature of space. But the tismess, that being who had summoned the helix, knew boldness was required, here and now at the final moments. And it stood boldly forth, waiting for the inevitable. All three—there were no others—were at the terminus of uncountable multiple trillions of eons, and weary.
Heaviness hung, a dire swaddling.

"What is there to fear?" the tismess said, rather more nastily than it had intended. *Reify*, it had thought, urgently.

Heaviness hung, undiminished.

"What is there to fear?" Again, trying to flense the tone of nastiness, chagrined at its incivility, the velv whimpered and stared at the great helix, receptors clouding as the brightness fattened. The point of alarm had been reached and abandoned long since. "I am the last," it said.

"As is each of us," thought the ostren. "We are, each of us, the end of the line. Out of time, all time, the last. But why are you frightened?"

"Because ... it is the end. The question at last answered. There will be no more. No more I, no more you, no more of any living species. Does that not terrify you?"

"Yes," thought the ostren. "Yes. Yes, it does."

The tismess was silent.

"...NO MORE I, NO MORE YOU, NO MORE OF ANY LIVING SPECIES. DOES THAT NOT TERRIFY YOU?"

And the great helix solidified, its colors steadied, and the last three stared as only they were able, looking into the future, for the past and present were now gone, looking to see what would overwhelm them as they were vaporized, gone like their kind, gone forever, not even motes, not even memories. And they saw, the three last, absolutely perfect, beings; they saw what was to come.

"Oh, how good," whispered the velv, her tissues roiling most golden. "How wonderful. And I'm not afraid ... not now."

The ostren made the sound that very little children had once made when they had truly learned where

IN THAT INSTANT, HE SAW BACKWARD INTO MEMORY, BACKWARD INTO THE NIGHT THAT HAD PRECEDED THE FIRST THOUGHT.

the puppy farm is. But there was no fear, either, in the ostren.
For the tismess, as it was all coming to an end, suddenly there was what there was to be seen.

What was on the other side.

Before him, immediately before him, was the darkness. Heavy, breathing yet silent; it seemed to go on forever. But that *was* the other side. And beyond that darkness was something: something he could *call* the "other side." Could he see it, could he even imagine it, there had to *be* another side beyond this side. He reveled in the moment of knowledge that all there had ever been would go on, would start anew perhaps, would roll on through the final night, no matter how long. There *was* an "other side."

But, of course, in truth, what he was seeing was only another aspect of the only darkness—and not even darkness; nothing.

What he was seeing was every thought he had ever had, every song he had ever sung, everyone he had ever known, every moment of his trillion aeons, all and everything of memory; where he had stood, what he had done and what had been done around him, what there was and what there could ever have been.
In that instant, he saw backward into memory, backward into the night that had preceded the first thought.

Faraway, a galaxy became as dust, and vanished, leaving no print, no recollection, no residue. Then, one by one, in correct stately procession, the solitary stars went blind.

The question was answered: *Sat i sat bene.*

Running the unacceptable risk of writing an afterword oh by the way "note" a thousand times longer than the story itself, I sit down to explicate the "Bradbury connection" to this, perhaps my last-published story. Like Ray, I am now old, and there is an infinitude more to recollect and savor of links between Bradbury and Ellison. Truly, it should suffice for even the most marrowsucking obsessive fan that Ray and I have known each other close on forever.

Ray contends that in very short order he and I will be sitting down together cutting-up-touches with Dickens and Dorothy Parker, shuckin' n' jivin' with Aesop and Melville.

Uh... well, okay, Ray, if you say so.

(I am rather less condolent with that Hereafter stuff than is Ray. As has averred Nat Hentoff, I come from, and remain as one with, a grand and glorious tradition of stiff-necked Jewish Atheists. Ray and I have a long-standing wager on this one, which of us is on the money, and which is betting on a lame pony. Sadly, the winner will never collect.)

HARLAN ELLISON®
TALKS ABOUT
WEARINESS

La-dee-dah. Back where we began. Too many words, yet I'll attempt that undanceable rigadoon.

These days of the electronic babble, every doofus with some hand-held device calls every other male he knows "brother."

"Hey, Bro! Whussup, Bro? Howzit goin', Bro?"

Strangers: brother. Casual acquaintances: brother. Same skin color supermarket bagger: brother. Other skin-colored guy who tipped you when you parked his Beamer: brother. Much like the oafishly careless, empty, and repetitious whomping of the once-specific, cherished and singular word "awesome," the sacred word BROTHER has become in inept mouths, a dull and wearisome trope.

(Awesome is the word one uses for Eleanor Roosevelt, Mt. Kilimanjaro, and pitching a no-hit no-run ballgame. Not available for the crappy cheese quesadilla you had this afternoon, or for anybody who Dances with the Stars. With or without a wooden leg.) Same goes for yo **Bruth**-thuh.

I had only one sib, my late sister. The men of my lifelong existence whom I would countenance as my brother are less than the number of dactyls on my left hand, and they know who they are. Apparently, Ray Bradbury and I are *brothers*.

Not in some absurd catch-all absurdity of vacuous gibber, but actually and really "we are brothers." Whence cometh this assertion?

From Ray Bradbury. That's whence.

"You know, Harlan," he said to me, leaning in and grinning that Midwestern just-fell-off-the-turnip-truck grin, "we are brothers, y'know; you and I, together."

I grinned back at him with *my* hayseed Midwestern mien, onaccounta we are both paid liars, one from Waukegan and one from Cleveland, and I played his straight-man by responding, "How's that, Ray?" (The players freeze *in situ* as the Bloviating Narrator fills in the background data, thus slowing the movie and thus shamefacedly doing the necessary bricklaying:)

The table across which Ray was leaning was in a booth at one of my and Ray's all-time favorite restaurants, The Pacific Dining Car in downtown Los Angeles. The night was in 1965. Our dining companions had both gone off to the toilets. That is to say, she had gone off to one; her husband had gone off to another. Her name was Leigh Bracket; his name was Edmond Hamilton. The queen of fantasy writing. Great movies based on Hammett and Chandler. A legend in this life. The Eric John Stark Stories. A kind and imperially gracious woman. One of the best people ever known to me. Ed looked like something out of *American Gothic*. They called him Galaxy Smasher—the true creator of the space opera. Dozens and dozens of stories all the way back to the advent of Gernsbach: The Star King series. All those great comic books, and the Captain Future pulp novelettes. Droll, cosmically smart, one helluva plotter, and kind to tots like me and Ray. They were the Strophe and Antistrophe of our literary infancy. So, they're gone, Bradbury and I are alone, grinnin' & schmoosin' and he proceeds to explain to me that he and I are *brothers*. Not my word, *his* word. (Not to make this too clear, but I have a chasmlike abomination of bloviating SF fans who, upon the death of someone they once met in an elevator, begin to leak like WikiAnything, just to buy themselves the face-time at a memorial. "Oh, yes, I knew Isaac as if he were my 'brother...' / "Oh, lawdy, I pluckt up rootabuggas with Cliff Simak in de fields..." / "Yes, Octavia Butler and I were ever so close...") This unlikely story I tell actually happened. Go ask Bradbury if you think I'm fudging it. But better hurry...

Anyhow, I says back to him, "How's that, Ray?"

And he says back to me, "Them."

And I says to him, "Ed and Leigh?"

And he says back to me, "Our father and mother. They raised us." I have no memory of the rest of the actual verbiage,

Well, Sir, wasn't that a keen moment!

You see, I was working at Paramount at the time, on one or another of the crippled creations Rouse and Greene had hired me to do for vast sums of money (I was in my "hot 15" at the time.) And Leigh, whom I'd known since my teens in Ohio, was writing a dog for Howard Hawks called *Red Line 7000*, starring James Caan, (who, coincidentally, played the role of "Harlan Ellison" in an *Alfred Hitchcock Hour* based on my *Memos From Purgatory* only a year or so earlier). Also at Paramount.

Our offices were near to hand.

...ay doesn't drive. I drive. Every time we both got booked into the same lecture gig at some jerkwater literary potlatch, I drove. Bradbury lectured.

Me, he lectured. (Our politics are about as close as our faiths.)

So, I was always the wheelman on the caper.

Leigh didn't have (what she used to call, to mock James M. Cain) a "short" that night, and I can't remember what Ed's story was. But I wound up doing the driving down to the Pacific Dining Car, and we left straight from the studio. Ray must've come by cab: he met us at the Bronson Gate, and I did my thing downtown for a good big T-bone dinner. Also Bermuda onion, Rondo Hatton's-jaw sized tomatoes with Roquefort dressing, and Zucchini Florentine. Ray drank; I never touch the stuff. We had an

absolutely nova-squooshing dinner.

Thus, before I run on at greater length, the answer to the question "Can you reminisce a bit about your Ray Bradbury connection?" is frozen in Ray's asserveration: we're brothers.

He said so.

But, not to make a big foofaraw of it, Ray has trouble remembering who I am, and who Harlan Ellison is. And then, he'll remember, howl "Live Forever!" or somesuch impossibility at me, and recall me as "Ah, yes, the 'Terrible-Tempered Mr. Bang.'" And I'll smile wanly, and scream back at him, "*Nothing* lives forever, Ray, you crazy old coot! Not the Great Pyramid of Gizah, not the Polar ice caps, not a single blade of green grass, you nut-bag!"

And that is the link between us, the "connection." Nobody ever writ it large on the Northern massif of Mt. Shazam...

You gotta **agree** with your brother.

You just got to love him.

HARLAN ELLISON

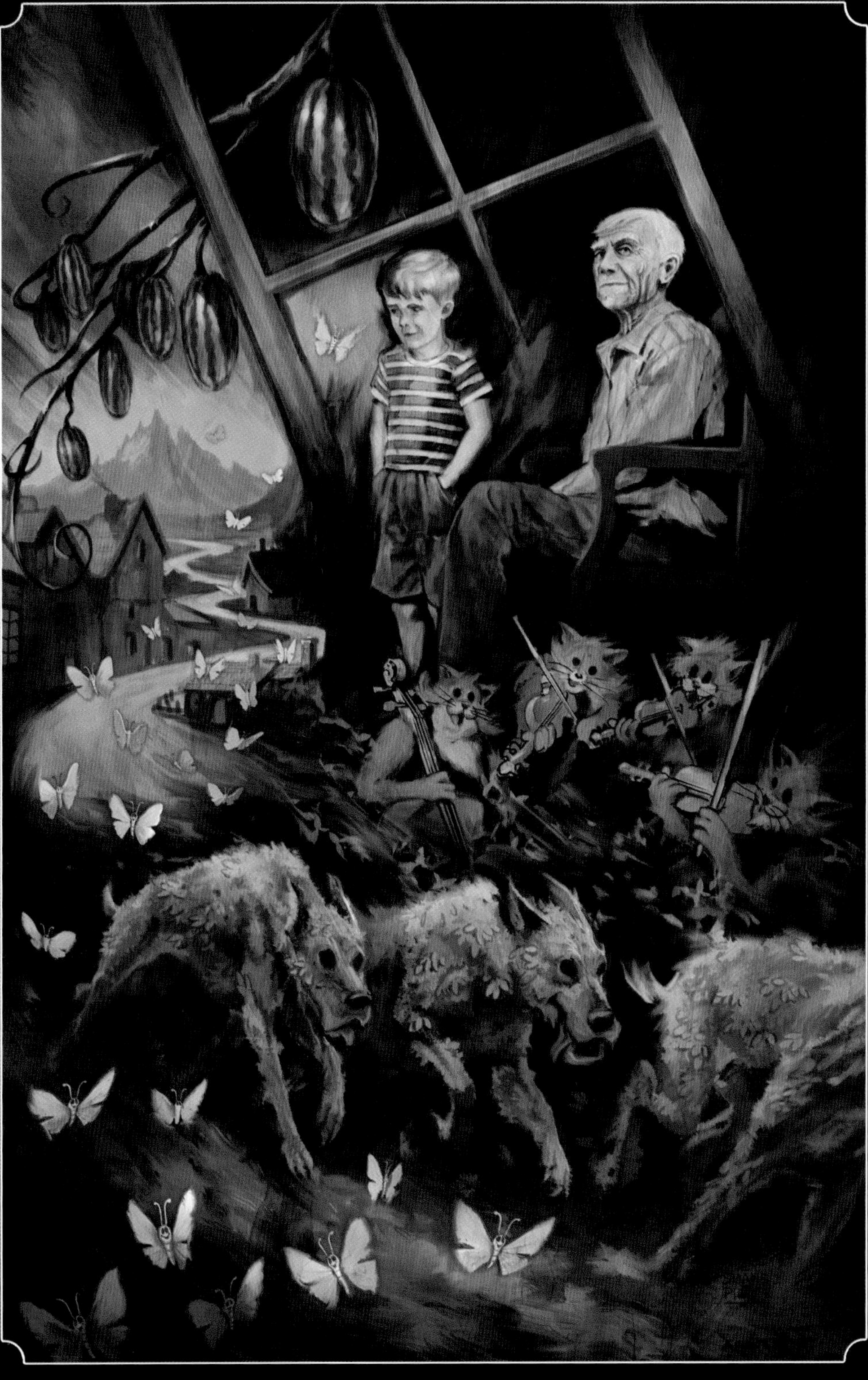

art by SHANE PIERCE

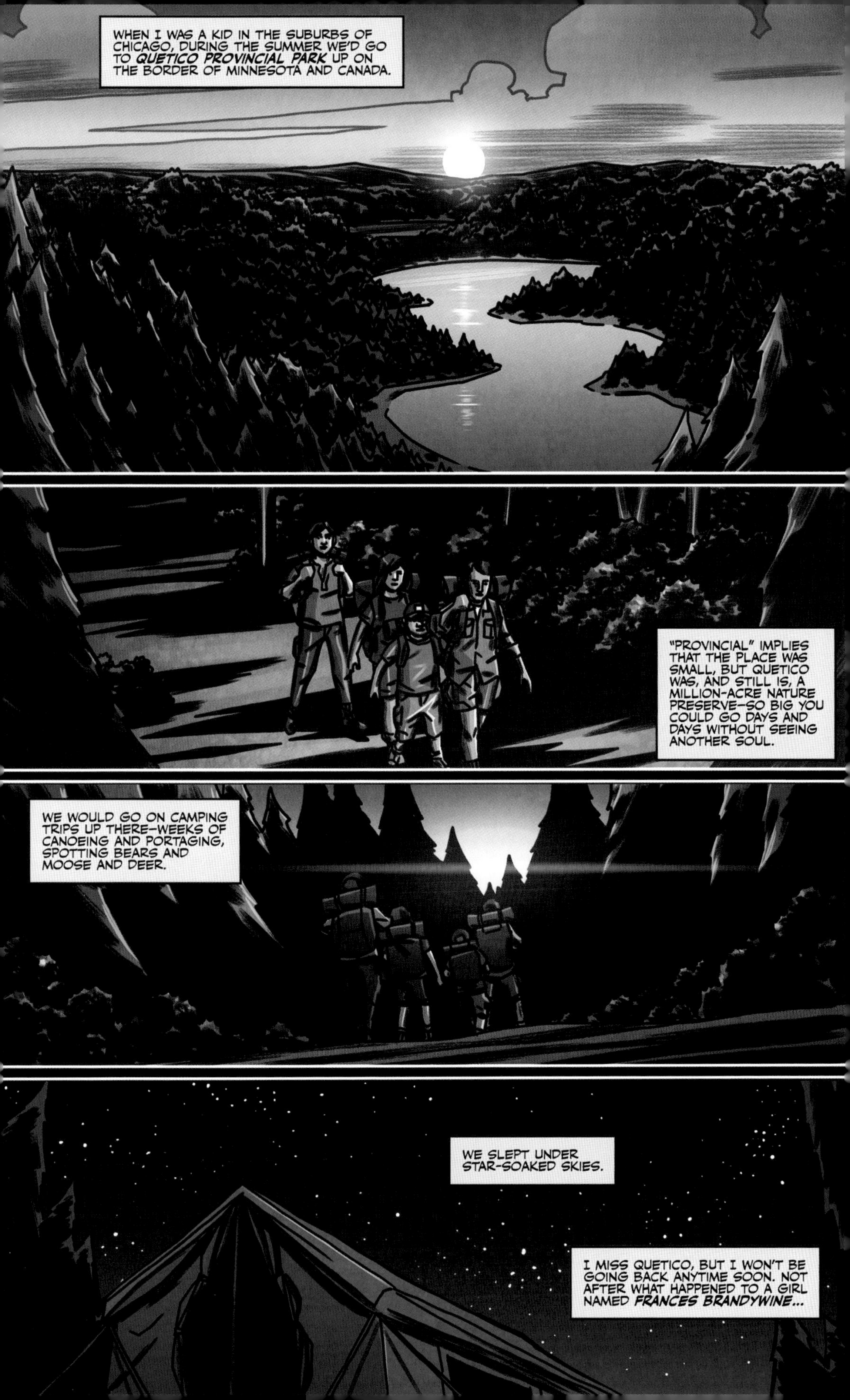
WHEN I WAS A KID IN THE SUBURBS OF CHICAGO, DURING THE SUMMER WE'D GO TO QUETICO PROVINCIAL PARK UP ON THE BORDER OF MINNESOTA AND CANADA.
"PROVINCIAL" IMPLIES THAT THE PLACE WAS SMALL, BUT QUETICO WAS, AND STILL IS, A MILLION-ACRE NATURE PRESERVE—SO BIG YOU COULD GO DAYS AND DAYS WITHOUT SEEING ANOTHER SOUL.
WE WOULD GO ON CAMPING TRIPS UP THERE—WEEKS OF CANOEING AND PORTAGING, SPOTTING BEARS AND MOOSE AND DEER.
WE SLEPT UNDER STAR-SOAKED SKIES.
I MISS QUETICO, BUT I WON'T BE GOING BACK ANYTIME SOON. NOT AFTER WHAT HAPPENED TO A GIRL NAMED FRANCES BRANDYWINE...

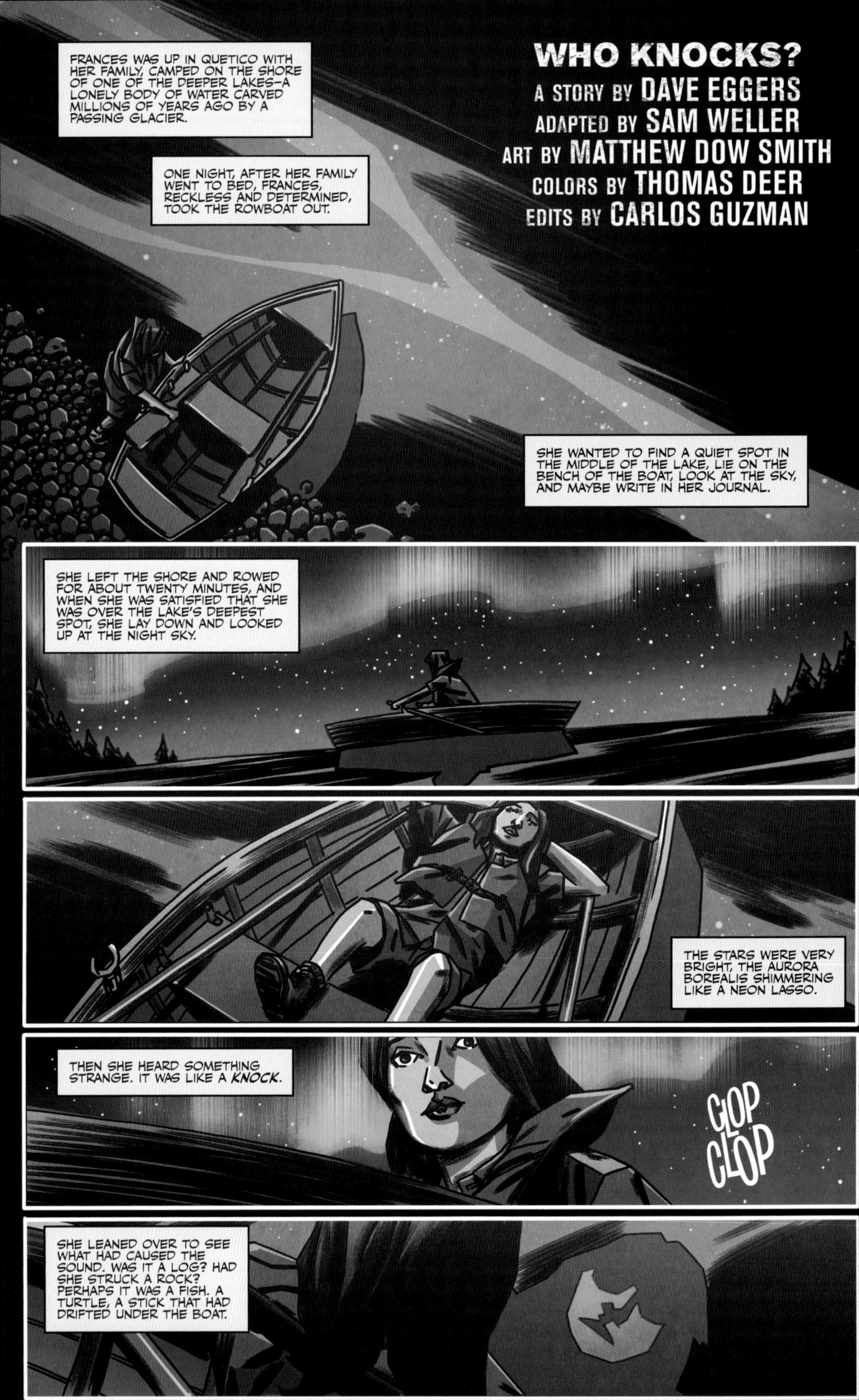
FRANCES WAS UP IN QUETICO WITH HER FAMILY, CAMPED ON THE SHORE OF ONE OF THE DEEPER LAKES—A LONELY BODY OF WATER CARVED MILLIONS OF YEARS AGO BY A PASSING GLACIER.
WHO KNOCKS?
A STORY BY DAVE EGGERS
ADAPTED BY SAM WELLER
ART BY MATTHEW DOW SMITH
COLORS BY THOMAS DEER
EDITS BY CARLOS GUZMAN
ONE NIGHT, AFTER HER FAMILY WENT TO BED, FRANCES, RECKLESS AND DETERMINED, TOOK THE ROWBOAT OUT.
SHE WANTED TO FIND A QUIET SPOT IN THE MIDDLE OF THE LAKE, LIE ON THE BENCH OF THE BOAT, LOOK AT THE SKY, AND MAYBE WRITE IN HER JOURNAL.
SHE LEFT THE SHORE AND ROWED FOR ABOUT TWENTY MINUTES, AND WHEN SHE WAS SATISFIED THAT SHE WAS OVER THE LAKE'S DEEPEST SPOT, SHE LAY DOWN AND LOOKED UP AT THE NIGHT SKY.
THE STARS WERE VERY BRIGHT, THE AURORA BOREALIS SHIMMERING LIKE A NEON LASSO.
THEN SHE HEARD SOMETHING STRANGE. IT WAS LIKE A *KNOCK*.
CLOP CLOP
SHE LEANED OVER TO SEE WHAT HAD CAUSED THE SOUND. WAS IT A LOG? HAD SHE STRUCK A ROCK? PERHAPS IT WAS A FISH. A TURTLE, A STICK THAT HAD DRIFTED UNDER THE BOAT.

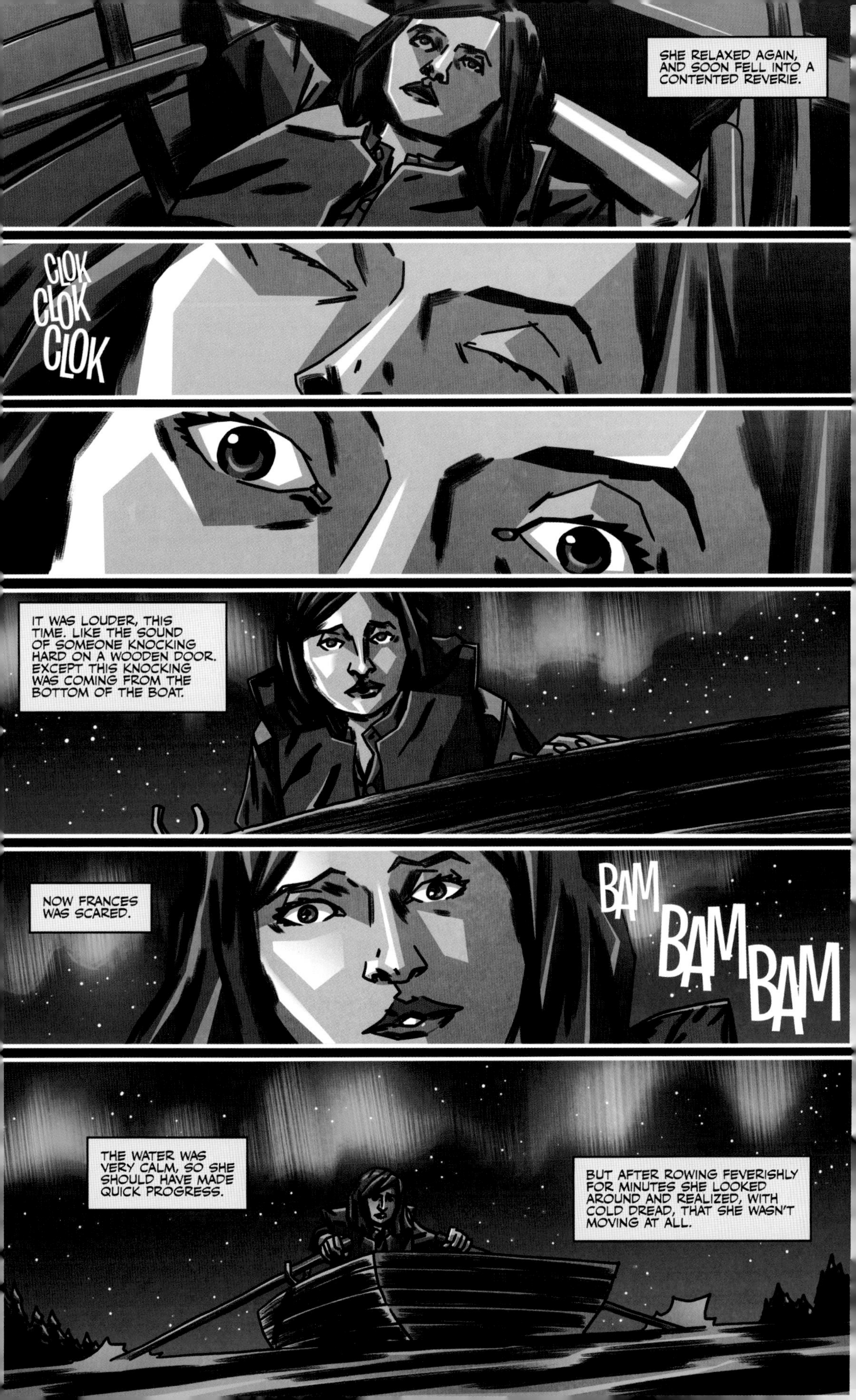
SHE RELAXED AGAIN, AND SOON FELL INTO A CONTENTED REVERIE.
CLOK CLOK CLOK
IT WAS LOUDER, THIS TIME. LIKE THE SOUND OF SOMEONE KNOCKING HARD ON A WOODEN DOOR. EXCEPT THIS KNOCKING WAS COMING FROM THE BOTTOM OF THE BOAT.
NOW FRANCES WAS SCARED.
BAM BAM BAM
THE WATER WAS VERY CALM, SO SHE SHOULD HAVE MADE QUICK PROGRESS.
BUT AFTER ROWING FEVERISHLY FOR MINUTES SHE LOOKED AROUND AND REALIZED, WITH COLD DREAD, THAT SHE WASN'T MOVING AT ALL.

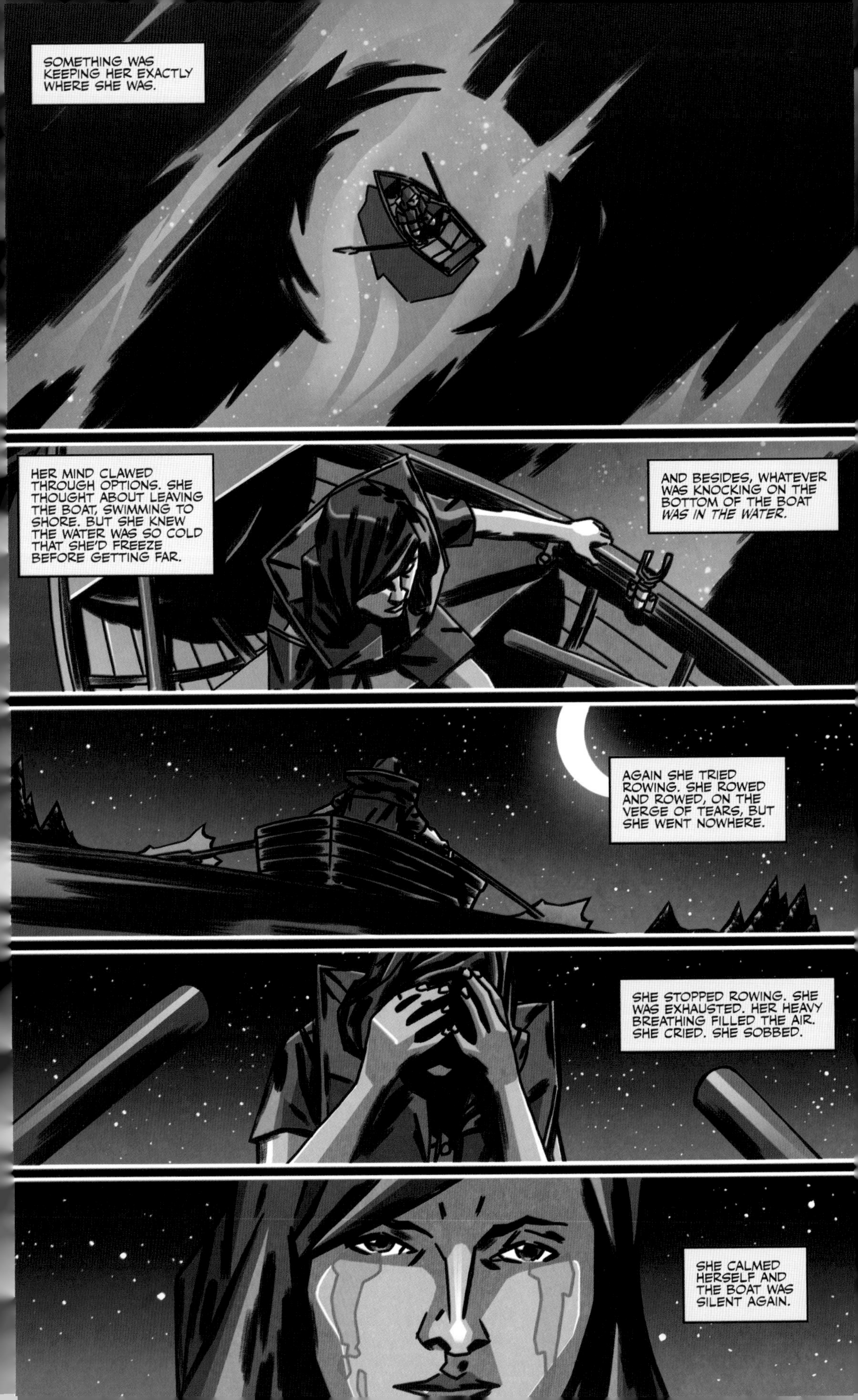
SOMETHING WAS KEEPING HER EXACTLY WHERE SHE WAS.
HER MIND CLAWED THROUGH OPTIONS. SHE THOUGHT ABOUT LEAVING THE BOAT, SWIMMING TO SHORE. BUT SHE KNEW THE WATER WAS SO COLD THAT SHE'D FREEZE BEFORE GETTING FAR.
AND BESIDES, WHATEVER WAS KNOCKING ON THE BOTTOM OF THE BOAT *WAS IN THE WATER.*
AGAIN SHE TRIED ROWING. SHE ROWED AND ROWED, ON THE VERGE OF TEARS, BUT SHE WENT NOWHERE.
SHE STOPPED ROWING. SHE WAS EXHAUSTED. HER HEAVY BREATHING FILLED THE AIR. SHE CRIED. SHE SOBBED.
SHE CALMED HERSELF AND THE BOAT WAS SILENT AGAIN.

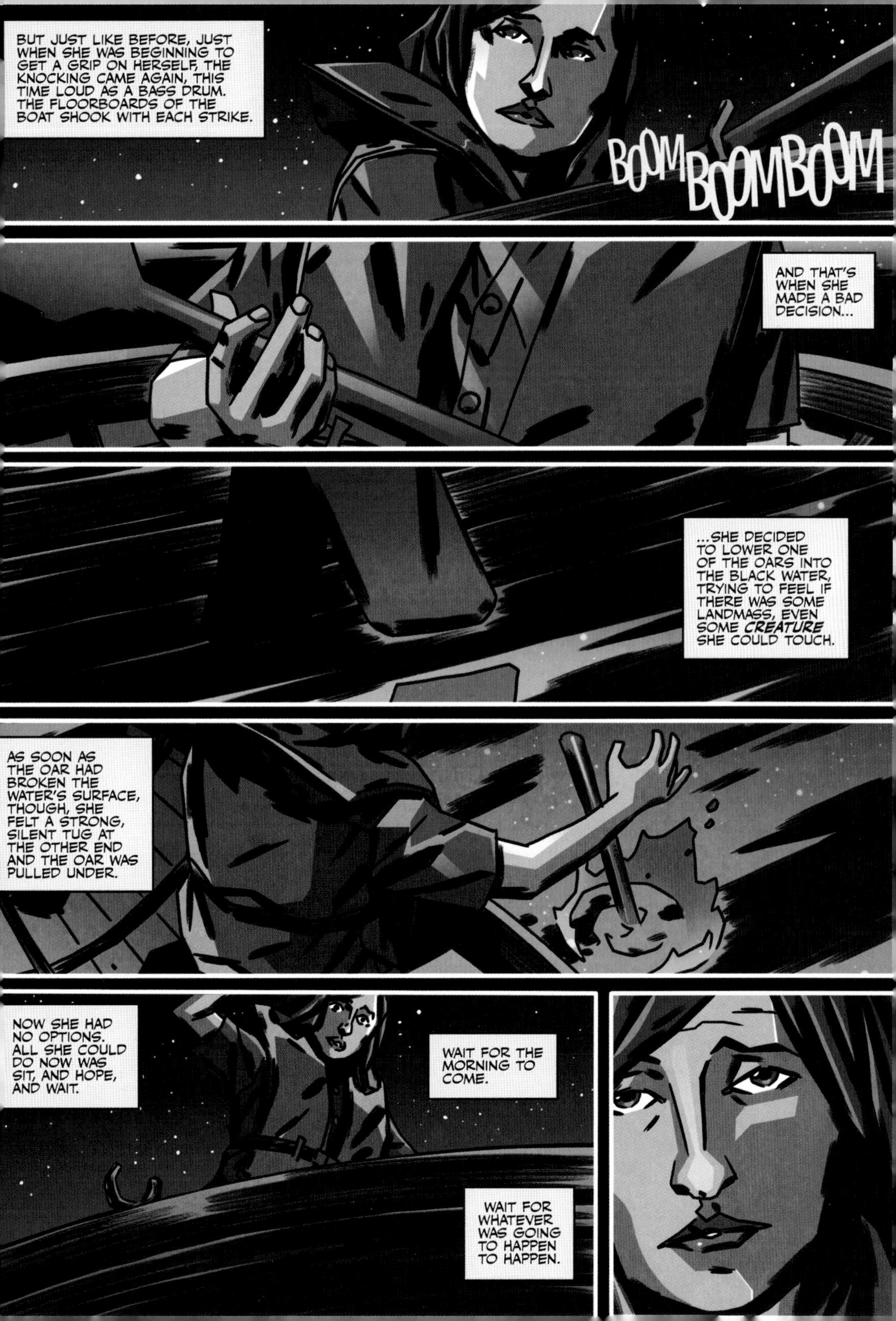

BUT JUST LIKE BEFORE, JUST WHEN SHE WAS BEGINNING TO GET A GRIP ON HERSELF, THE KNOCKING CAME AGAIN, THIS TIME LOUD AS A BASS DRUM. THE FLOORBOARDS OF THE BOAT SHOOK WITH EACH STRIKE.
BOOM BOOM BOOM
AND THAT'S WHEN SHE MADE A BAD DECISION...
...SHE DECIDED TO LOWER ONE OF THE OARS INTO THE BLACK WATER, TRYING TO FEEL IF THERE WAS SOME LANDMASS, EVEN SOME CREATURE SHE COULD TOUCH.
AS SOON AS THE OAR HAD BROKEN THE WATER'S SURFACE, THOUGH, SHE FELT A STRONG, SILENT TUG AT THE OTHER END AND THE OAR WAS PULLED UNDER.
NOW SHE HAD NO OPTIONS. ALL SHE COULD DO NOW WAS SIT, AND HOPE, AND WAIT.
WAIT FOR THE MORNING TO COME.
WAIT FOR WHATEVER WAS GOING TO HAPPEN TO HAPPEN.

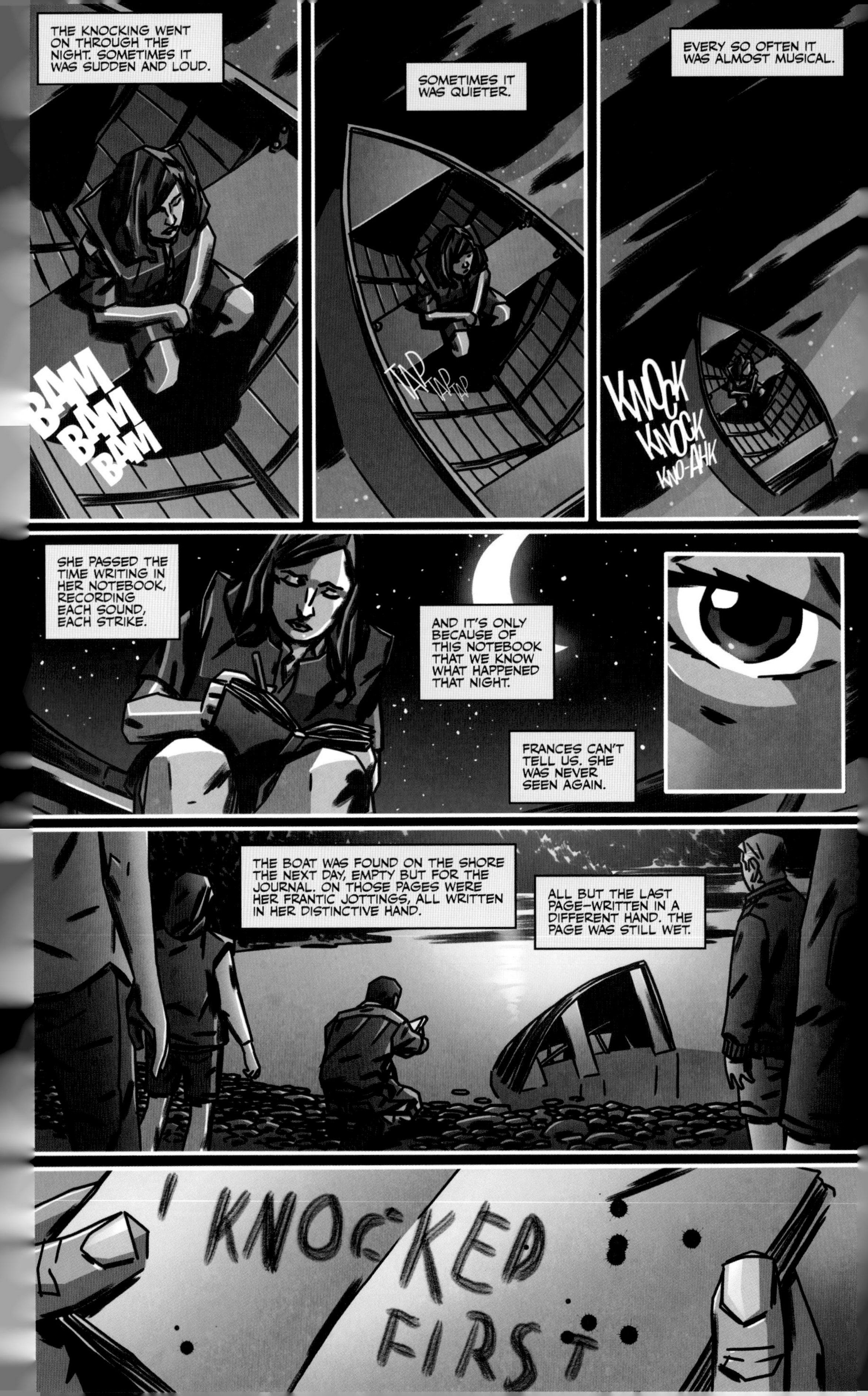
THE KNOCKING WENT ON THROUGH THE NIGHT. SOMETIMES IT WAS SUDDEN AND LOUD.
BAM BAM BAM
SOMETIMES IT WAS QUIETER.
TAP TAP TAP
EVERY SO OFTEN IT WAS ALMOST MUSICAL.
KNOCK KNOCK KNO-AHK
SHE PASSED THE TIME WRITING IN HER NOTEBOOK, RECORDING EACH SOUND, EACH STRIKE.
AND IT'S ONLY BECAUSE OF THIS NOTEBOOK THAT WE KNOW WHAT HAPPENED THAT NIGHT.
FRANCES CAN'T TELL US. SHE WAS NEVER SEEN AGAIN.
THE BOAT WAS FOUND ON THE SHORE THE NEXT DAY, EMPTY BUT FOR THE JOURNAL. ON THOSE PAGES WERE HER FRANTIC JOTTINGS, ALL WRITTEN IN HER DISTINCTIVE HAND.
ALL BUT THE LAST PAGE—WRITTEN IN A DIFFERENT HAND. THE PAGE WAS STILL WET.
I KNOCKED FIRST

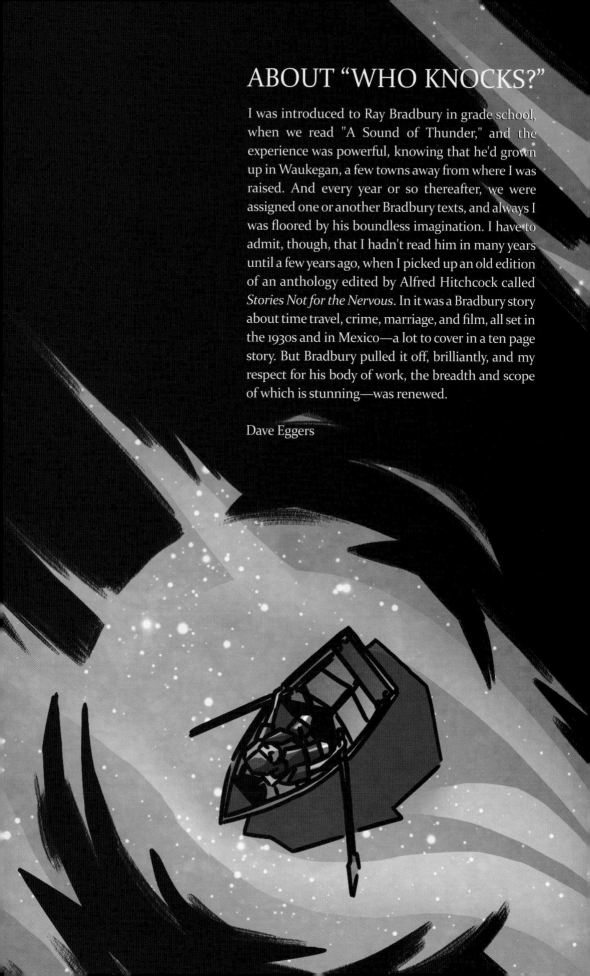

ABOUT "WHO KNOCKS?"

I was introduced to Ray Bradbury in grade school, when we read "A Sound of Thunder," and the experience was powerful, knowing that he'd grown up in Waukegan, a few towns away from where I was raised. And every year or so thereafter, we were assigned one or another Bradbury texts, and always I was floored by his boundless imagination. I have to admit, though, that I hadn't read him in many years until a few years ago, when I picked up an old edition of an anthology edited by Alfred Hitchcock called *Stories Not for the Nervous*. In it was a Bradbury story about time travel, crime, marriage, and film, all set in the 1930s and in Mexico—a lot to cover in a ten page story. But Bradbury pulled it off, brilliantly, and my respect for his body of work, the breadth and scope of which is stunning—was renewed.

Dave Eggers

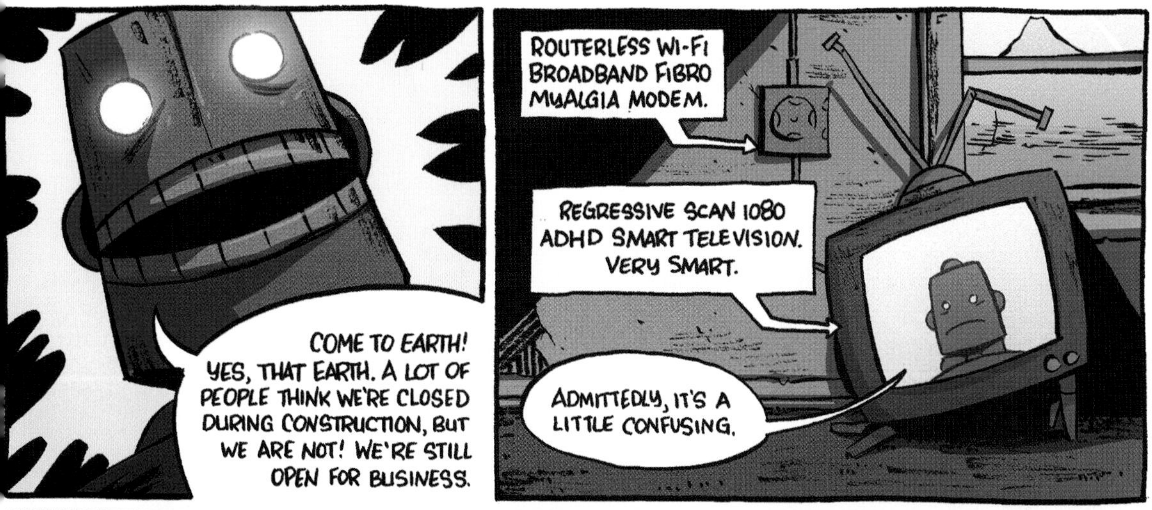
COME TO EARTH! YES, THAT EARTH. A LOT OF PEOPLE THINK WE'RE CLOSED DURING CONSTRUCTION, BUT WE ARE NOT! WE'RE STILL OPEN FOR BUSINESS.
ROUTERLESS WI-FI BROADBAND FIBRO MYALGIA MODEM.
REGRESSIVE SCAN 1080 ADHD SMART TELEVISION. VERY SMART.
ADMITTEDLY, IT'S A LITTLE CONFUSING.

HOKUM HOWKUM HISTORY PRESENTS:

EARTH: A GIFT SHOP

STORY BY CHARLES YU
SCRIPT BY MORT CASTLE
ART BY CHRISTINE LARSEN

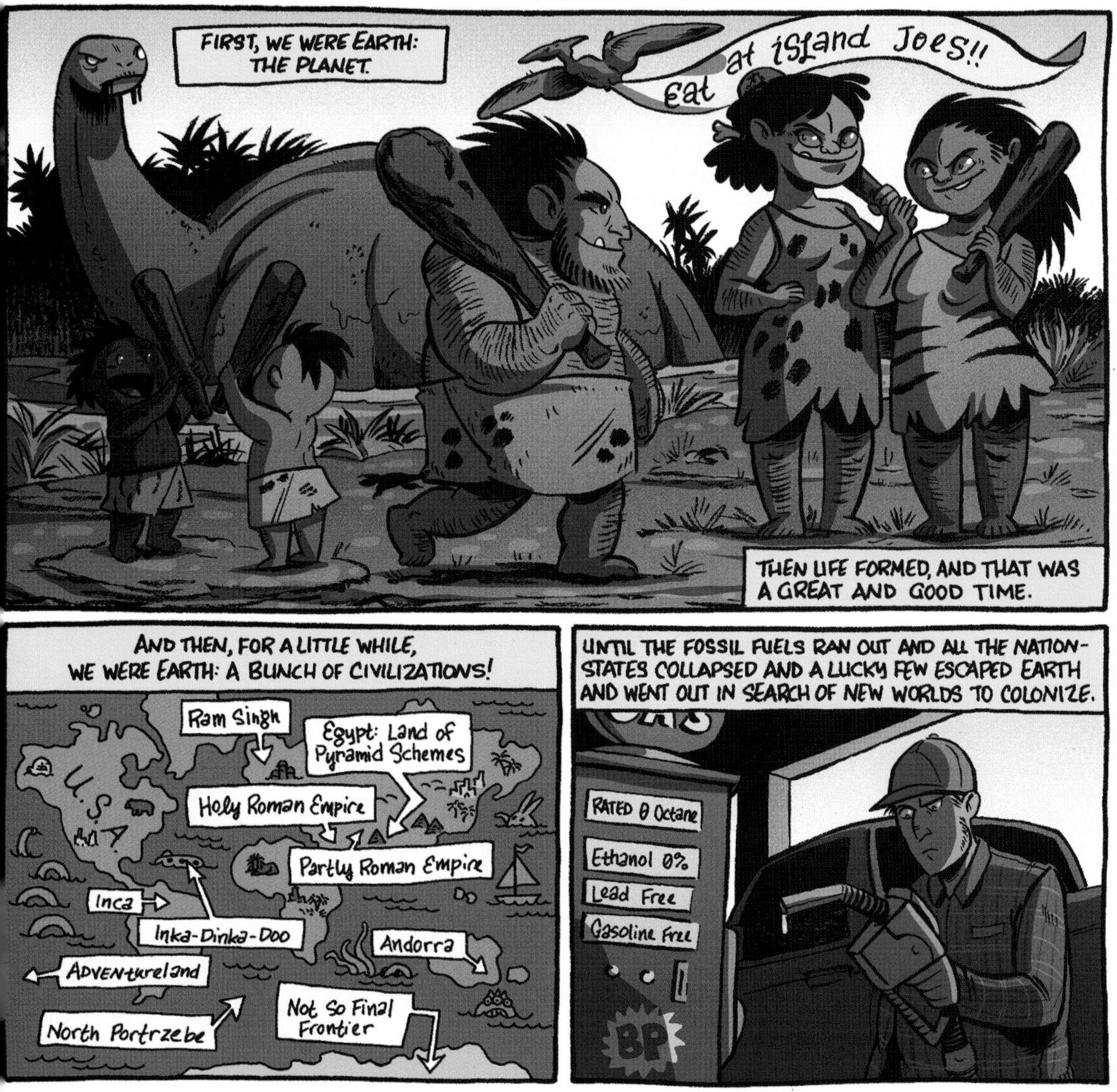
FIRST, WE WERE EARTH: THE PLANET.
eat at isLand Joes!!
THEN LIFE FORMED, AND THAT WAS A GREAT AND GOOD TIME.
AND THEN, FOR A LITTLE WHILE, WE WERE EARTH: A BUNCH OF CIVILIZATIONS!
Ram Singh
Egypt: Land of Pyramid Schemes
U.S.A.
Holy Roman Empire
Partly Roman Empire
Inca
Inka-Dinka-Doo
Andorra
Adventureland
Not So Final Frontier
North Portrzebe
UNTIL THE FOSSIL FUELS RAN OUT AND ALL THE NATION-STATES COLLAPSED AND A LUCKY FEW ESCAPED EARTH AND WENT OUT IN SEARCH OF NEW WORLDS TO COLONIZE.
RATED 0 Octane
Ethanol 0%
Lead Free
Gasoline Free
BP

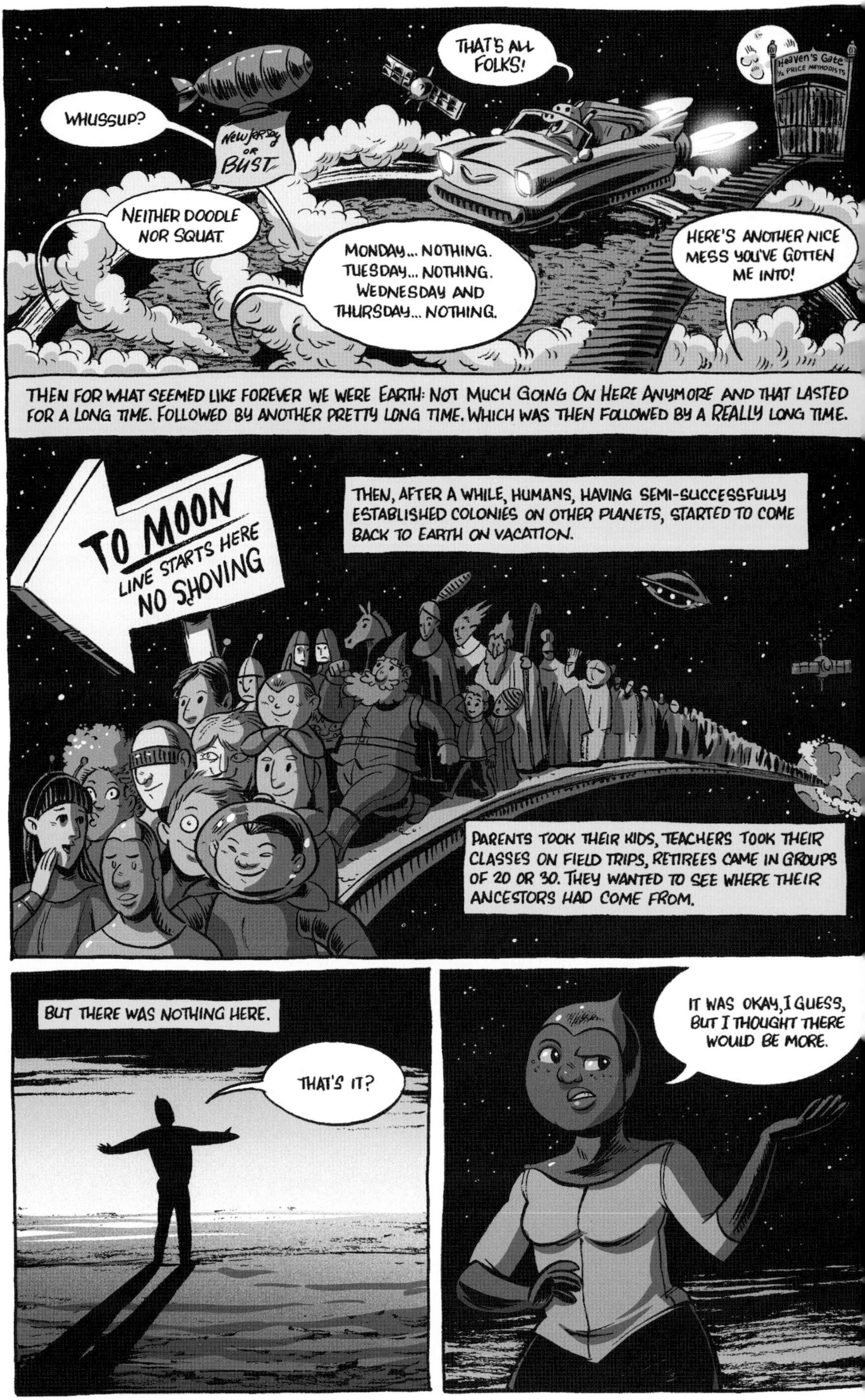
WHUSSUP?
New Jersey or BUST
NEITHER DOODLE NOR SQUAT.
THAT'S ALL FOLKS!
Heaven's Gate ½ PRICE METHODISTS
MONDAY... NOTHING. TUESDAY... NOTHING. WEDNESDAY AND THURSDAY... NOTHING.
HERE'S ANOTHER NICE MESS YOU'VE GOTTEN ME INTO!
THEN FOR WHAT SEEMED LIKE FOREVER WE WERE EARTH: NOT MUCH GOING ON HERE ANYMORE AND THAT LASTED FOR A LONG TIME. FOLLOWED BY ANOTHER PRETTY LONG TIME. WHICH WAS THEN FOLLOWED BY A REALLY LONG TIME.
TO MOON
LINE STARTS HERE
NO SHOVING
THEN, AFTER A WHILE, HUMANS, HAVING SEMI-SUCCESSFULLY ESTABLISHED COLONIES ON OTHER PLANETS, STARTED TO COME BACK TO EARTH ON VACATION.
PARENTS TOOK THEIR KIDS, TEACHERS TOOK THEIR CLASSES ON FIELD TRIPS, RETIREES CAME IN GROUPS OF 20 OR 30. THEY WANTED TO SEE WHERE THEIR ANCESTORS HAD COME FROM.
BUT THERE WAS NOTHING HERE.
THAT'S IT?
IT WAS OKAY, I GUESS, BUT I THOUGHT THERE WOULD BE MORE.

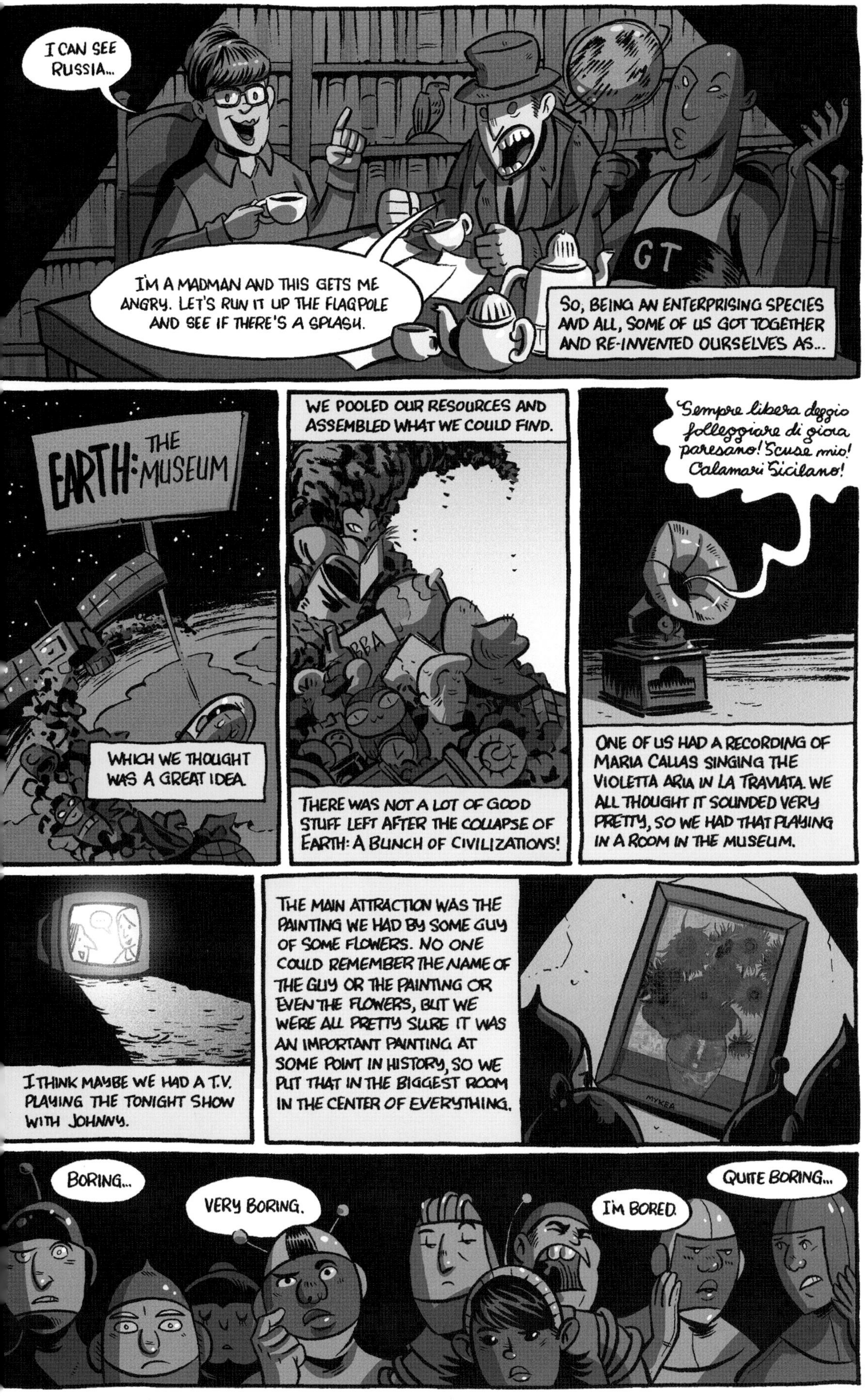
I CAN SEE RUSSIA...
I'M A MADMAN AND THIS GETS ME ANGRY. LET'S RUN IT UP THE FLAGPOLE AND SEE IF THERE'S A SPLASH.
GT
SO, BEING AN ENTERPRISING SPECIES AND ALL, SOME OF US GOT TOGETHER AND RE-INVENTED OURSELVES AS...
EARTH: THE MUSEUM
WHICH WE THOUGHT WAS A GREAT IDEA.
WE POOLED OUR RESOURCES AND ASSEMBLED WHAT WE COULD FIND.
THERE WAS NOT A LOT OF GOOD STUFF LEFT AFTER THE COLLAPSE OF EARTH: A BUNCH OF CIVILIZATIONS!
Sempre libera deggio folleggiare di gioia paresano! Scuse mio! Calamari Sicilano!
ONE OF US HAD A RECORDING OF MARIA CALLAS SINGING THE VIOLETTA ARIA IN LA TRAVIATA. WE ALL THOUGHT IT SOUNDED VERY PRETTY, SO WE HAD THAT PLAYING IN A ROOM IN THE MUSEUM.
I THINK MAYBE WE HAD A T.V. PLAYING THE TONIGHT SHOW WITH JOHNNY.
THE MAIN ATTRACTION WAS THE PAINTING WE HAD BY SOME GUY OF SOME FLOWERS. NO ONE COULD REMEMBER THE NAME OF THE GUY OR THE PAINTING OR EVEN THE FLOWERS, BUT WE WERE ALL PRETTY SURE IT WAS AN IMPORTANT PAINTING AT SOME POINT IN HISTORY, SO WE PUT THAT IN THE BIGGEST ROOM IN THE CENTER OF EVERYTHING.
MYKEA
BORING...
VERY BORING.
I'M BORED.
QUITE BORING...

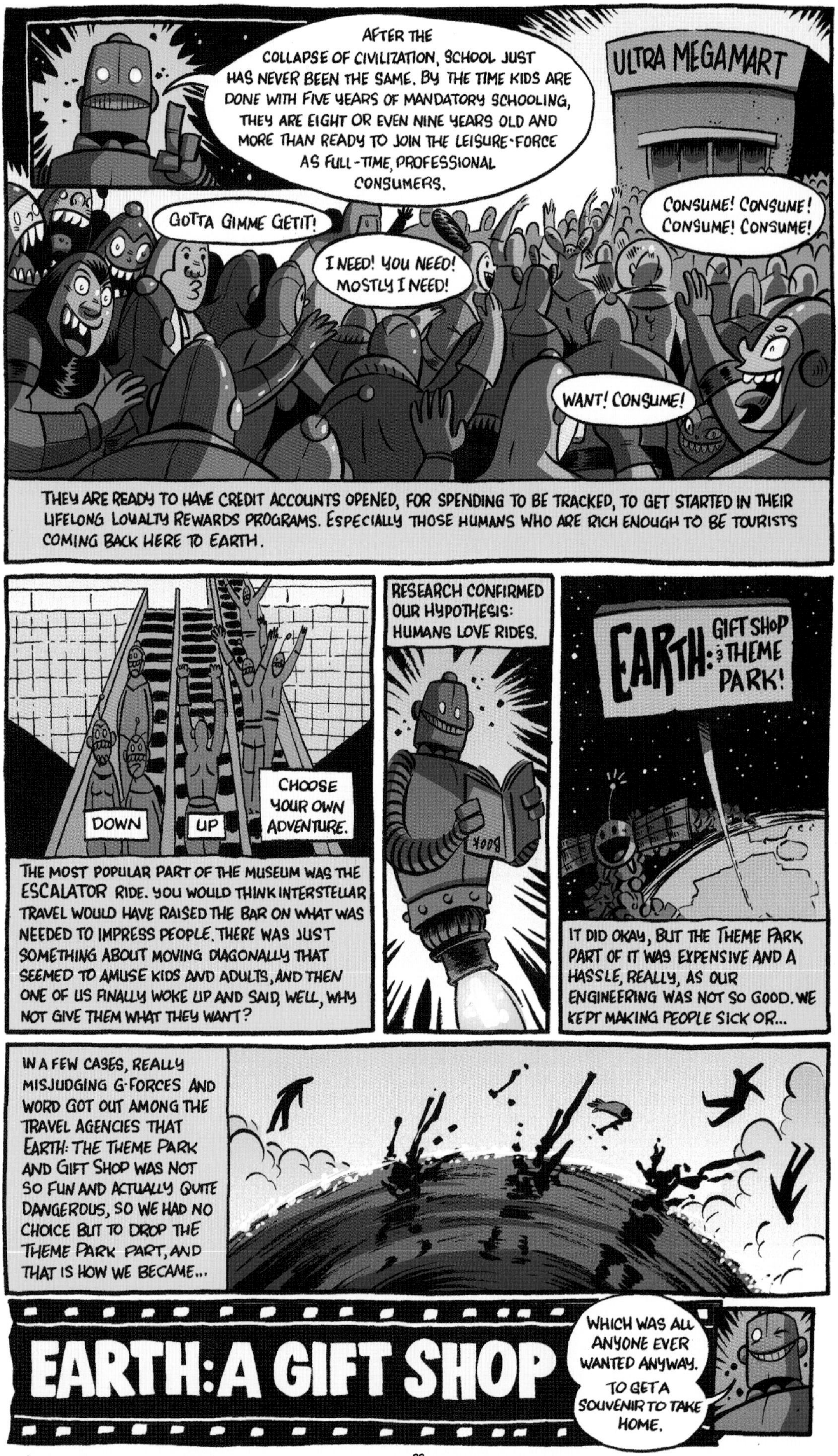
AFTER THE COLLAPSE OF CIVILIZATION, SCHOOL JUST HAS NEVER BEEN THE SAME. BY THE TIME KIDS ARE DONE WITH FIVE YEARS OF MANDATORY SCHOOLING, THEY ARE EIGHT OR EVEN NINE YEARS OLD AND MORE THAN READY TO JOIN THE LEISURE-FORCE AS FULL-TIME, PROFESSIONAL CONSUMERS.
ULTRA MEGAMART
GOTTA GIMME GETIT!
I NEED! YOU NEED! MOSTLY I NEED!
CONSUME! CONSUME! CONSUME! CONSUME!
WANT! CONSUME!
THEY ARE READY TO HAVE CREDIT ACCOUNTS OPENED, FOR SPENDING TO BE TRACKED, TO GET STARTED IN THEIR LIFELONG LOYALTY REWARDS PROGRAMS. ESPECIALLY THOSE HUMANS WHO ARE RICH ENOUGH TO BE TOURISTS COMING BACK HERE TO EARTH.
DOWN
UP
CHOOSE YOUR OWN ADVENTURE.
THE MOST POPULAR PART OF THE MUSEUM WAS THE ESCALATOR RIDE. YOU WOULD THINK INTERSTELLAR TRAVEL WOULD HAVE RAISED THE BAR ON WHAT WAS NEEDED TO IMPRESS PEOPLE. THERE WAS JUST SOMETHING ABOUT MOVING DIAGONALLY THAT SEEMED TO AMUSE KIDS AND ADULTS, AND THEN ONE OF US FINALLY WOKE UP AND SAID, WELL, WHY NOT GIVE THEM WHAT THEY WANT?
RESEARCH CONFIRMED OUR HYPOTHESIS: HUMANS LOVE RIDES.
BOOK
EARTH: GIFT SHOP & THEME PARK!
IT DID OKAY, BUT THE THEME PARK PART OF IT WAS EXPENSIVE AND A HASSLE, REALLY, AS OUR ENGINEERING WAS NOT SO GOOD. WE KEPT MAKING PEOPLE SICK OR...
IN A FEW CASES, REALLY MISJUDGING G-FORCES AND WORD GOT OUT AMONG THE TRAVEL AGENCIES THAT EARTH: THE THEME PARK AND GIFT SHOP WAS NOT SO FUN AND ACTUALLY QUITE DANGEROUS, SO WE HAD NO CHOICE BUT TO DROP THE THEME PARK PART, AND THAT IS HOW WE BECAME...
EARTH: A GIFT SHOP
WHICH WAS ALL ANYONE EVER WANTED ANYWAY.
TO GET A SOUVENIR TO TAKE HOME.

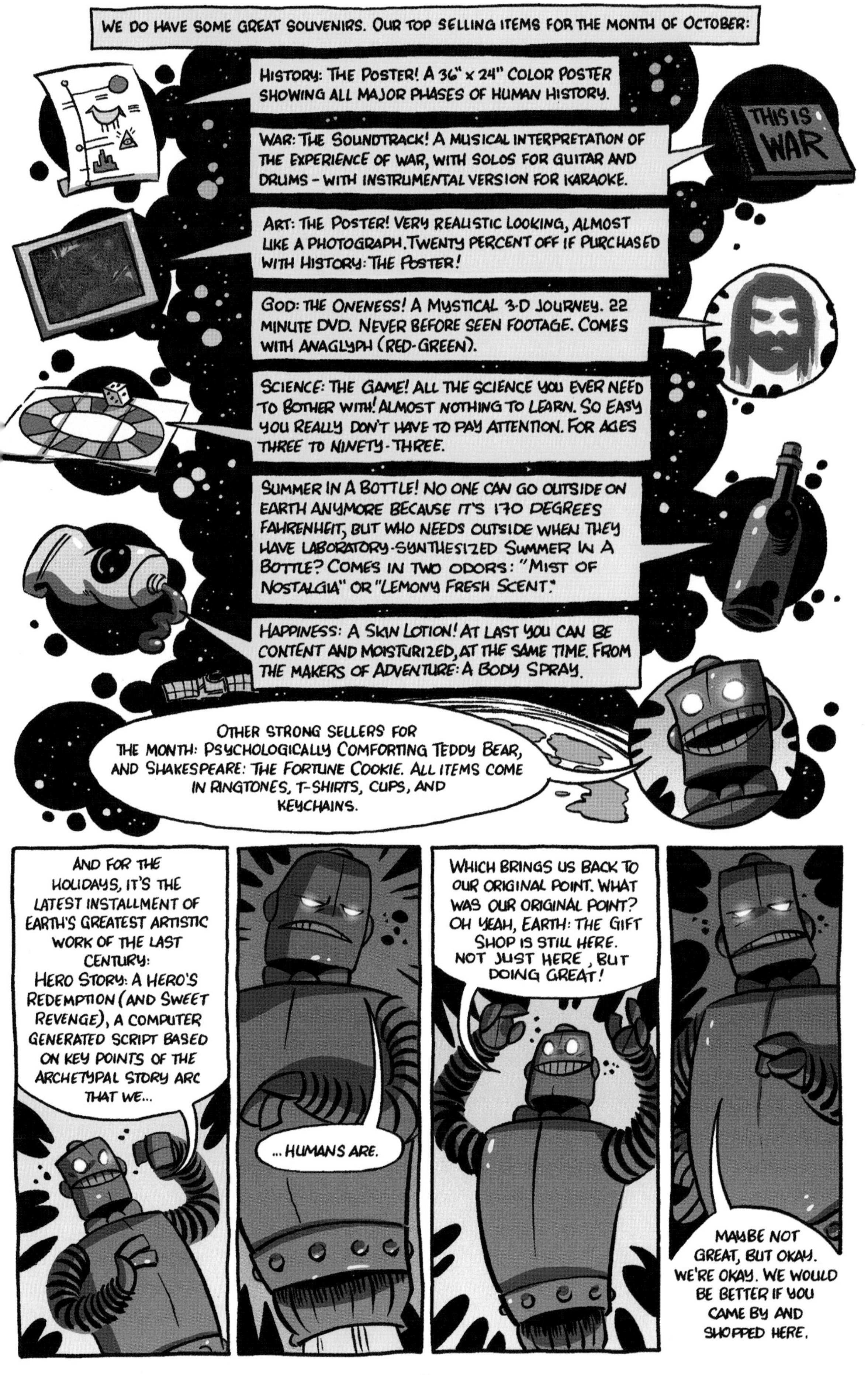

WE DO HAVE SOME GREAT SOUVENIRS. OUR TOP SELLING ITEMS FOR THE MONTH OF OCTOBER:
HISTORY: THE POSTER! A 36" x 24" COLOR POSTER SHOWING ALL MAJOR PHASES OF HUMAN HISTORY.
WAR: THE SOUNDTRACK! A MUSICAL INTERPRETATION OF THE EXPERIENCE OF WAR, WITH SOLOS FOR GUITAR AND DRUMS - WITH INSTRUMENTAL VERSION FOR KARAOKE.
THIS IS WAR
ART: THE POSTER! VERY REALISTIC LOOKING, ALMOST LIKE A PHOTOGRAPH. TWENTY PERCENT OFF IF PURCHASED WITH HISTORY: THE POSTER!
GOD: THE ONENESS! A MYSTICAL 3-D JOURNEY. 22 MINUTE DVD. NEVER BEFORE SEEN FOOTAGE. COMES WITH ANAGLYPH (RED-GREEN).
SCIENCE: THE GAME! ALL THE SCIENCE YOU EVER NEED TO BOTHER WITH! ALMOST NOTHING TO LEARN. SO EASY YOU REALLY DON'T HAVE TO PAY ATTENTION. FOR AGES THREE TO NINETY-THREE.
SUMMER IN A BOTTLE! NO ONE CAN GO OUTSIDE ON EARTH ANYMORE BECAUSE IT'S 170 DEGREES FAHRENHEIT, BUT WHO NEEDS OUTSIDE WHEN THEY HAVE LABORATORY-SYNTHESIZED SUMMER IN A BOTTLE? COMES IN TWO ODORS: "MIST OF NOSTALGIA" OR "LEMONY FRESH SCENT."
HAPPINESS: A SKIN LOTION! AT LAST YOU CAN BE CONTENT AND MOISTURIZED, AT THE SAME TIME. FROM THE MAKERS OF ADVENTURE: A BODY SPRAY.
OTHER STRONG SELLERS FOR THE MONTH: PSYCHOLOGICALLY COMFORTING TEDDY BEAR, AND SHAKESPEARE: THE FORTUNE COOKIE. ALL ITEMS COME IN RINGTONES, T-SHIRTS, CUPS, AND KEYCHAINS.
AND FOR THE HOLIDAYS, IT'S THE LATEST INSTALLMENT OF EARTH'S GREATEST ARTISTIC WORK OF THE LAST CENTURY: HERO STORY: A HERO'S REDEMPTION (AND SWEET REVENGE), A COMPUTER GENERATED SCRIPT BASED ON KEY POINTS OF THE ARCHETYPAL STORY ARC THAT WE...
... HUMANS ARE.
WHICH BRINGS US BACK TO OUR ORIGINAL POINT. WHAT WAS OUR ORIGINAL POINT? OH YEAH, EARTH: THE GIFT SHOP IS STILL HERE. NOT JUST HERE, BUT DOING GREAT!
MAYBE NOT GREAT, BUT OKAY. WE'RE OKAY. WE WOULD BE BETTER IF YOU CAME BY AND SHOPPED HERE.

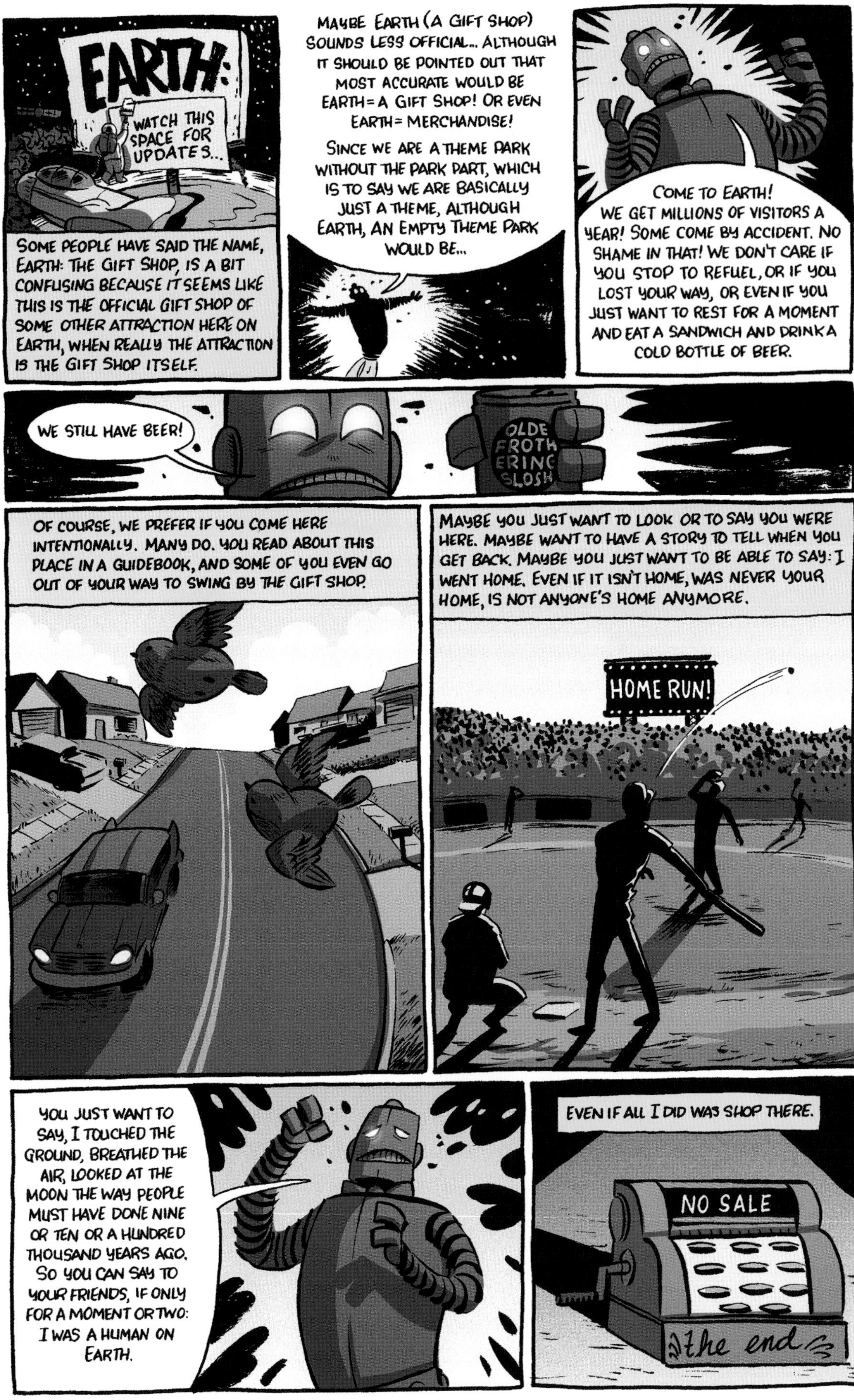
EARTH:
WATCH THIS SPACE FOR UPDATES...
SOME PEOPLE HAVE SAID THE NAME, EARTH: THE GIFT SHOP, IS A BIT CONFUSING BECAUSE IT SEEMS LIKE THIS IS THE OFFICIAL GIFT SHOP OF SOME OTHER ATTRACTION HERE ON EARTH, WHEN REALLY THE ATTRACTION IS THE GIFT SHOP ITSELF.
MAYBE EARTH (A GIFT SHOP) SOUNDS LESS OFFICIAL... ALTHOUGH IT SHOULD BE POINTED OUT THAT MOST ACCURATE WOULD BE EARTH = A GIFT SHOP! OR EVEN EARTH = MERCHANDISE!
SINCE WE ARE A THEME PARK WITHOUT THE PARK PART, WHICH IS TO SAY WE ARE BASICALLY JUST A THEME, ALTHOUGH EARTH, AN EMPTY THEME PARK WOULD BE...
COME TO EARTH! WE GET MILLIONS OF VISITORS A YEAR! SOME COME BY ACCIDENT. NO SHAME IN THAT! WE DON'T CARE IF YOU STOP TO REFUEL, OR IF YOU LOST YOUR WAY, OR EVEN IF YOU JUST WANT TO REST FOR A MOMENT AND EAT A SANDWICH AND DRINK A COLD BOTTLE OF BEER.
WE STILL HAVE BEER!
OLDE FROTHERING SLOSH
OF COURSE, WE PREFER IF YOU COME HERE INTENTIONALLY. MANY DO. YOU READ ABOUT THIS PLACE IN A GUIDEBOOK, AND SOME OF YOU EVEN GO OUT OF YOUR WAY TO SWING BY THE GIFT SHOP.
MAYBE YOU JUST WANT TO LOOK OR TO SAY YOU WERE HERE. MAYBE WANT TO HAVE A STORY TO TELL WHEN YOU GET BACK. MAYBE YOU JUST WANT TO BE ABLE TO SAY: I WENT HOME. EVEN IF IT ISN'T HOME, WAS NEVER YOUR HOME, IS NOT ANYONE'S HOME ANYMORE.
HOME RUN!
YOU JUST WANT TO SAY, I TOUCHED THE GROUND, BREATHED THE AIR, LOOKED AT THE MOON THE WAY PEOPLE MUST HAVE DONE NINE OR TEN OR A HUNDRED THOUSAND YEARS AGO. SO YOU CAN SAY TO YOUR FRIENDS, IF ONLY FOR A MOMENT OR TWO: I WAS A HUMAN ON EARTH.
EVEN IF ALL I DID WAS SHOP THERE.
NO SALE
the end

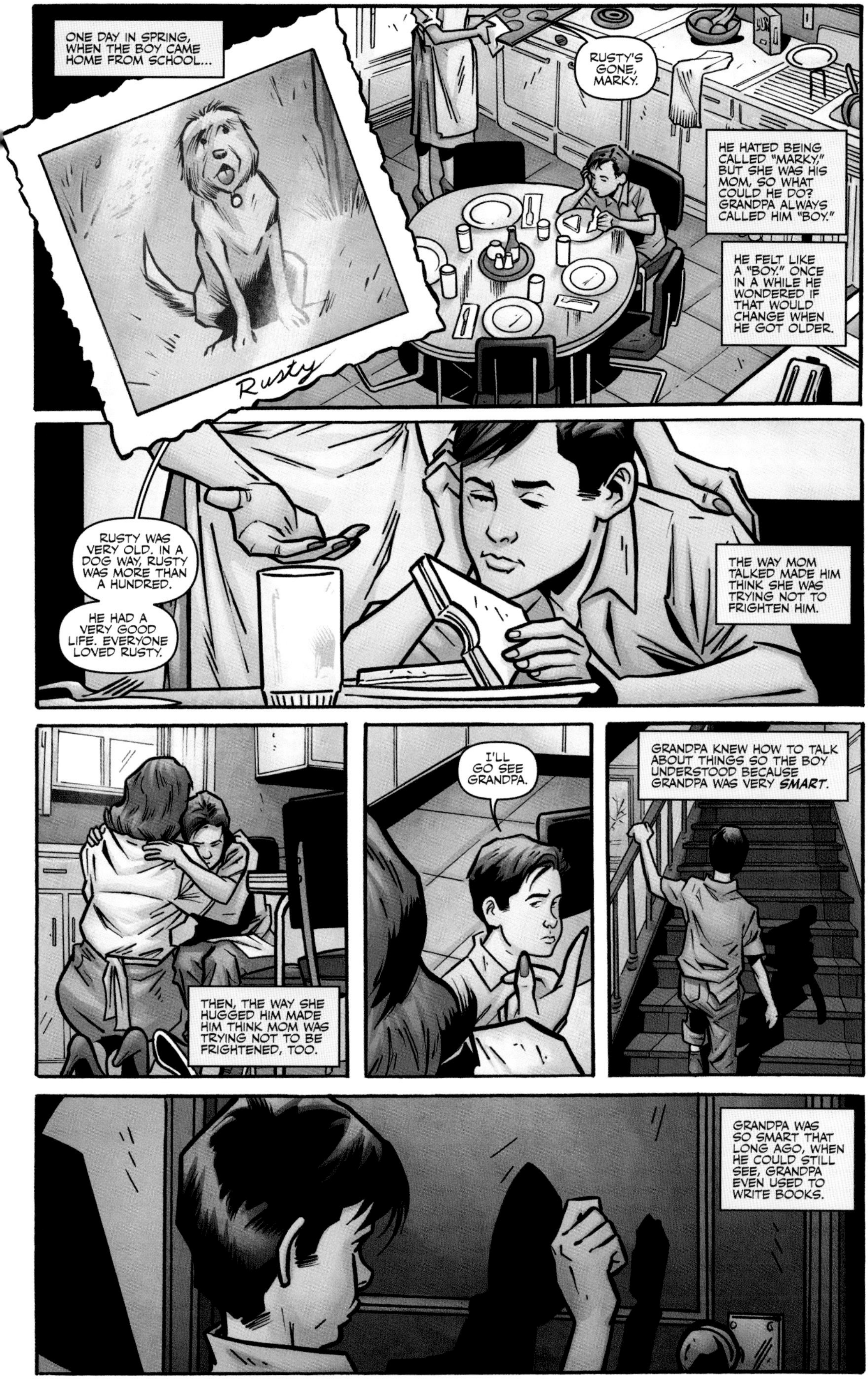
ONE DAY IN SPRING, WHEN THE BOY CAME HOME FROM SCHOOL...
Rusty
RUSTY'S GONE, MARKY.
HE HATED BEING CALLED "MARKY," BUT SHE WAS HIS MOM, SO WHAT COULD HE DO? GRANDPA ALWAYS CALLED HIM "BOY."
HE FELT LIKE A "BOY." ONCE IN A WHILE HE WONDERED IF THAT WOULD CHANGE WHEN HE GOT OLDER.
RUSTY WAS VERY OLD. IN A DOG WAY, RUSTY WAS MORE THAN A HUNDRED.
HE HAD A VERY GOOD LIFE. EVERYONE LOVED RUSTY.
THE WAY MOM TALKED MADE HIM THINK SHE WAS TRYING NOT TO FRIGHTEN HIM.
THEN, THE WAY SHE HUGGED HIM MADE HIM THINK MOM WAS TRYING NOT TO BE FRIGHTENED, TOO.
I'LL GO SEE GRANDPA.
GRANDPA KNEW HOW TO TALK ABOUT THINGS SO THE BOY UNDERSTOOD BECAUSE GRANDPA WAS VERY SMART.
GRANDPA WAS SO SMART THAT LONG AGO, WHEN HE COULD STILL SEE, GRANDPA EVEN USED TO WRITE BOOKS.

TUNK

TUNK

TUNK

HE KNOCKED ONE-TWO-THREE.
NEVER JUST ONE OR ONE-TWO,
OR ONE-TWO-THREE-FOUR. THAT
WAS THEIR SPECIAL KNOCK.

ENTER.

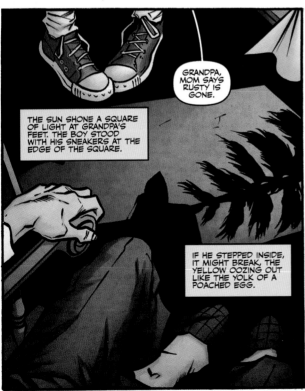

GRANDPA,
MOM SAYS
RUSTY IS
GONE.

THE SUN SHONE A SQUARE
OF LIGHT AT GRANDPA'S
FEET. THE BOY STOOD
WITH HIS SNEAKERS AT THE
EDGE OF THE SQUARE.

IF HE STEPPED INSIDE,
IT MIGHT BREAK, THE
YELLOW OOZING OUT
LIKE THE YOLK OF A
POACHED EGG.

YOUR MOTHER
IS TRUTHFUL
ENOUGH, THOUGH
SO SADLY LACKING
IN IMAGINATION IT'S
OFTEN DIFFICULT
FOR ME TO
ACKNOWLEDGE
HER AS MY
DAUGHTER.

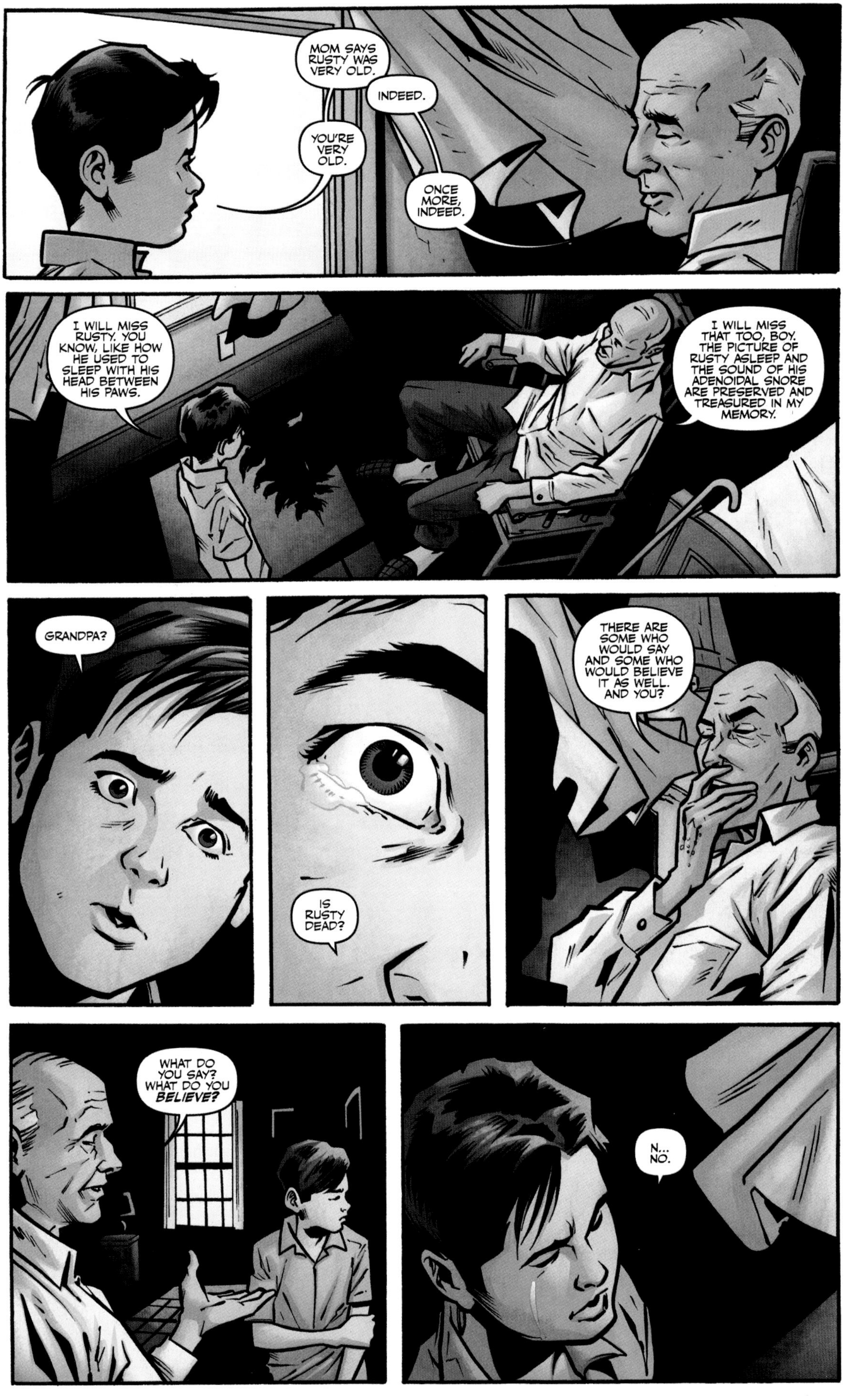
MOM SAYS RUSTY WAS VERY OLD.
INDEED.
YOU'RE VERY OLD.
ONCE MORE, INDEED.
I WILL MISS RUSTY. YOU KNOW, LIKE HOW HE USED TO SLEEP WITH HIS HEAD BETWEEN HIS PAWS.
I WILL MISS THAT TOO, BOY. THE PICTURE OF RUSTY ASLEEP AND THE SOUND OF HIS ADENOIDAL SNORE ARE PRESERVED AND TREASURED IN MY MEMORY.
GRANDPA?
IS RUSTY DEAD?
THERE ARE SOME WHO WOULD SAY AND SOME WHO WOULD BELIEVE IT AS WELL. AND YOU?
WHAT DO YOU SAY? WHAT DO YOU *BELIEVE?*
N... NO.

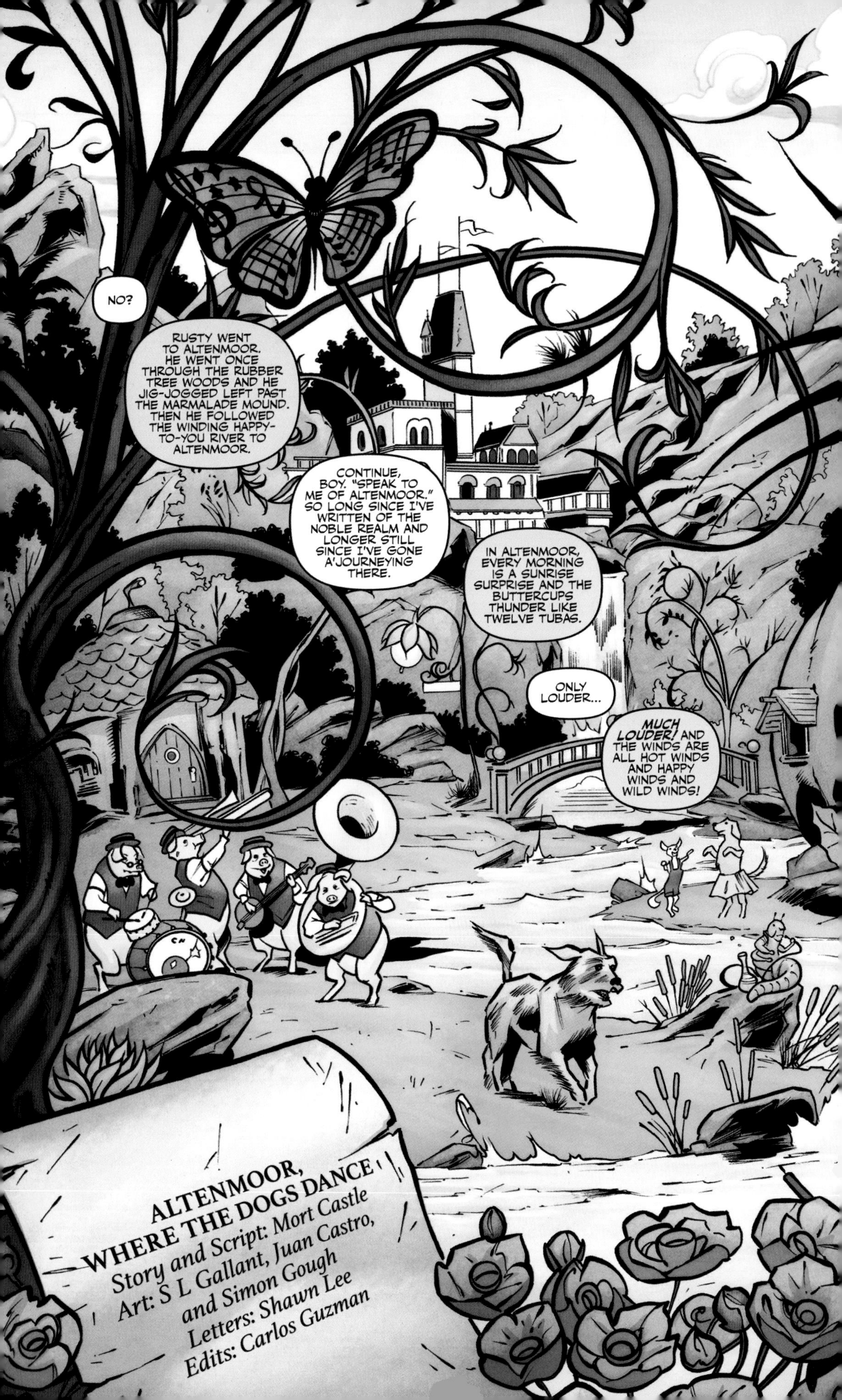

NO?
RUSTY WENT TO ALTENMOOR. HE WENT ONCE THROUGH THE RUBBER TREE WOODS AND HE JIG-JOGGED LEFT PAST THE MARMALADE MOUND. THEN HE FOLLOWED THE WINDING HAPPY-TO-YOU RIVER TO ALTENMOOR.
CONTINUE, BOY. "SPEAK TO ME OF ALTENMOOR." SO LONG SINCE I'VE WRITTEN OF THE NOBLE REALM AND LONGER STILL SINCE I'VE GONE A'JOURNEYING THERE.
IN ALTENMOOR, EVERY MORNING IS A SUNRISE SURPRISE AND THE BUTTERCUPS THUNDER LIKE TWELVE TUBAS.
ONLY LOUDER...
MUCH LOUDER! AND THE WINDS ARE ALL HOT WINDS AND HAPPY WINDS AND WILD WINDS!
ALTENMOOR, WHERE THE DOGS DANCE
Story and Script: Mort Castle
Art: S L Gallant, Juan Castro, and Simon Gough
Letters: Shawn Lee
Edits: Carlos Guzman

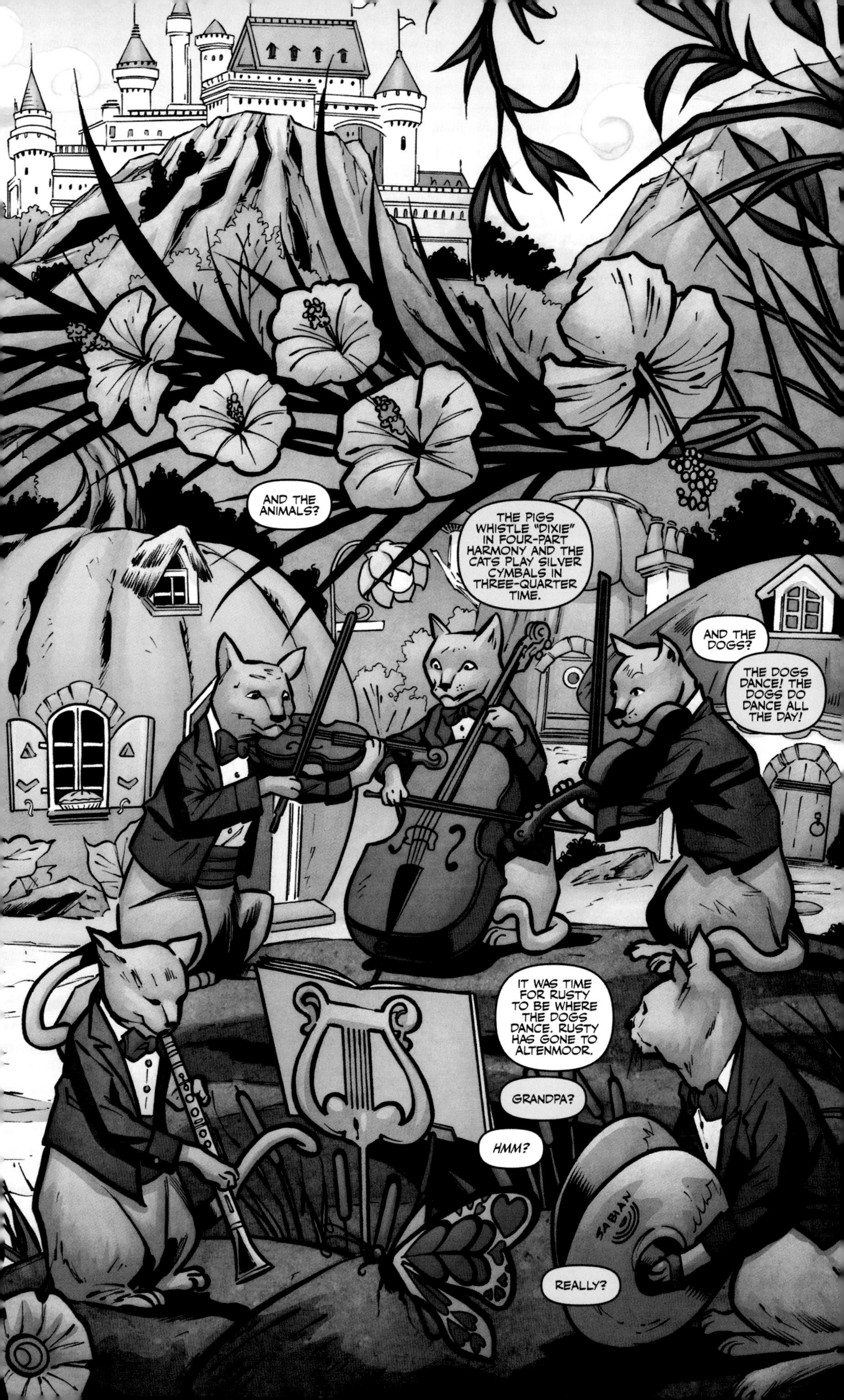
AND THE ANIMALS?
THE PIGS WHISTLE "DIXIE" IN FOUR-PART HARMONY AND THE CATS PLAY SILVER CYMBALS IN THREE-QUARTER TIME.
AND THE DOGS?
THE DOGS DANCE! THE DOGS DO DANCE ALL THE DAY!
IT WAS TIME FOR RUSTY TO BE WHERE THE DOGS DANCE. RUSTY HAS GONE TO ALTENMOOR.
GRANDPA?
HMM?
REALLY?
SABIAN

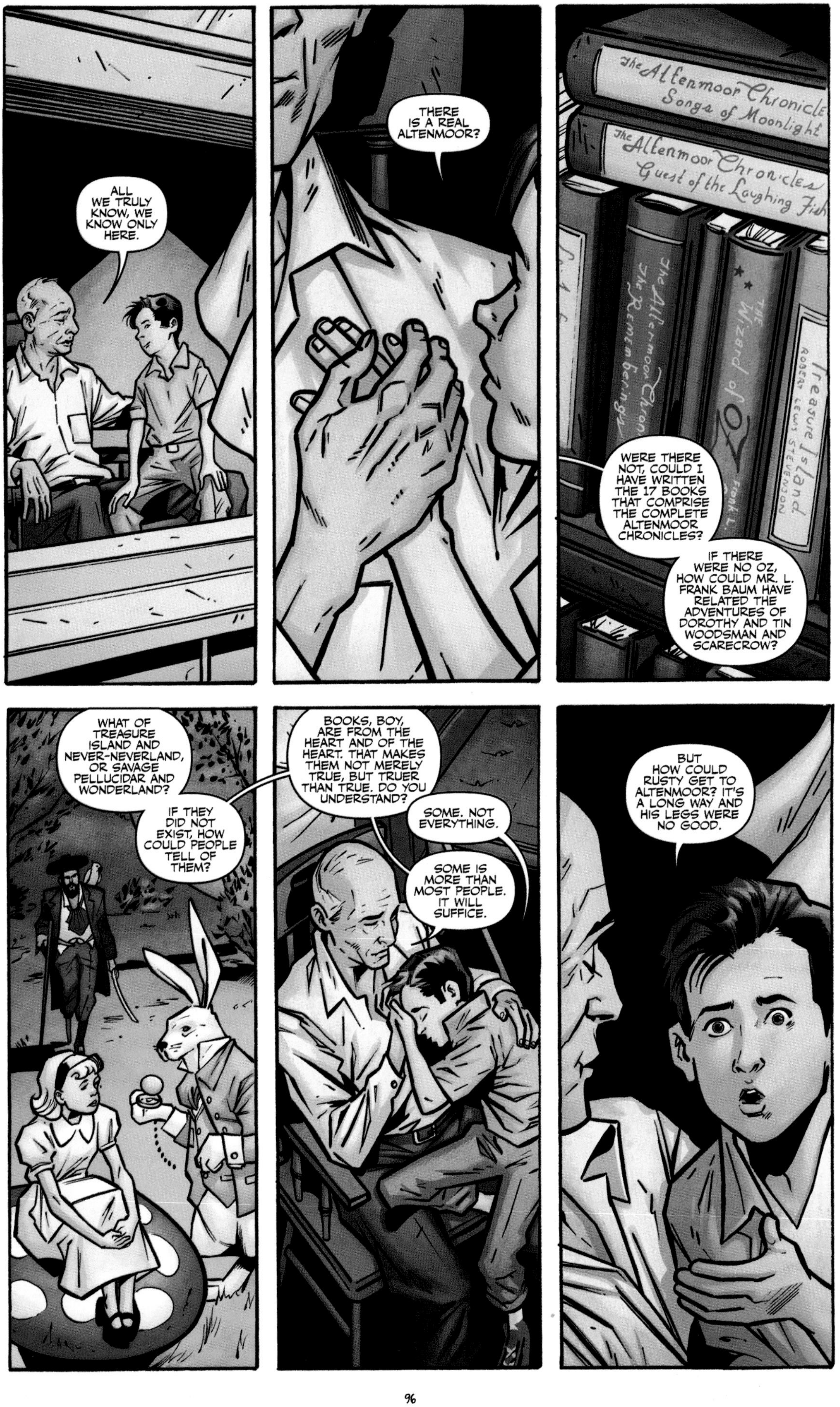

ALL WE TRULY KNOW, WE KNOW ONLY HERE.
THERE IS A REAL ALTENMOOR?
The Altenmoor Chronicle
Songs of Moonlight
The Altenmoor Chronicles
Guest of the Laughing Fish
The Wizard of Oz
Treasure Island
WERE THERE NOT, COULD I HAVE WRITTEN THE 17 BOOKS THAT COMPRISE THE COMPLETE ALTENMOOR CHRONICLES?
IF THERE WERE NO OZ, HOW COULD MR. L. FRANK BAUM HAVE RELATED THE ADVENTURES OF DOROTHY AND TIN WOODSMAN AND SCARECROW?
WHAT OF TREASURE ISLAND AND NEVER-NEVERLAND, OR SAVAGE PELLUCIDAR AND WONDERLAND?
IF THEY DID NOT EXIST, HOW COULD PEOPLE TELL OF THEM?
BOOKS, BOY, ARE FROM THE HEART AND OF THE HEART. THAT MAKES THEM NOT MERELY TRUE, BUT TRUER THAN TRUE. DO YOU UNDERSTAND?
SOME. NOT EVERYTHING.
SOME IS MORE THAN MOST PEOPLE. IT WILL SUFFICE.
BUT HOW COULD RUSTY GET TO ALTENMOOR? IT'S A LONG WAY AND HIS LEGS WERE NO GOOD.

I TOUCHED RUSTY. I PATTED THAT BONY KNOB AT THE BACK OF HIS SKULL AND TICKLED BETWEEN HIS EARS. I TOUCHED HIM, AND ALL THE STRENGTH I COULD GIVE, I GAVE TO RUSTY SO HE COULD MAKE THE TREK TO ALTENMOOR.

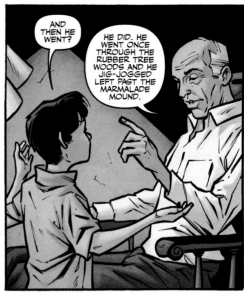

AND THEN HE WENT?

HE DID. HE WENT ONCE THROUGH THE RUBBER TREE WOODS AND HE JIG-JOGGED LEFT PAST THE MARMALADE MOUND.

THEN HE FOLLOWED THE WINDING HAPPY-TO-YOU RIVER TO ALTENMOOR!

NOW RUSTY IS DANCING WHERE THE DOGS DANCE. I BELIEVE THAT.

I DO, TOO.

ON A WINTER NIGHT SO COLD THAT THE HOUSE COULD NOT KEEP OUT ALL THE WINTER CHILL, THE BOY AWOKE.

AT FIRST, HE THOUGHT A DREAM HAD FRIGHTENED HIM AWAKE, BUT HE REALIZED HE WAS NOT FRIGHTENED.

TUNK TUNK TUNK

THEN THE BOY KNEW IT WAS A THOUGHT THAT HAD PULLED HIM FROM HIS SLEEP.

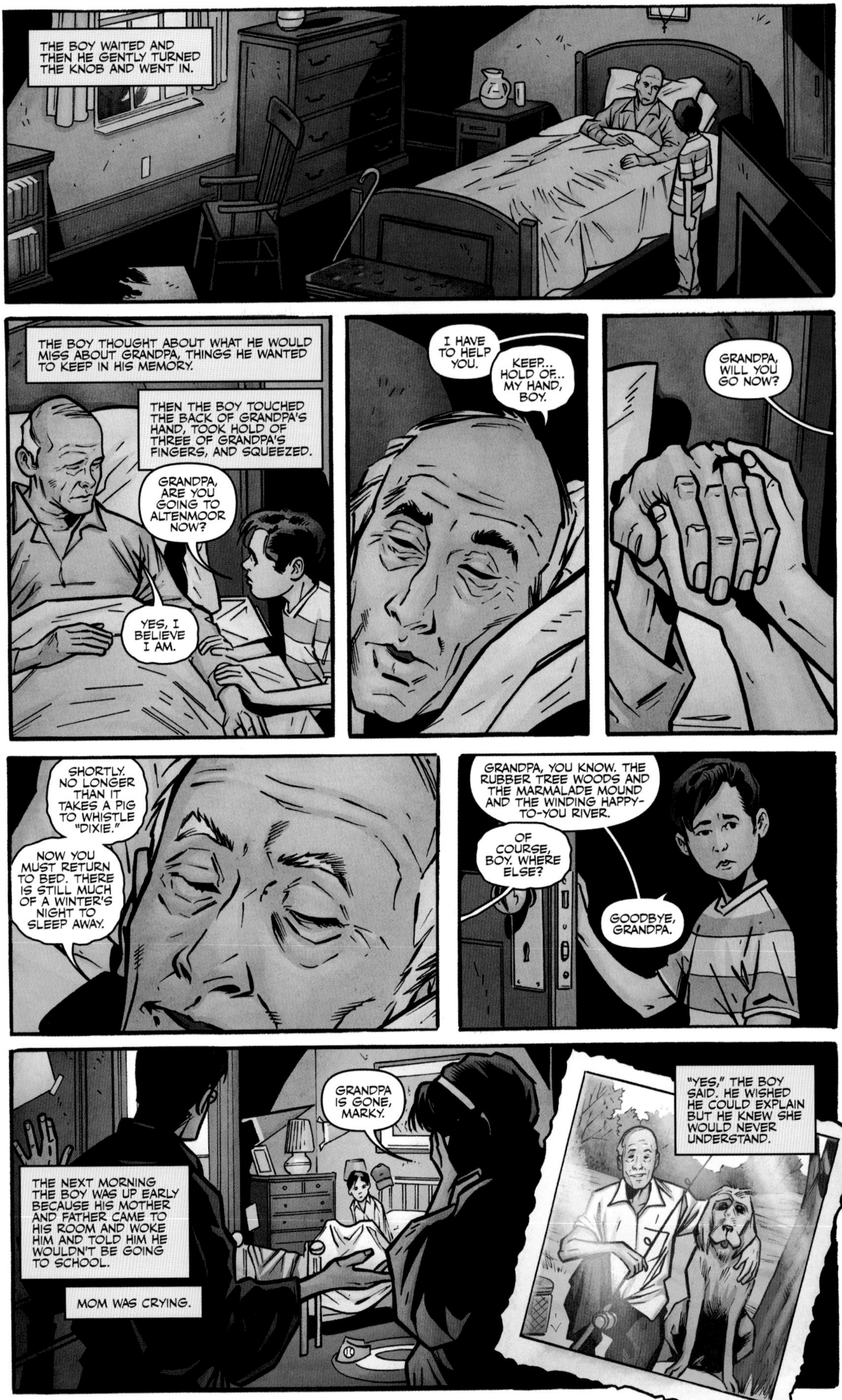
THE BOY WAITED AND THEN HE GENTLY TURNED THE KNOB AND WENT IN.
THE BOY THOUGHT ABOUT WHAT HE WOULD MISS ABOUT GRANDPA, THINGS HE WANTED TO KEEP IN HIS MEMORY.
THEN THE BOY TOUCHED THE BACK OF GRANDPA'S HAND, TOOK HOLD OF THREE OF GRANDPA'S FINGERS, AND SQUEEZED.
GRANDPA, ARE YOU GOING TO ALTENMOOR NOW?
YES, I BELIEVE I AM.
I HAVE TO HELP YOU.
KEEP... HOLD OF... MY HAND, BOY.
GRANDPA, WILL YOU GO NOW?
SHORTLY. NO LONGER THAN IT TAKES A PIG TO WHISTLE "DIXIE."
NOW YOU MUST RETURN TO BED. THERE IS STILL MUCH OF A WINTER'S NIGHT TO SLEEP AWAY.
GRANDPA, YOU KNOW. THE RUBBER TREE WOODS AND THE MARMALADE MOUND AND THE WINDING HAPPY-TO-YOU RIVER.
OF COURSE, BOY. WHERE ELSE?
GOODBYE, GRANDPA.
THE NEXT MORNING THE BOY WAS UP EARLY BECAUSE HIS MOTHER AND FATHER CAME TO HIS ROOM AND WOKE HIM AND TOLD HIM HE WOULDN'T BE GOING TO SCHOOL.
MOM WAS CRYING.
GRANDPA IS GONE, MARKY.
"YES," THE BOY SAID. HE WISHED HE COULD EXPLAIN BUT HE KNEW SHE WOULD NEVER UNDERSTAND.

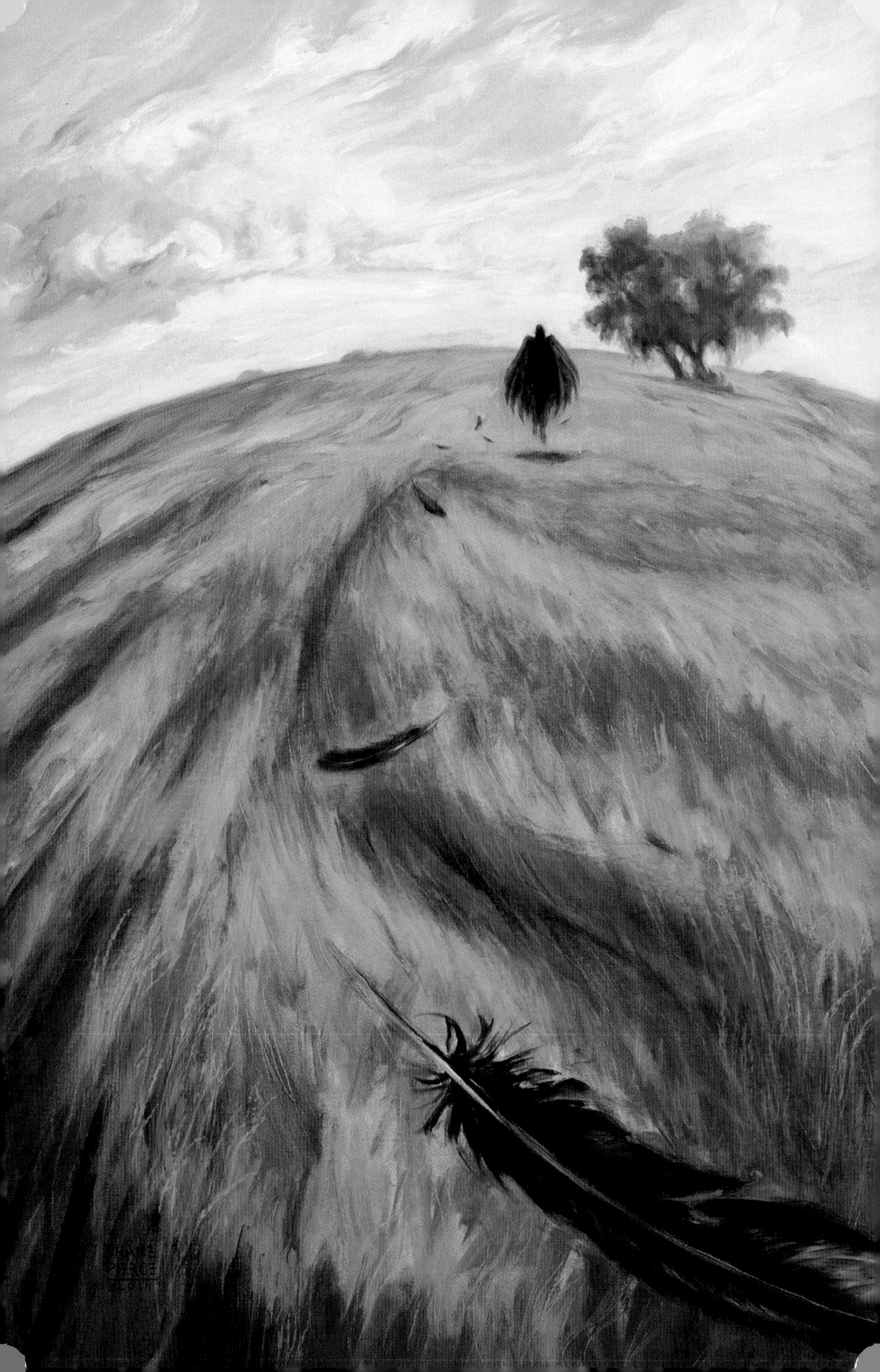

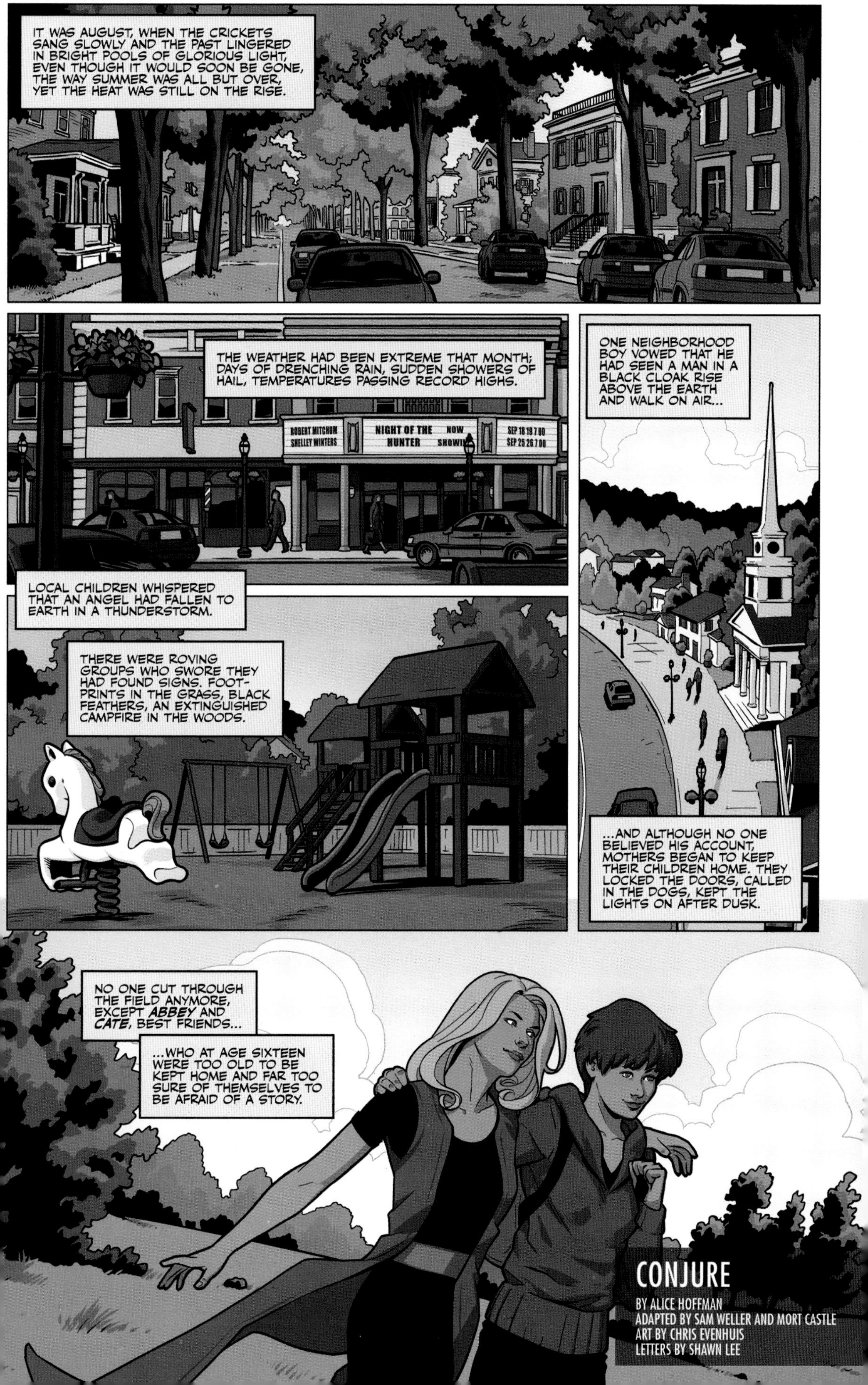
IT WAS AUGUST, WHEN THE CRICKETS SANG SLOWLY AND THE PAST LINGERED IN BRIGHT POOLS OF GLORIOUS LIGHT, EVEN THOUGH IT WOULD SOON BE GONE, THE WAY SUMMER WAS ALL BUT OVER, YET THE HEAT WAS STILL ON THE RISE.
THE WEATHER HAD BEEN EXTREME THAT MONTH; DAYS OF DRENCHING RAIN, SUDDEN SHOWERS OF HAIL, TEMPERATURES PASSING RECORD HIGHS.
ROBERT MITCHUM SHELLEY WINTERS
NIGHT OF THE HUNTER
NOW SHOWI
SEP 18 19 7 00 SEP 25 26 7 00
ONE NEIGHBORHOOD BOY VOWED THAT HE HAD SEEN A MAN IN A BLACK CLOAK RISE ABOVE THE EARTH AND WALK ON AIR...
LOCAL CHILDREN WHISPERED THAT AN ANGEL HAD FALLEN TO EARTH IN A THUNDERSTORM.
THERE WERE ROVING GROUPS WHO SWORE THEY HAD FOUND SIGNS. FOOT-PRINTS IN THE GRASS, BLACK FEATHERS, AN EXTINGUISHED CAMPFIRE IN THE WOODS.
...AND ALTHOUGH NO ONE BELIEVED HIS ACCOUNT, MOTHERS BEGAN TO KEEP THEIR CHILDREN HOME. THEY LOCKED THE DOORS, CALLED IN THE DOGS, KEPT THE LIGHTS ON AFTER DUSK.
NO ONE CUT THROUGH THE FIELD ANYMORE, EXCEPT *ABBEY* AND *CATE*, BEST FRIENDS...
...WHO AT AGE SIXTEEN WERE TOO OLD TO BE KEPT HOME AND FAR TOO SURE OF THEMSELVES TO BE AFRAID OF A STORY.
CONJURE
BY ALICE HOFFMAN
ADAPTED BY SAM WELLER AND MORT CASTLE
ART BY CHRIS EVENHUIS
LETTERS BY SHAWN LEE

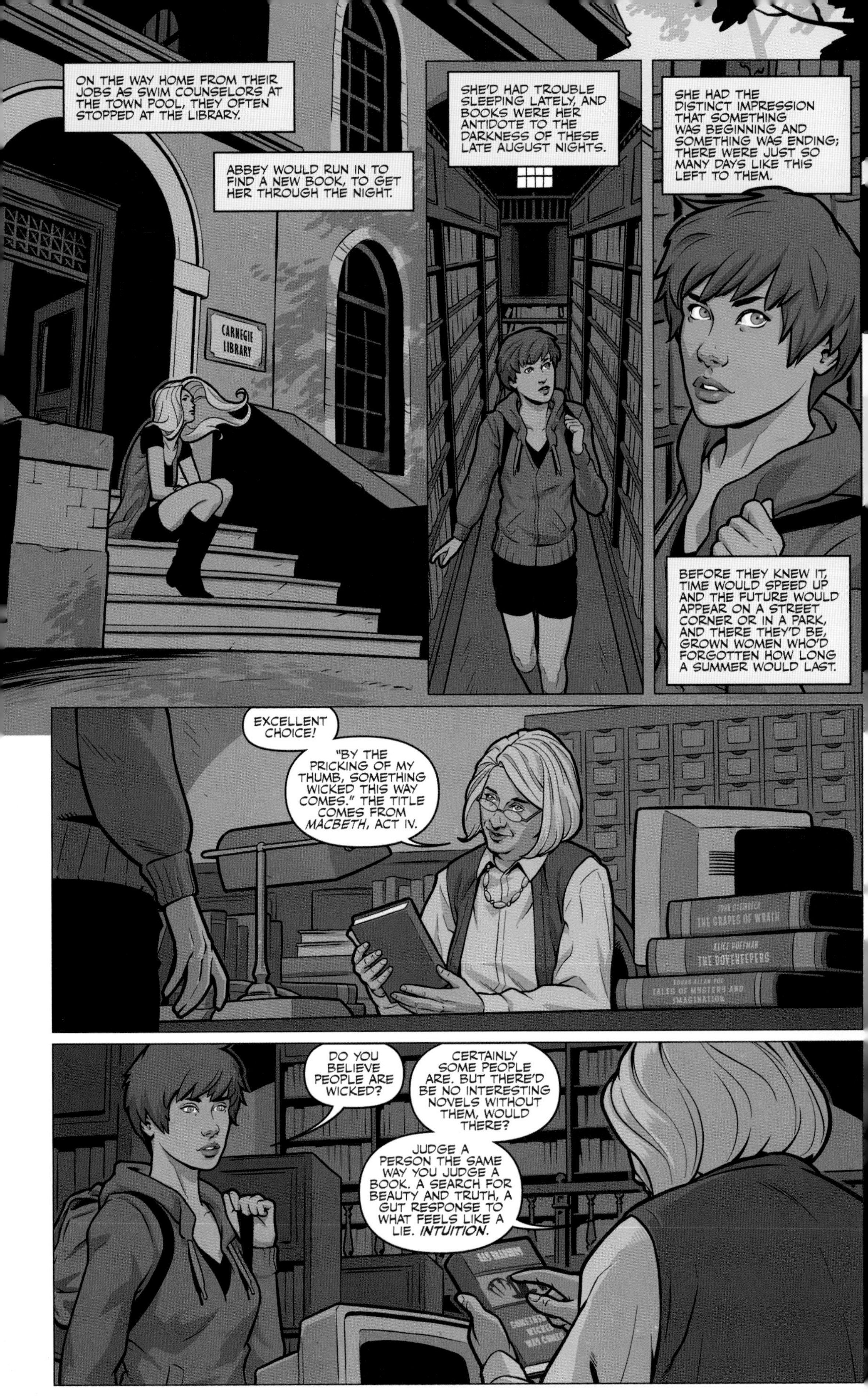

ON THE WAY HOME FROM THEIR JOBS AS SWIM COUNSELORS AT THE TOWN POOL, THEY OFTEN STOPPED AT THE LIBRARY.
ABBEY WOULD RUN IN TO FIND A NEW BOOK, TO GET HER THROUGH THE NIGHT.
CARNEGIE LIBRARY
SHE'D HAD TROUBLE SLEEPING LATELY, AND BOOKS WERE HER ANTIDOTE TO THE DARKNESS OF THESE LATE AUGUST NIGHTS.
SHE HAD THE DISTINCT IMPRESSION THAT SOMETHING WAS BEGINNING AND SOMETHING WAS ENDING; THERE WERE JUST SO MANY DAYS LIKE THIS LEFT TO THEM.
BEFORE THEY KNEW IT, TIME WOULD SPEED UP AND THE FUTURE WOULD APPEAR ON A STREET CORNER OR IN A PARK, AND THERE THEY'D BE, GROWN WOMEN WHO'D FORGOTTEN HOW LONG A SUMMER WOULD LAST.
EXCELLENT CHOICE!
"BY THE PRICKING OF MY THUMB, SOMETHING WICKED THIS WAY COMES." THE TITLE COMES FROM *MACBETH*, ACT IV.
JOHN STEINBECK THE GRAPES OF WRATH
ALICE HOFFMAN THE DOVEKEEPERS
EDGAR ALLAN POE TALES OF MYSTERY AND IMAGINATION
DO YOU BELIEVE PEOPLE ARE WICKED?
CERTAINLY SOME PEOPLE ARE. BUT THERE'D BE NO INTERESTING NOVELS WITHOUT THEM, WOULD THERE?
JUDGE A PERSON THE SAME WAY YOU JUDGE A BOOK. A SEARCH FOR BEAUTY AND TRUTH, A GUT RESPONSE TO WHAT FEELS LIKE A LIE. *INTUITION*.

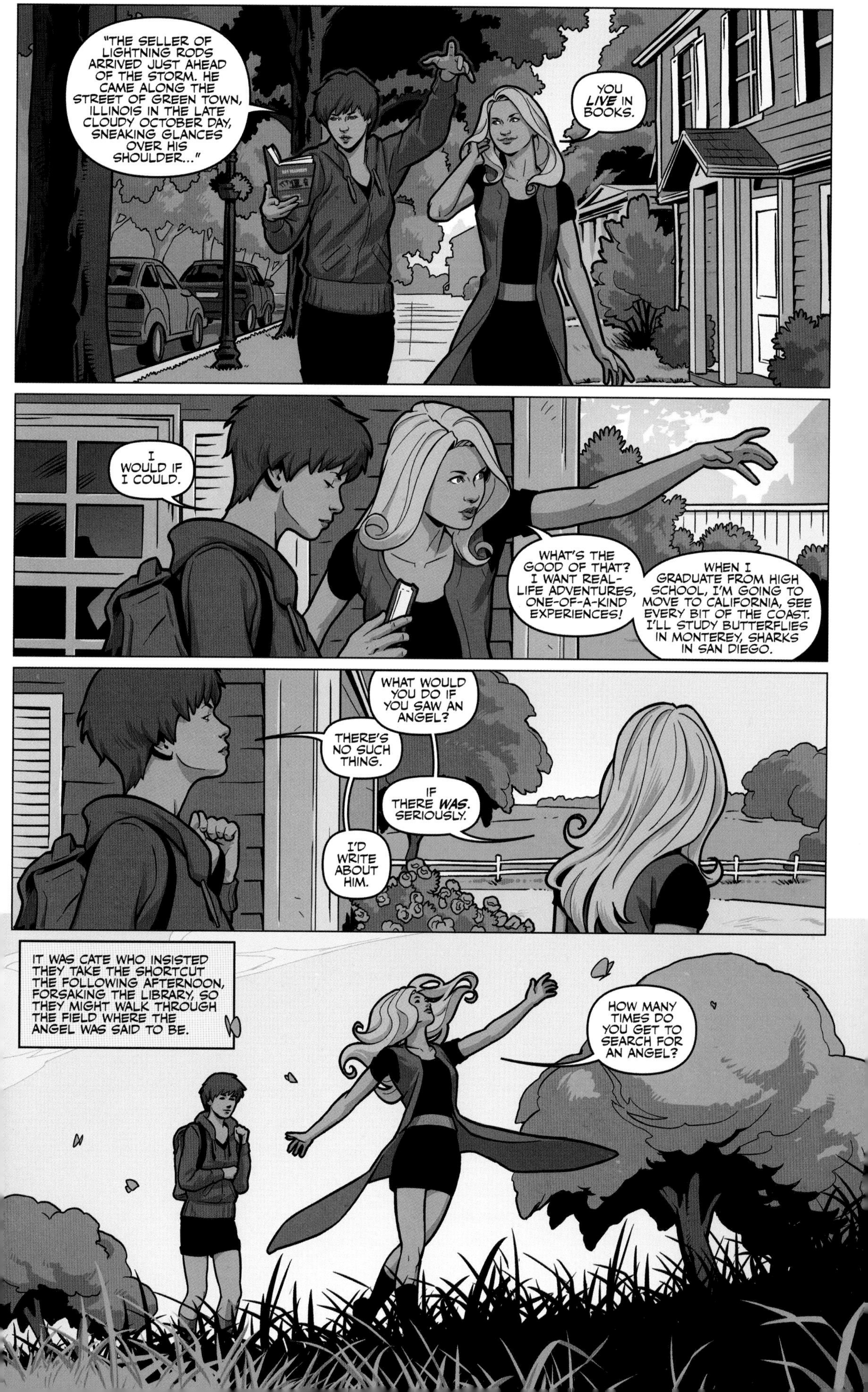

"THE SELLER OF LIGHTNING RODS ARRIVED JUST AHEAD OF THE STORM. HE CAME ALONG THE STREET OF GREEN TOWN, ILLINOIS IN THE LATE CLOUDY OCTOBER DAY, SNEAKING GLANCES OVER HIS SHOULDER..."
YOU *LIVE* IN BOOKS.
I WOULD IF I COULD.
WHAT'S THE GOOD OF THAT? I WANT REAL-LIFE ADVENTURES, ONE-OF-A-KIND EXPERIENCES!
WHEN I GRADUATE FROM HIGH SCHOOL, I'M GOING TO MOVE TO CALIFORNIA, SEE EVERY BIT OF THE COAST. I'LL STUDY BUTTERFLIES IN MONTEREY, SHARKS IN SAN DIEGO.
WHAT WOULD YOU DO IF YOU SAW AN ANGEL?
THERE'S NO SUCH THING.
IF THERE *WAS*. SERIOUSLY.
I'D WRITE ABOUT HIM.
IT WAS CATE WHO INSISTED THEY TAKE THE SHORTCUT THE FOLLOWING AFTERNOON, FORSAKING THE LIBRARY, SO THEY MIGHT WALK THROUGH THE FIELD WHERE THE ANGEL WAS SAID TO BE.
HOW MANY TIMES DO YOU GET TO SEARCH FOR AN ANGEL?

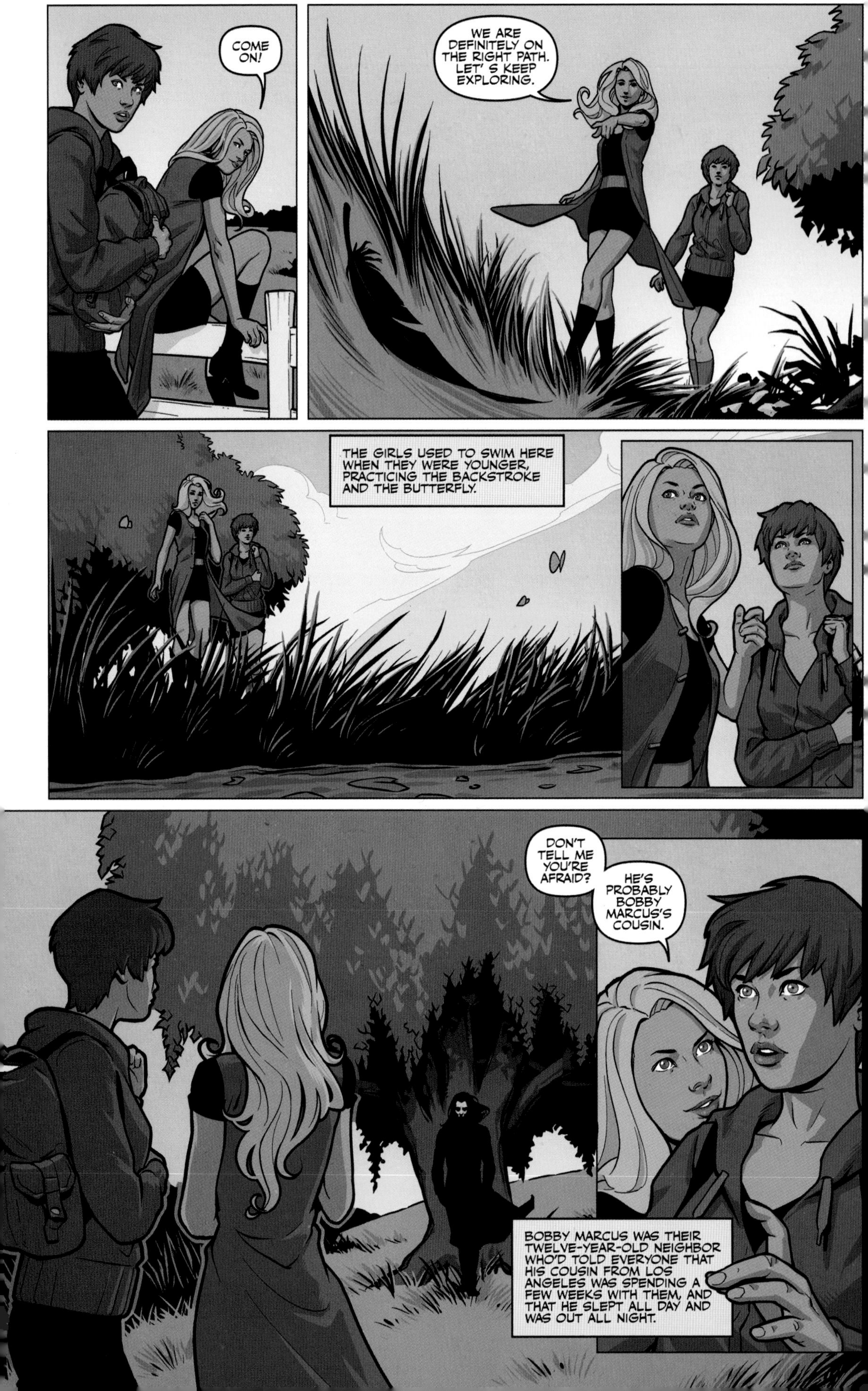
COME ON!
WE ARE DEFINITELY ON THE RIGHT PATH. LET'S KEEP EXPLORING.
THE GIRLS USED TO SWIM HERE WHEN THEY WERE YOUNGER, PRACTICING THE BACKSTROKE AND THE BUTTERFLY.
DON'T TELL ME YOU'RE AFRAID?
HE'S PROBABLY BOBBY MARCUS'S COUSIN.
BOBBY MARCUS WAS THEIR TWELVE-YEAR-OLD NEIGHBOR WHO'D TOLD EVERYONE THAT HIS COUSIN FROM LOS ANGELES WAS SPENDING A FEW WEEKS WITH THEM, AND THAT HE SLEPT ALL DAY AND WAS OUT ALL NIGHT.

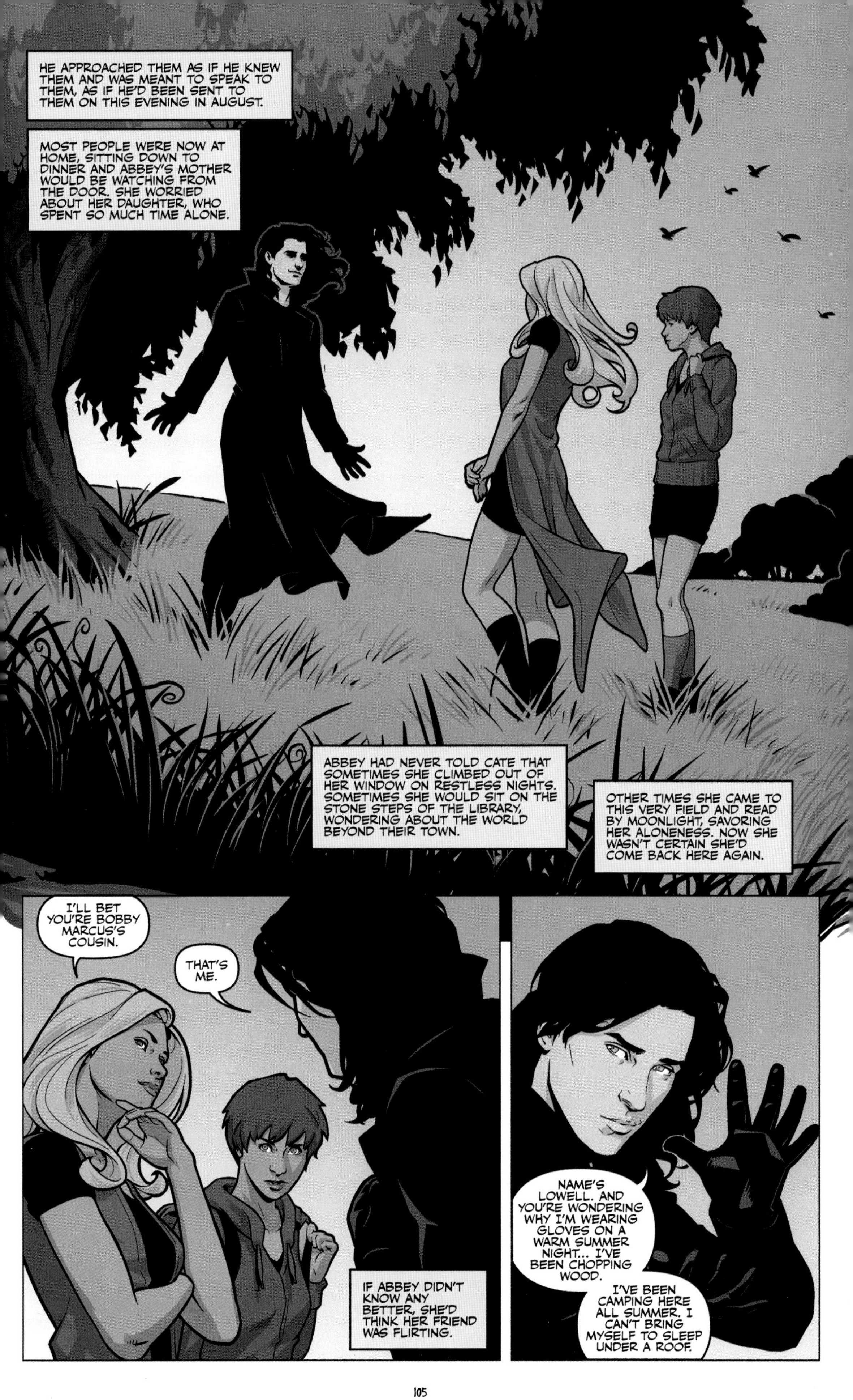
HE APPROACHED THEM AS IF HE KNEW THEM AND WAS MEANT TO SPEAK TO THEM, AS IF HE'D BEEN SENT TO THEM ON THIS EVENING IN AUGUST.
MOST PEOPLE WERE NOW AT HOME, SITTING DOWN TO DINNER AND ABBEY'S MOTHER WOULD BE WATCHING FROM THE DOOR. SHE WORRIED ABOUT HER DAUGHTER, WHO SPENT SO MUCH TIME ALONE.
ABBEY HAD NEVER TOLD CATE THAT SOMETIMES SHE CLIMBED OUT OF HER WINDOW ON RESTLESS NIGHTS. SOMETIMES SHE WOULD SIT ON THE STONE STEPS OF THE LIBRARY, WONDERING ABOUT THE WORLD BEYOND THEIR TOWN.
OTHER TIMES SHE CAME TO THIS VERY FIELD AND READ BY MOONLIGHT, SAVORING HER ALONENESS. NOW SHE WASN'T CERTAIN SHE'D COME BACK HERE AGAIN.
I'LL BET YOU'RE BOBBY MARCUS'S COUSIN.
THAT'S ME.
IF ABBEY DIDN'T KNOW ANY BETTER, SHE'D THINK HER FRIEND WAS FLIRTING.
NAME'S LOWELL. AND YOU'RE WONDERING WHY I'M WEARING GLOVES ON A WARM SUMMER NIGHT... I'VE BEEN CHOPPING WOOD.
I'VE BEEN CAMPING HERE ALL SUMMER. I CAN'T BRING MYSELF TO SLEEP UNDER A ROOF.

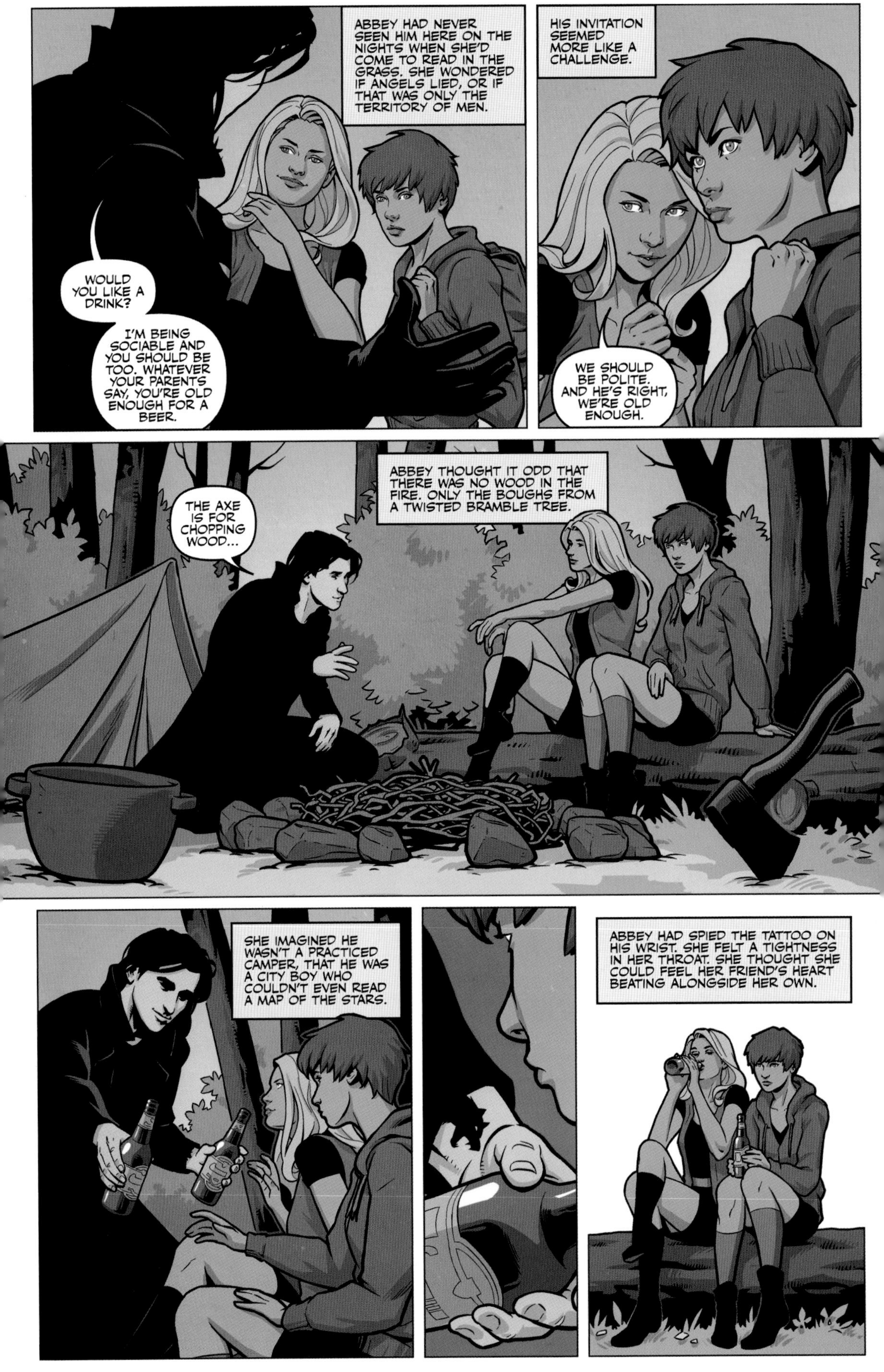

ABBEY HAD NEVER SEEN HIM HERE ON THE NIGHTS WHEN SHE'D COME TO READ IN THE GRASS. SHE WONDERED IF ANGELS LIED, OR IF THAT WAS ONLY THE TERRITORY OF MEN.
WOULD YOU LIKE A DRINK?
I'M BEING SOCIABLE AND YOU SHOULD BE TOO. WHATEVER YOUR PARENTS SAY, YOU'RE OLD ENOUGH FOR A BEER.
HIS INVITATION SEEMED MORE LIKE A CHALLENGE.
WE SHOULD BE POLITE. AND HE'S RIGHT, WE'RE OLD ENOUGH.
ABBEY THOUGHT IT ODD THAT THERE WAS NO WOOD IN THE FIRE. ONLY THE BOUGHS FROM A TWISTED BRAMBLE TREE.
THE AXE IS FOR CHOPPING WOOD...
SHE IMAGINED HE WASN'T A PRACTICED CAMPER, THAT HE WAS A CITY BOY WHO COULDN'T EVEN READ A MAP OF THE STARS.
ABBEY HAD SPIED THE TATTOO ON HIS WRIST. SHE FELT A TIGHTNESS IN HER THROAT. SHE THOUGHT SHE COULD FEEL HER FRIEND'S HEART BEATING ALONGSIDE HER OWN.

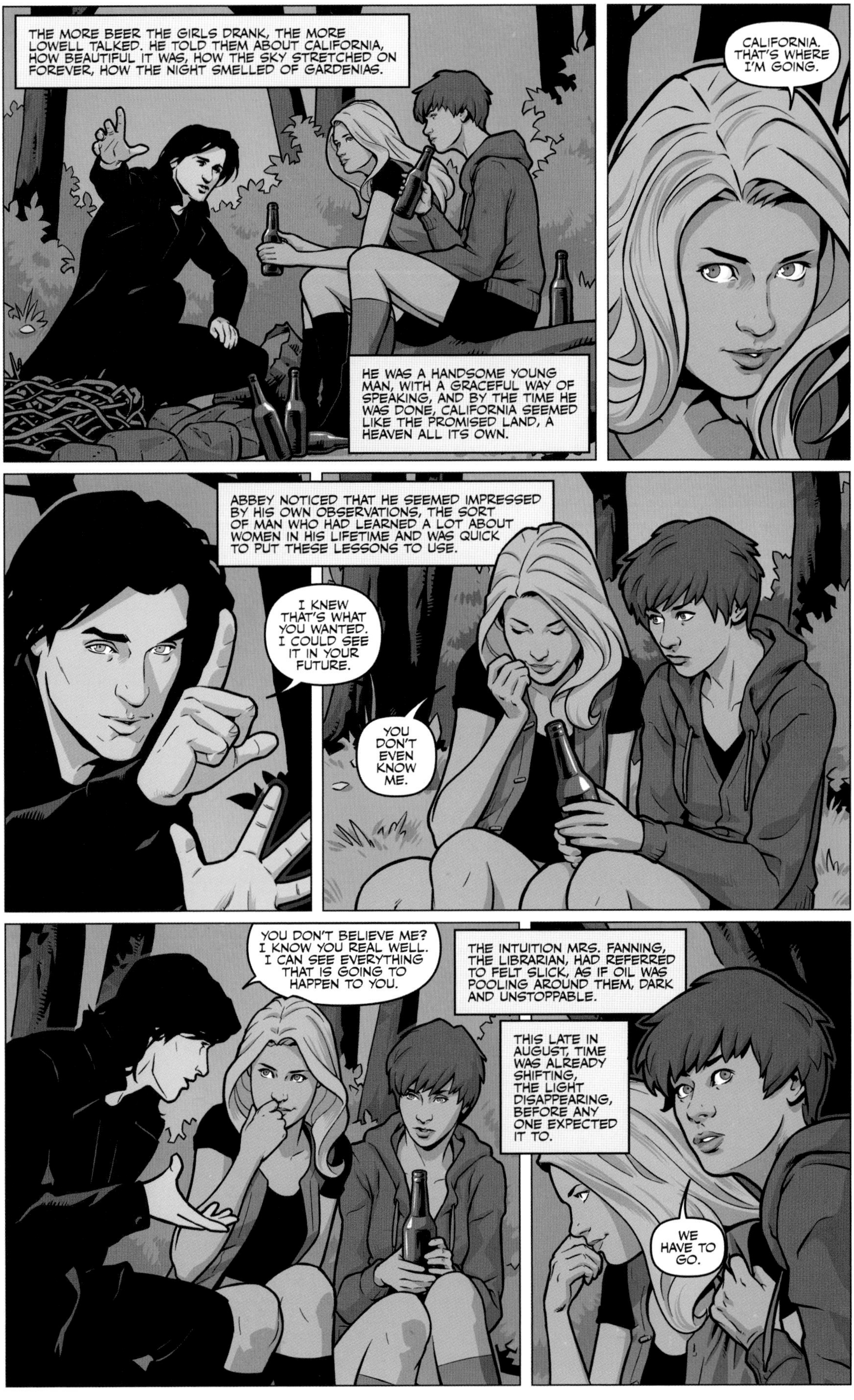

THE MORE BEER THE GIRLS DRANK, THE MORE LOWELL TALKED. HE TOLD THEM ABOUT CALIFORNIA, HOW BEAUTIFUL IT WAS, HOW THE SKY STRETCHED ON FOREVER, HOW THE NIGHT SMELLED OF GARDENIAS.
HE WAS A HANDSOME YOUNG MAN, WITH A GRACEFUL WAY OF SPEAKING, AND BY THE TIME HE WAS DONE, CALIFORNIA SEEMED LIKE THE PROMISED LAND, A HEAVEN ALL ITS OWN.
CALIFORNIA. THAT'S WHERE I'M GOING.
ABBEY NOTICED THAT HE SEEMED IMPRESSED BY HIS OWN OBSERVATIONS, THE SORT OF MAN WHO HAD LEARNED A LOT ABOUT WOMEN IN HIS LIFETIME AND WAS QUICK TO PUT THESE LESSONS TO USE.
I KNEW THAT'S WHAT YOU WANTED. I COULD SEE IT IN YOUR FUTURE.
YOU DON'T EVEN KNOW ME.
YOU DON'T BELIEVE ME? I KNOW YOU REAL WELL. I CAN SEE EVERYTHING THAT IS GOING TO HAPPEN TO YOU.
THE INTUITION MRS. FANNING, THE LIBRARIAN, HAD REFERRED TO FELT SLICK, AS IF OIL WAS POOLING AROUND THEM, DARK AND UNSTOPPABLE.
THIS LATE IN AUGUST, TIME WAS ALREADY SHIFTING, THE LIGHT DISAPPEARING, BEFORE ANY ONE EXPECTED IT TO.
WE HAVE TO GO.

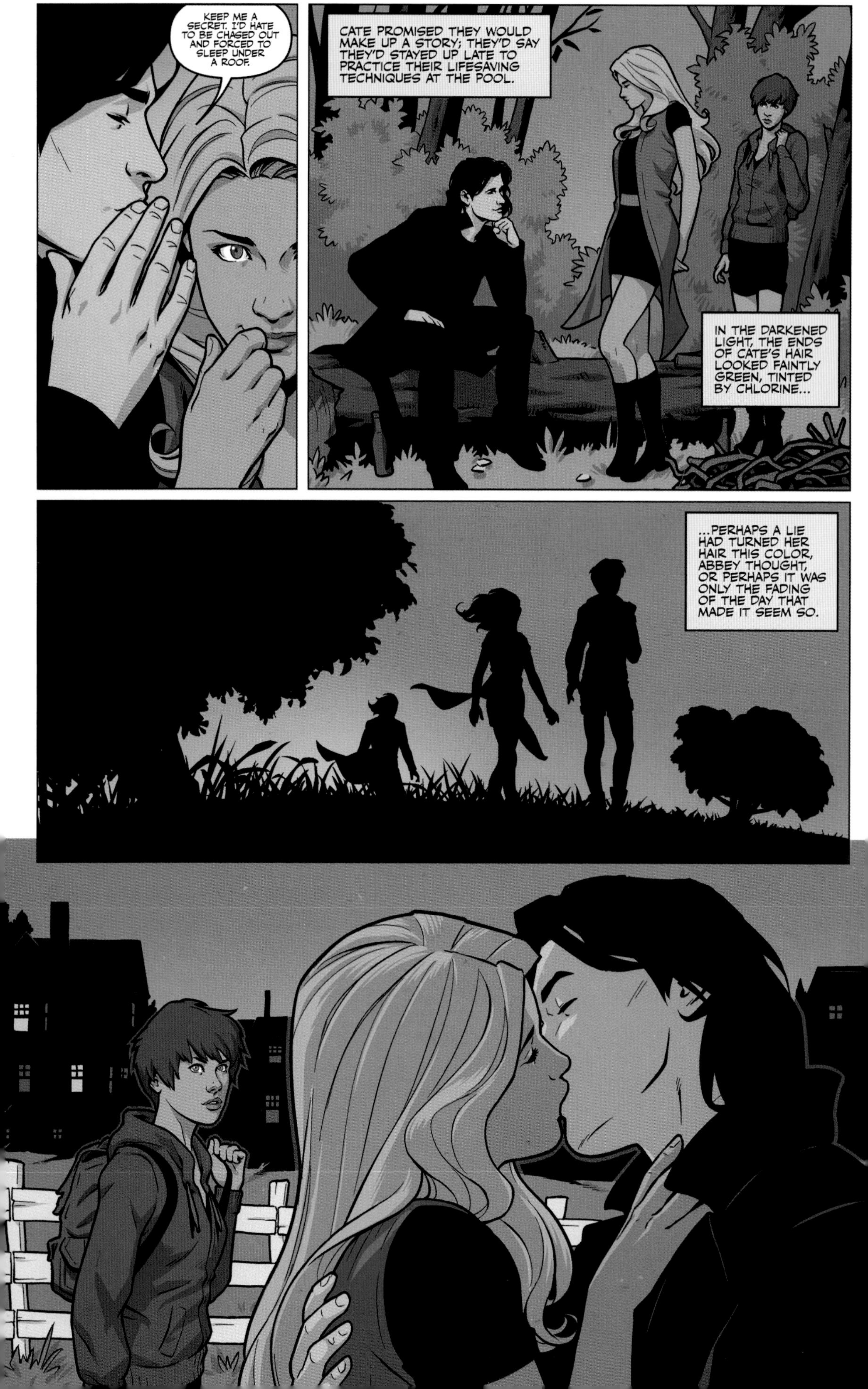
KEEP ME A SECRET. I'D HATE TO BE CHASED OUT AND FORCED TO SLEEP UNDER A ROOF.
CATE PROMISED THEY WOULD MAKE UP A STORY; THEY'D SAY THEY'D STAYED UP LATE TO PRACTICE THEIR LIFESAVING TECHNIQUES AT THE POOL.
IN THE DARKENED LIGHT, THE ENDS OF CATE'S HAIR LOOKED FAINTLY GREEN, TINTED BY CHLORINE...
...PERHAPS A LIE HAD TURNED HER HAIR THIS COLOR, ABBEY THOUGHT, OR PERHAPS IT WAS ONLY THE FADING OF THE DAY THAT MADE IT SEEM SO.

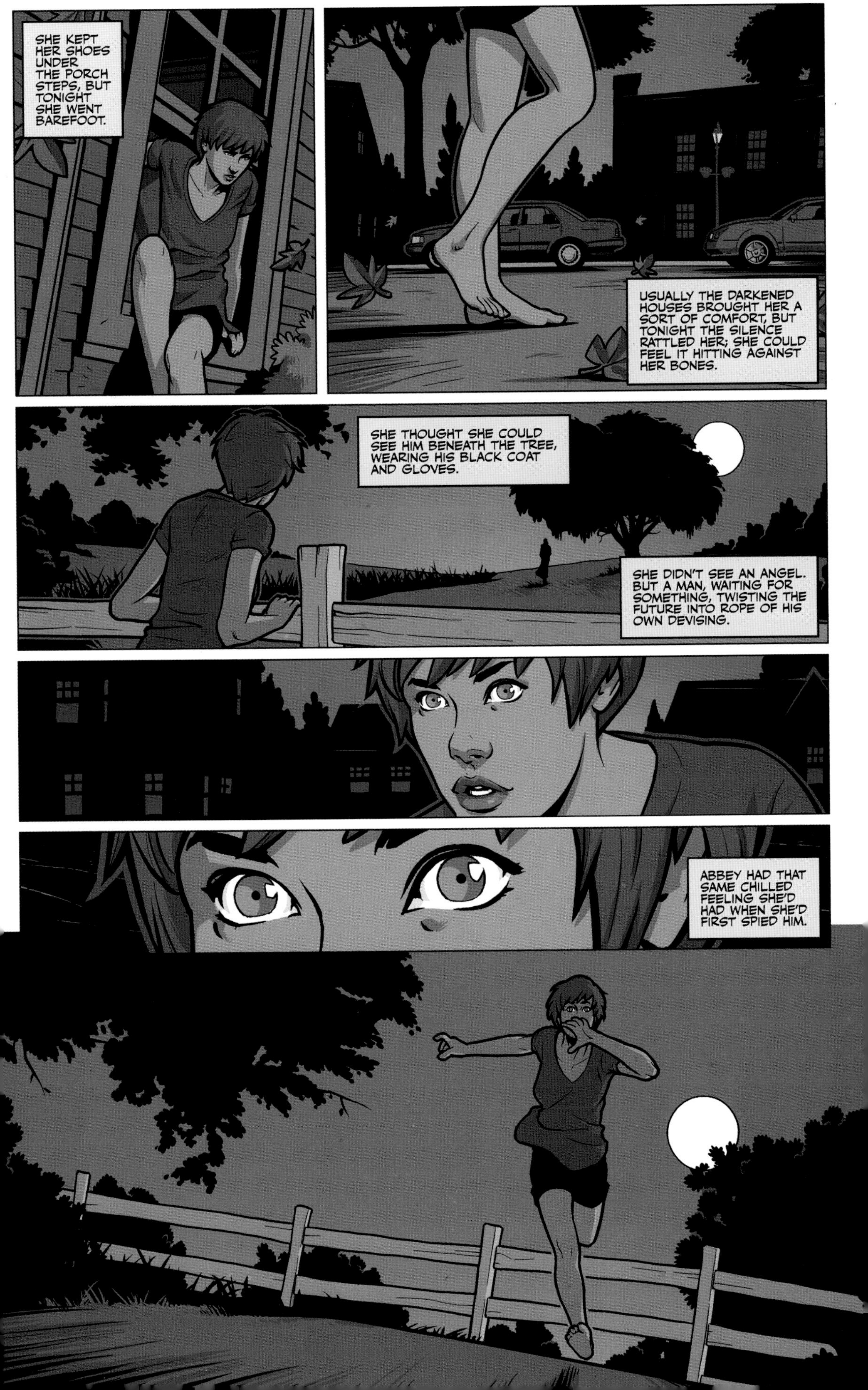
SHE KEPT HER SHOES UNDER THE PORCH STEPS, BUT TONIGHT SHE WENT BAREFOOT.
USUALLY THE DARKENED HOUSES BROUGHT HER A SORT OF COMFORT, BUT TONIGHT THE SILENCE RATTLED HER; SHE COULD FEEL IT HITTING AGAINST HER BONES.
SHE THOUGHT SHE COULD SEE HIM BENEATH THE TREE, WEARING HIS BLACK COAT AND GLOVES.
SHE DIDN'T SEE AN ANGEL. BUT A MAN, WAITING FOR SOMETHING, TWISTING THE FUTURE INTO ROPE OF HIS OWN DEVISING.
ABBEY HAD THAT SAME CHILLED FEELING SHE'D HAD WHEN SHE'D FIRST SPIED HIM.

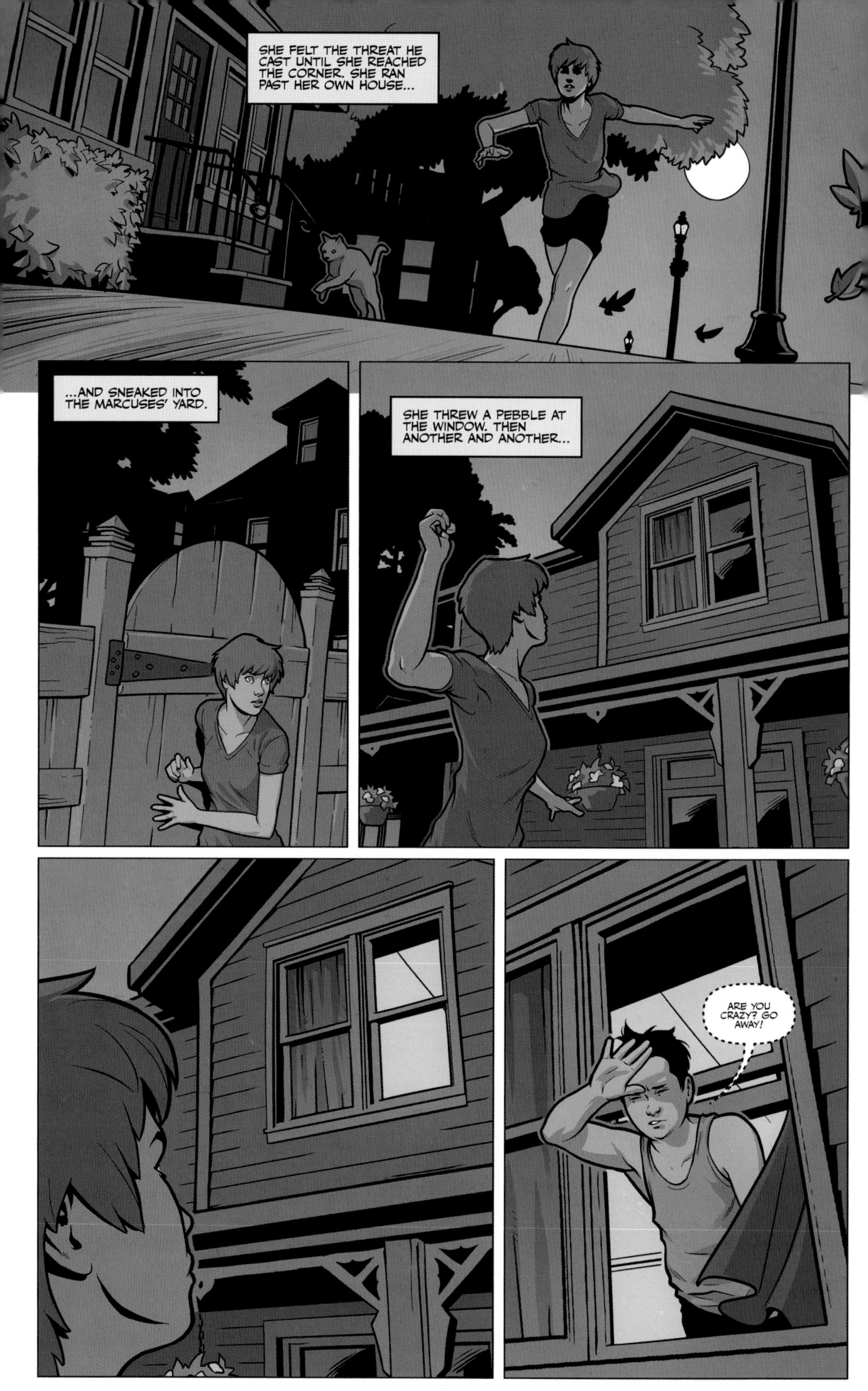
SHE FELT THE THREAT HE CAST UNTIL SHE REACHED THE CORNER. SHE RAN PAST HER OWN HOUSE...
...AND SNEAKED INTO THE MARCUSES' YARD.
SHE THREW A PEBBLE AT THE WINDOW. THEN ANOTHER AND ANOTHER...
ARE YOU CRAZY? GO AWAY!

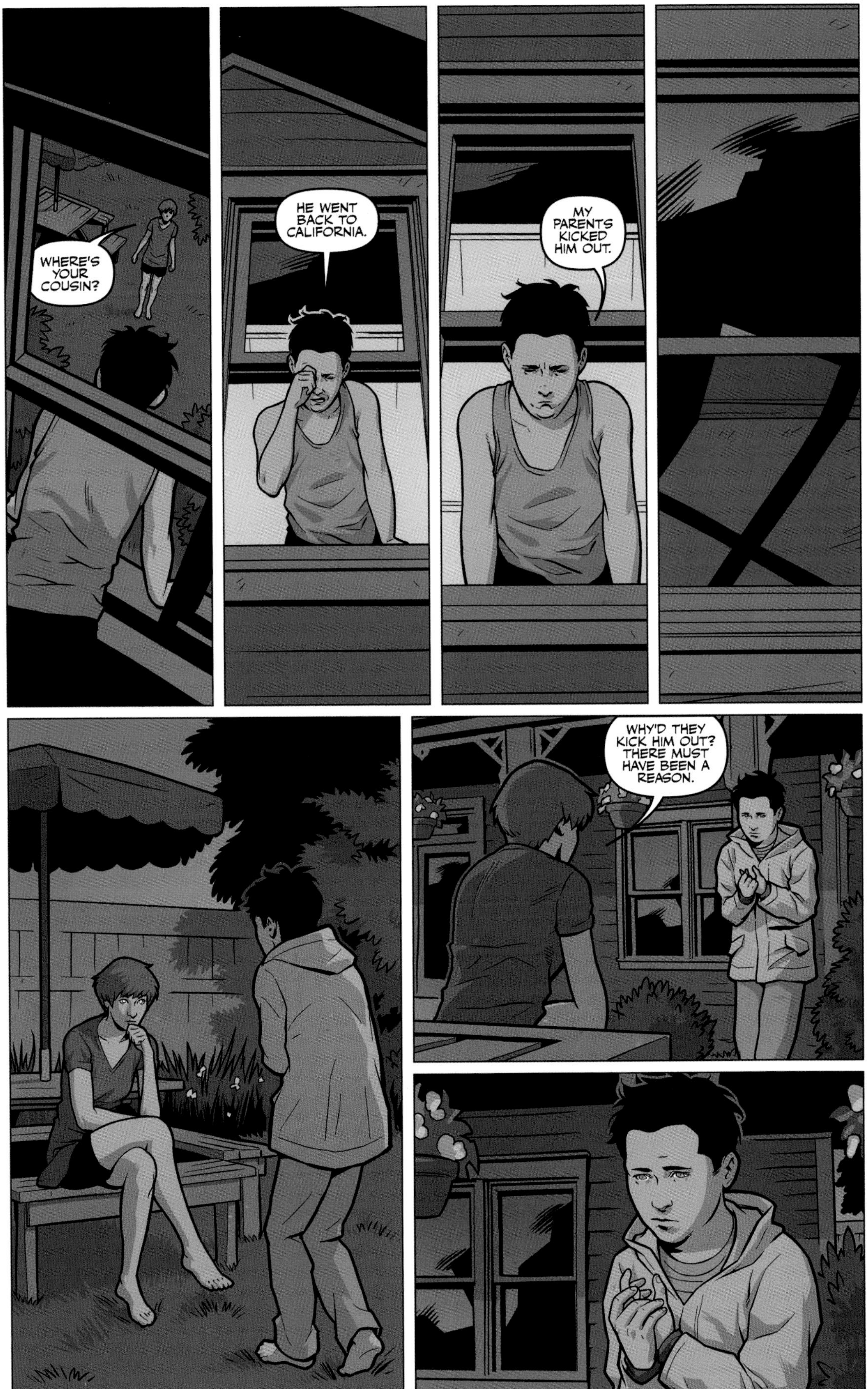
WHERE'S YOUR COUSIN?
HE WENT BACK TO CALIFORNIA.
MY PARENTS KICKED HIM OUT.
WHY'D THEY KICK HIM OUT? THERE MUST HAVE BEEN A REASON.

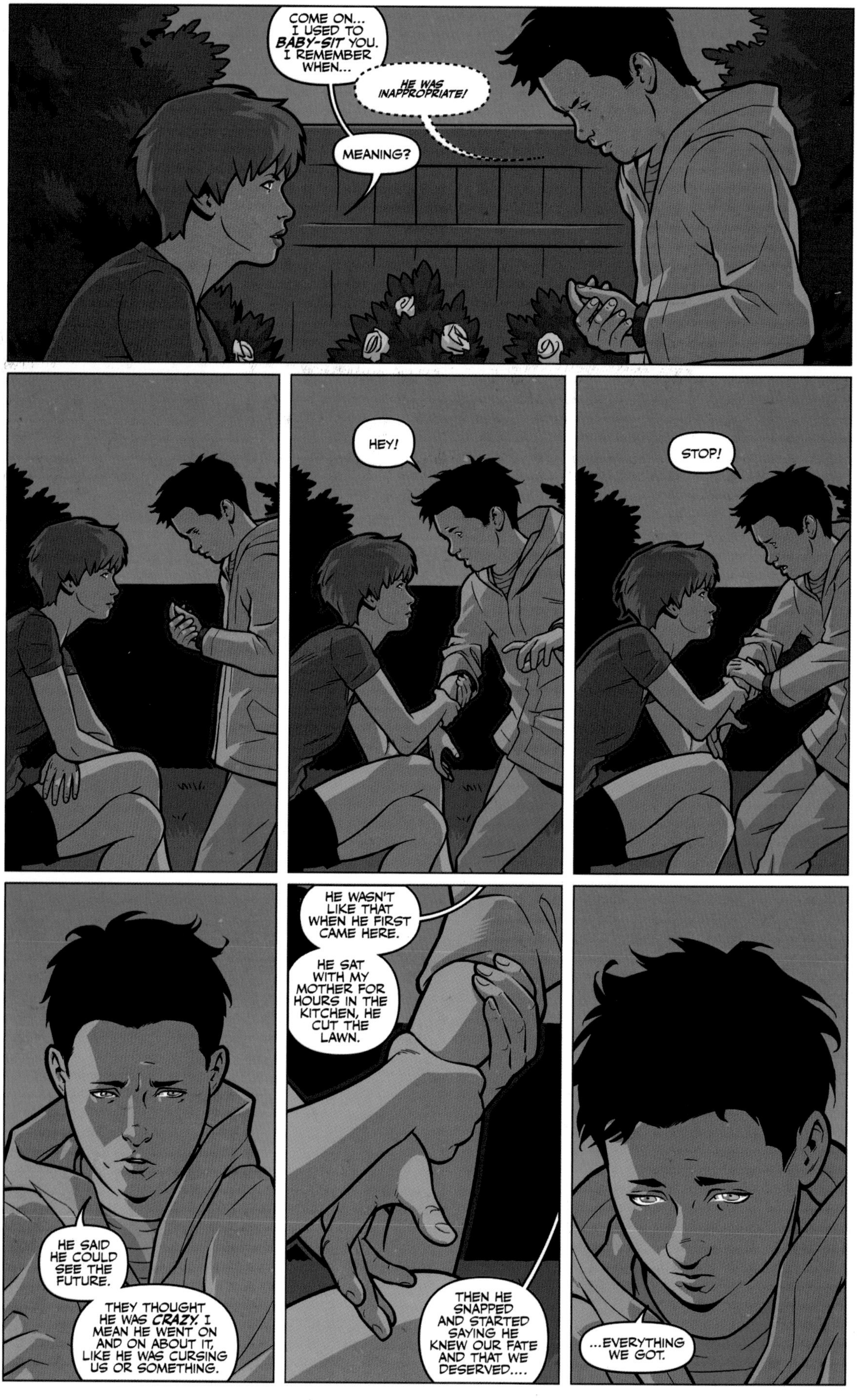
COME ON... I USED TO BABY-SIT YOU. I REMEMBER WHEN...
HE WAS INAPPROPRIATE!
MEANING?
HEY!
STOP!
HE SAID HE COULD SEE THE FUTURE.
THEY THOUGHT HE WAS CRAZY. I MEAN HE WENT ON AND ON ABOUT IT, LIKE HE WAS CURSING US OR SOMETHING.
HE WASN'T LIKE THAT WHEN HE FIRST CAME HERE.
HE SAT WITH MY MOTHER FOR HOURS IN THE KITCHEN, HE CUT THE LAWN.
THEN HE SNAPPED AND STARTED SAYING HE KNEW OUR FATE AND THAT WE DESERVED....
...EVERYTHING WE GOT.

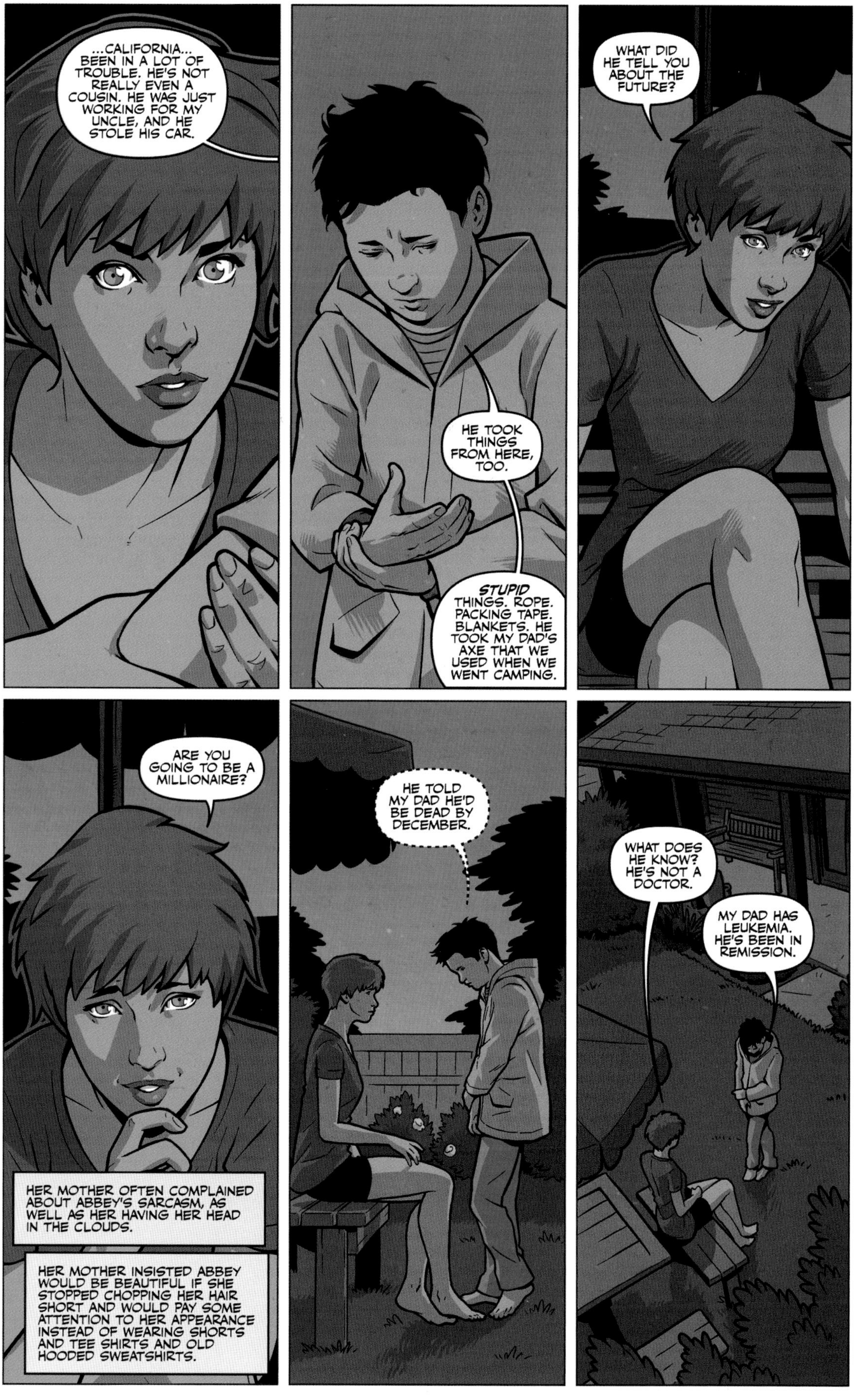
...CALIFORNIA... BEEN IN A LOT OF TROUBLE. HE'S NOT REALLY EVEN A COUSIN. HE WAS JUST WORKING FOR MY UNCLE, AND HE STOLE HIS CAR.
HE TOOK THINGS FROM HERE, TOO.
STUPID THINGS. ROPE. PACKING TAPE. BLANKETS. HE TOOK MY DAD'S AXE THAT WE USED WHEN WE WENT CAMPING.
WHAT DID HE TELL YOU ABOUT THE FUTURE?
ARE YOU GOING TO BE A MILLIONAIRE?
HER MOTHER OFTEN COMPLAINED ABOUT ABBEY'S SARCASM, AS WELL AS HER HAVING HER HEAD IN THE CLOUDS.
HER MOTHER INSISTED ABBEY WOULD BE BEAUTIFUL IF SHE STOPPED CHOPPING HER HAIR SHORT AND WOULD PAY SOME ATTENTION TO HER APPEARANCE INSTEAD OF WEARING SHORTS AND TEE SHIRTS AND OLD HOODED SWEATSHIRTS.
HE TOLD MY DAD HE'D BE DEAD BY DECEMBER.
WHAT DOES HE KNOW? HE'S NOT A DOCTOR.
MY DAD HAS LEUKEMIA. HE'S BEEN IN REMISSION.

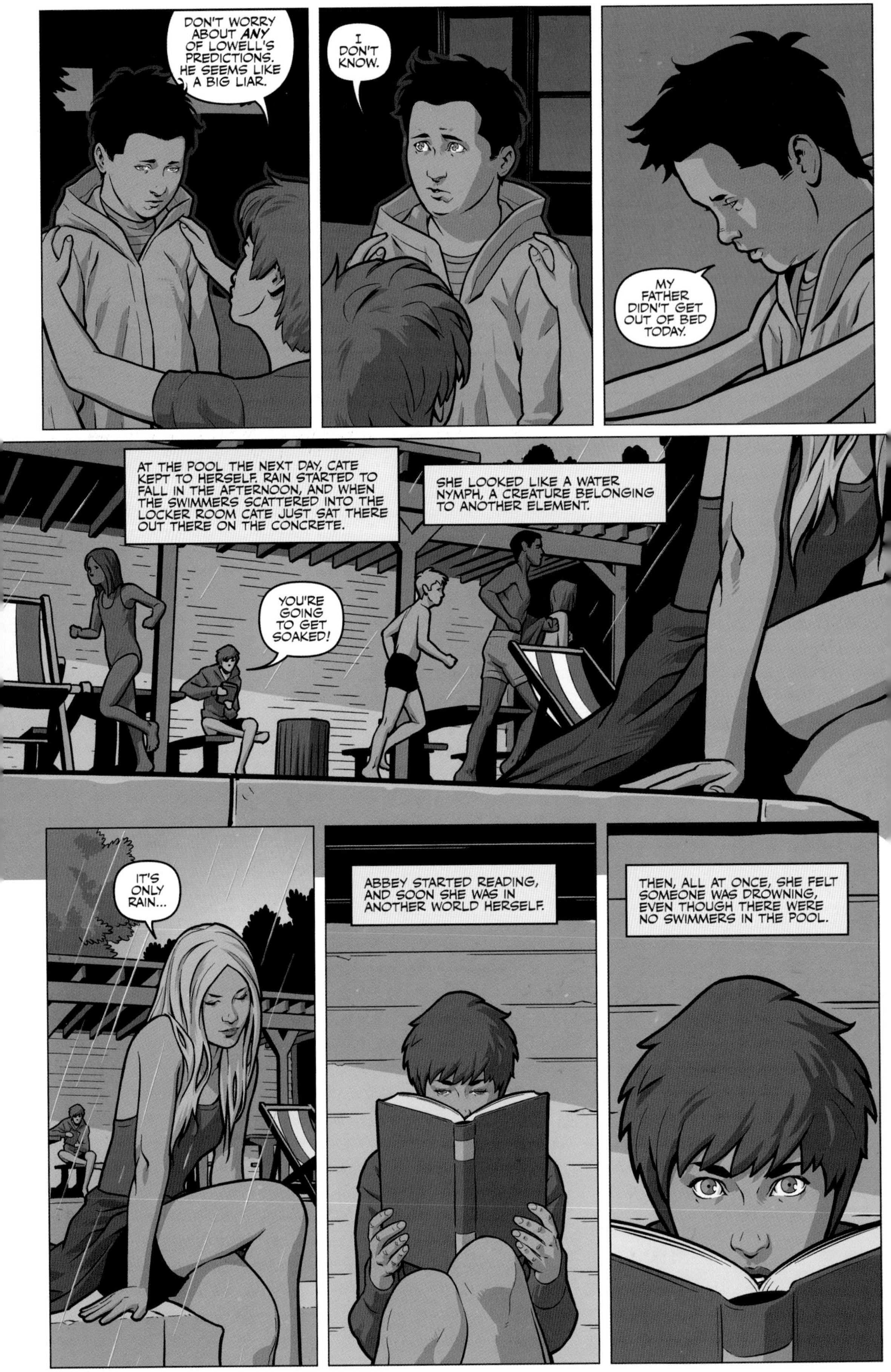
DON'T WORRY ABOUT ANY OF LOWELL'S PREDICTIONS. HE SEEMS LIKE A BIG LIAR.
I DON'T KNOW.
MY FATHER DIDN'T GET OUT OF BED TODAY.
AT THE POOL THE NEXT DAY, CATE KEPT TO HERSELF. RAIN STARTED TO FALL IN THE AFTERNOON, AND WHEN THE SWIMMERS SCATTERED INTO THE LOCKER ROOM CATE JUST SAT THERE OUT THERE ON THE CONCRETE.
SHE LOOKED LIKE A WATER NYMPH, A CREATURE BELONGING TO ANOTHER ELEMENT.
YOU'RE GOING TO GET SOAKED!
IT'S ONLY RAIN...
ABBEY STARTED READING, AND SOON SHE WAS IN ANOTHER WORLD HERSELF.
THEN, ALL AT ONCE, SHE FELT SOMEONE WAS DROWNING, EVEN THOUGH THERE WERE NO SWIMMERS IN THE POOL.

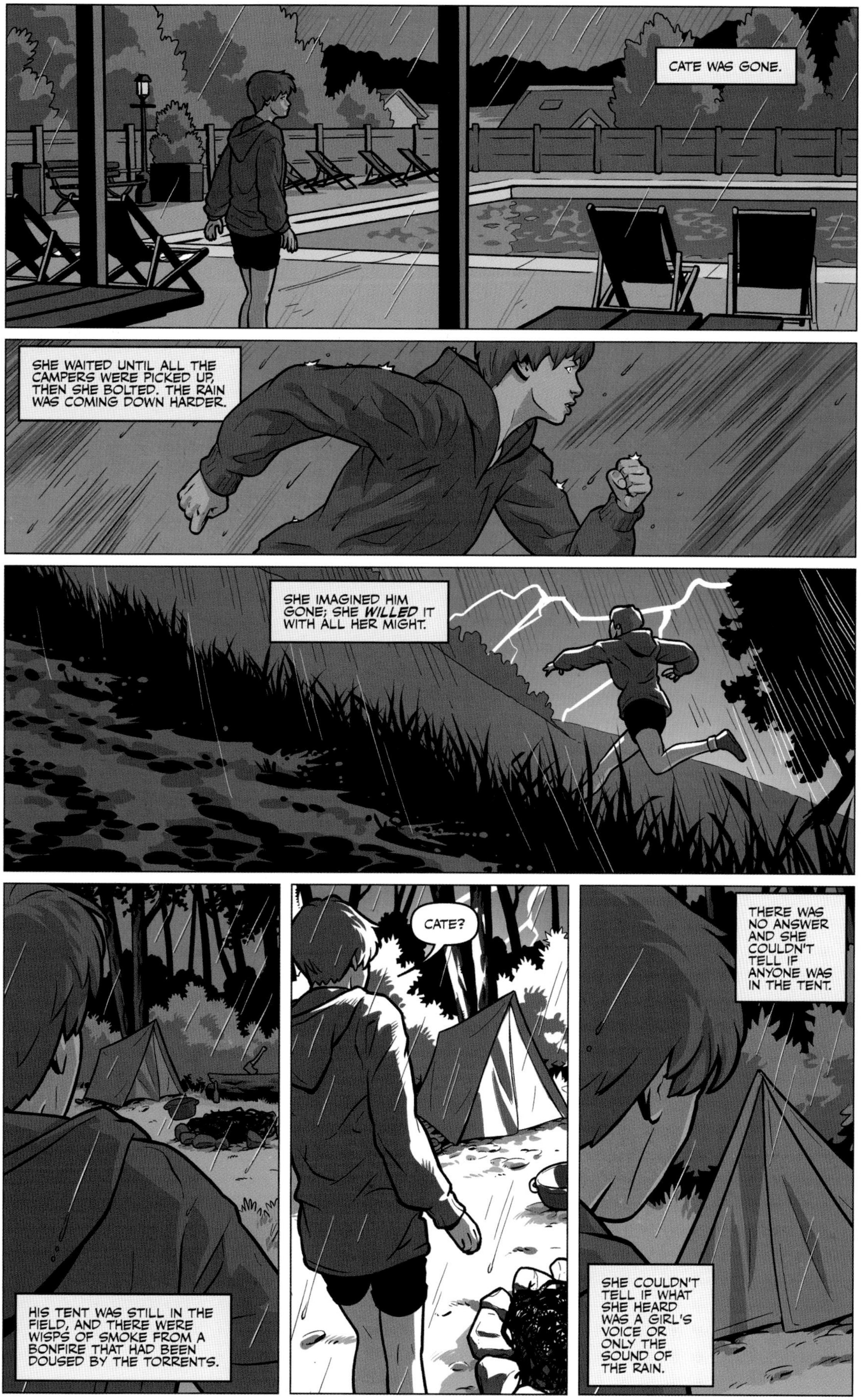
CATE WAS GONE.
SHE WAITED UNTIL ALL THE CAMPERS WERE PICKED UP, THEN SHE BOLTED. THE RAIN WAS COMING DOWN HARDER.
SHE IMAGINED HIM GONE; SHE WILLED IT WITH ALL HER MIGHT.
HIS TENT WAS STILL IN THE FIELD, AND THERE WERE WISPS OF SMOKE FROM A BONFIRE THAT HAD BEEN DOUSED BY THE TORRENTS.
CATE?
THERE WAS NO ANSWER AND SHE COULDN'T TELL IF ANYONE WAS IN THE TENT.
SHE COULDN'T TELL IF WHAT SHE HEARD WAS A GIRL'S VOICE OR ONLY THE SOUND OF THE RAIN.

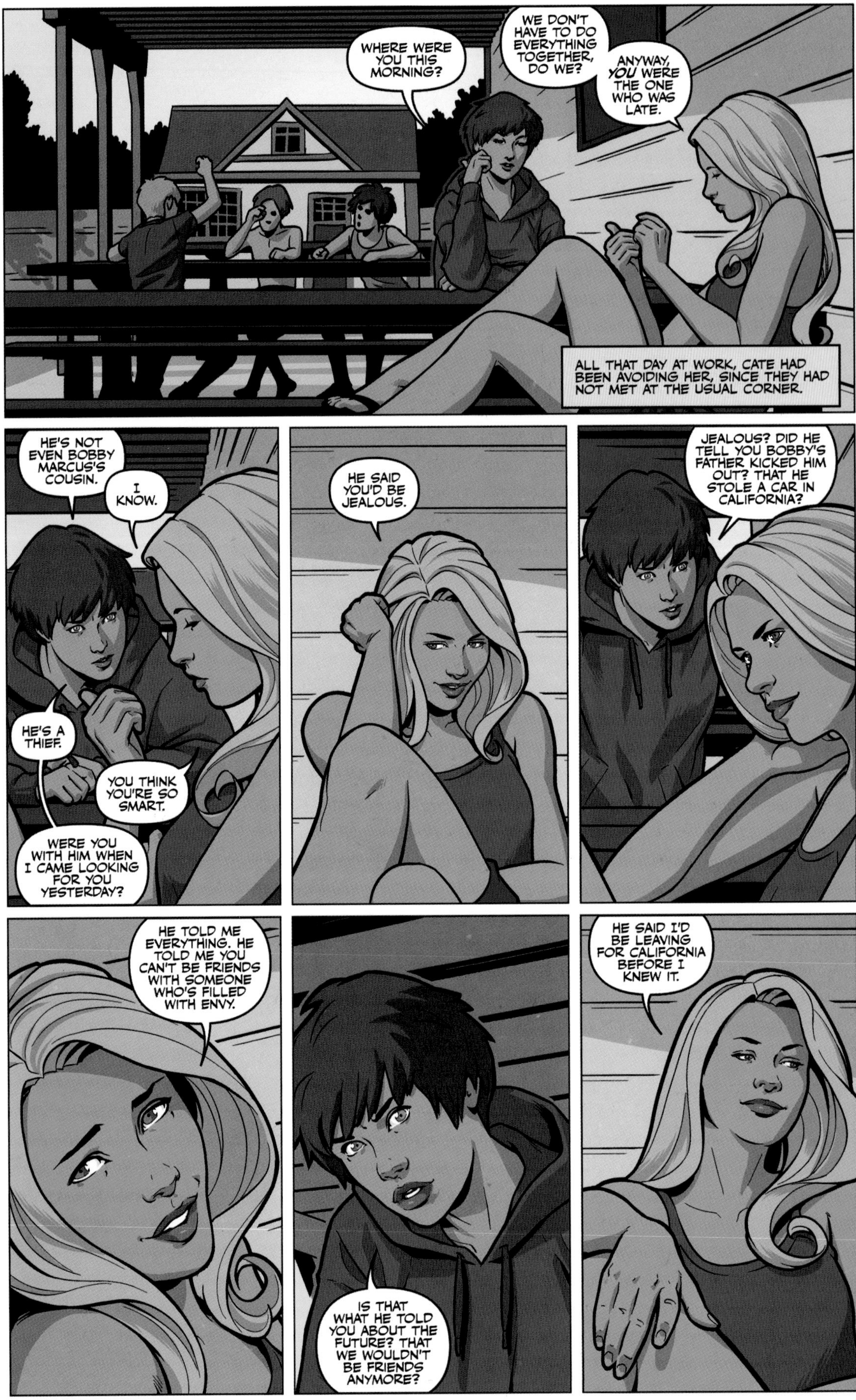
WHERE WERE YOU THIS MORNING?
WE DON'T HAVE TO DO EVERYTHING TOGETHER, DO WE?
ANYWAY, *YOU* WERE THE ONE WHO WAS LATE.
ALL THAT DAY AT WORK, CATE HAD BEEN AVOIDING HER, SINCE THEY HAD NOT MET AT THE USUAL CORNER.
HE'S NOT EVEN BOBBY MARCUS'S COUSIN.
I KNOW.
HE'S A THIEF.
YOU THINK YOU'RE SO SMART.
WERE YOU WITH HIM WHEN I CAME LOOKING FOR YOU YESTERDAY?
HE SAID YOU'D BE JEALOUS.
JEALOUS? DID HE TELL YOU BOBBY'S FATHER KICKED HIM OUT? THAT HE STOLE A CAR IN CALIFORNIA?
HE TOLD ME EVERYTHING. HE TOLD ME YOU CAN'T BE FRIENDS WITH SOMEONE WHO'S FILLED WITH ENVY.
IS THAT WHAT HE TOLD YOU ABOUT THE FUTURE? THAT WE WOULDN'T BE FRIENDS ANYMORE?
HE SAID I'D BE LEAVING FOR CALIFORNIA BEFORE I KNEW IT.

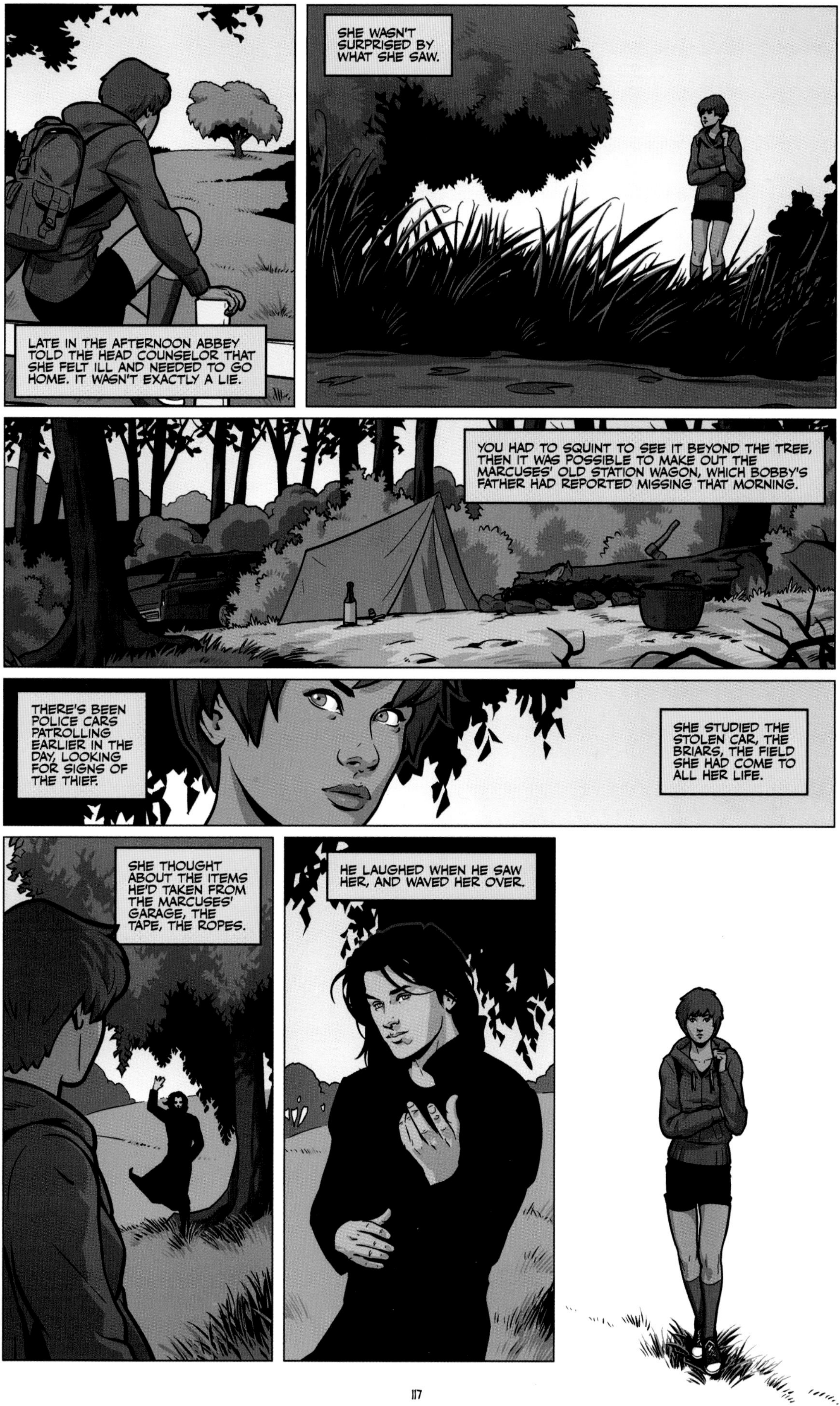
LATE IN THE AFTERNOON ABBEY TOLD THE HEAD COUNSELOR THAT SHE FELT ILL AND NEEDED TO GO HOME. IT WASN'T EXACTLY A LIE.
SHE WASN'T SURPRISED BY WHAT SHE SAW.
YOU HAD TO SQUINT TO SEE IT BEYOND THE TREE, THEN IT WAS POSSIBLE TO MAKE OUT THE MARCUSES' OLD STATION WAGON, WHICH BOBBY'S FATHER HAD REPORTED MISSING THAT MORNING.
THERE'S BEEN POLICE CARS PATROLLING EARLIER IN THE DAY, LOOKING FOR SIGNS OF THE THIEF.
SHE STUDIED THE STOLEN CAR, THE BRIARS, THE FIELD SHE HAD COME TO ALL HER LIFE.
SHE THOUGHT ABOUT THE ITEMS HE'D TAKEN FROM THE MARCUSES' GARAGE, THE TAPE, THE ROPES.
HE LAUGHED WHEN HE SAW HER, AND WAVED HER OVER.

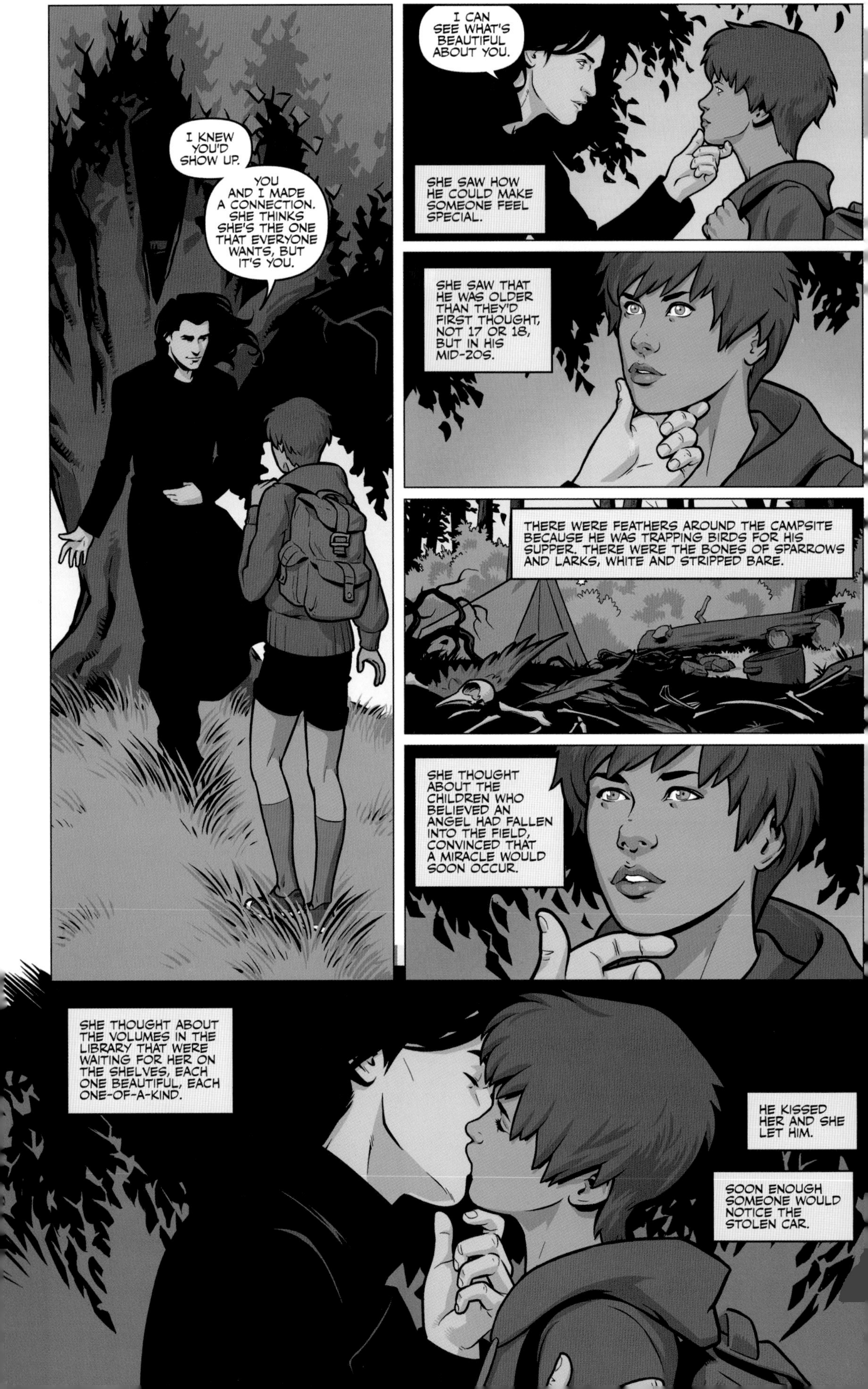

I KNEW YOU'D SHOW UP.
YOU AND I MADE A CONNECTION. SHE THINKS SHE'S THE ONE THAT EVERYONE WANTS, BUT IT'S YOU.
I CAN SEE WHAT'S BEAUTIFUL ABOUT YOU.
SHE SAW HOW HE COULD MAKE SOMEONE FEEL SPECIAL.
SHE SAW THAT HE WAS OLDER THAN THEY'D FIRST THOUGHT, NOT 17 OR 18, BUT IN HIS MID-20S.
THERE WERE FEATHERS AROUND THE CAMPSITE BECAUSE HE WAS TRAPPING BIRDS FOR HIS SUPPER. THERE WERE THE BONES OF SPARROWS AND LARKS, WHITE AND STRIPPED BARE.
SHE THOUGHT ABOUT THE CHILDREN WHO BELIEVED AN ANGEL HAD FALLEN INTO THE FIELD, CONVINCED THAT A MIRACLE WOULD SOON OCCUR.
SHE THOUGHT ABOUT THE VOLUMES IN THE LIBRARY THAT WERE WAITING FOR HER ON THE SHELVES, EACH ONE BEAUTIFUL, EACH ONE-OF-A-KIND.
HE KISSED HER AND SHE LET HIM.
SOON ENOUGH SOMEONE WOULD NOTICE THE STOLEN CAR.

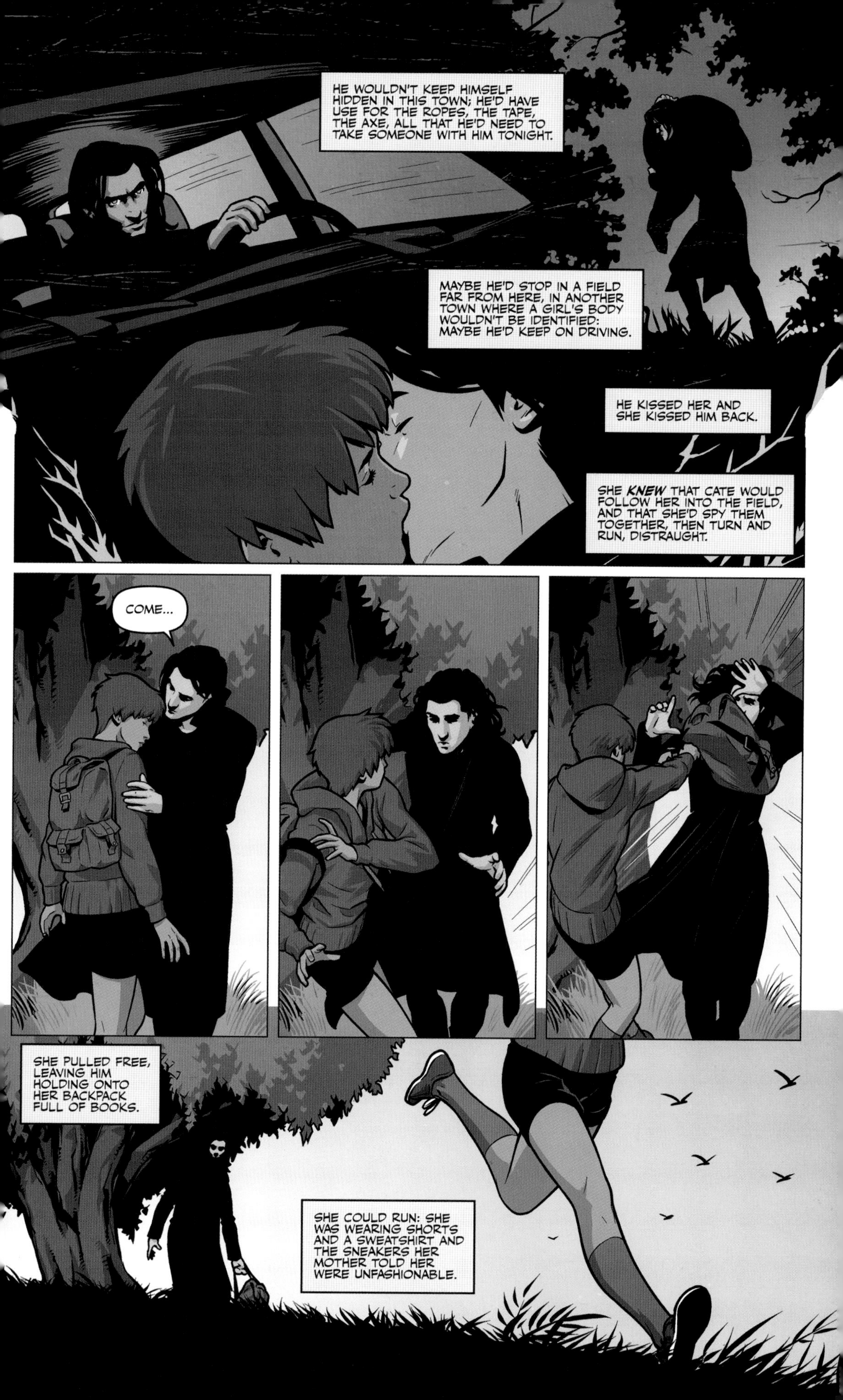
HE WOULDN'T KEEP HIMSELF HIDDEN IN THIS TOWN; HE'D HAVE USE FOR THE ROPES, THE TAPE, THE AXE, ALL THAT HE'D NEED TO TAKE SOMEONE WITH HIM TONIGHT.
MAYBE HE'D STOP IN A FIELD FAR FROM HERE, IN ANOTHER TOWN WHERE A GIRL'S BODY WOULDN'T BE IDENTIFIED: MAYBE HE'D KEEP ON DRIVING.
HE KISSED HER AND SHE KISSED HIM BACK.
SHE *KNEW* THAT CATE WOULD FOLLOW HER INTO THE FIELD, AND THAT SHE'D SPY THEM TOGETHER, THEN TURN AND RUN, DISTRAUGHT.
COME...
SHE PULLED FREE, LEAVING HIM HOLDING ONTO HER BACKPACK FULL OF BOOKS.
SHE COULD RUN: SHE WAS WEARING SHORTS AND A SWEATSHIRT AND THE SNEAKERS HER MOTHER TOLD HER WERE UNFASHIONABLE.

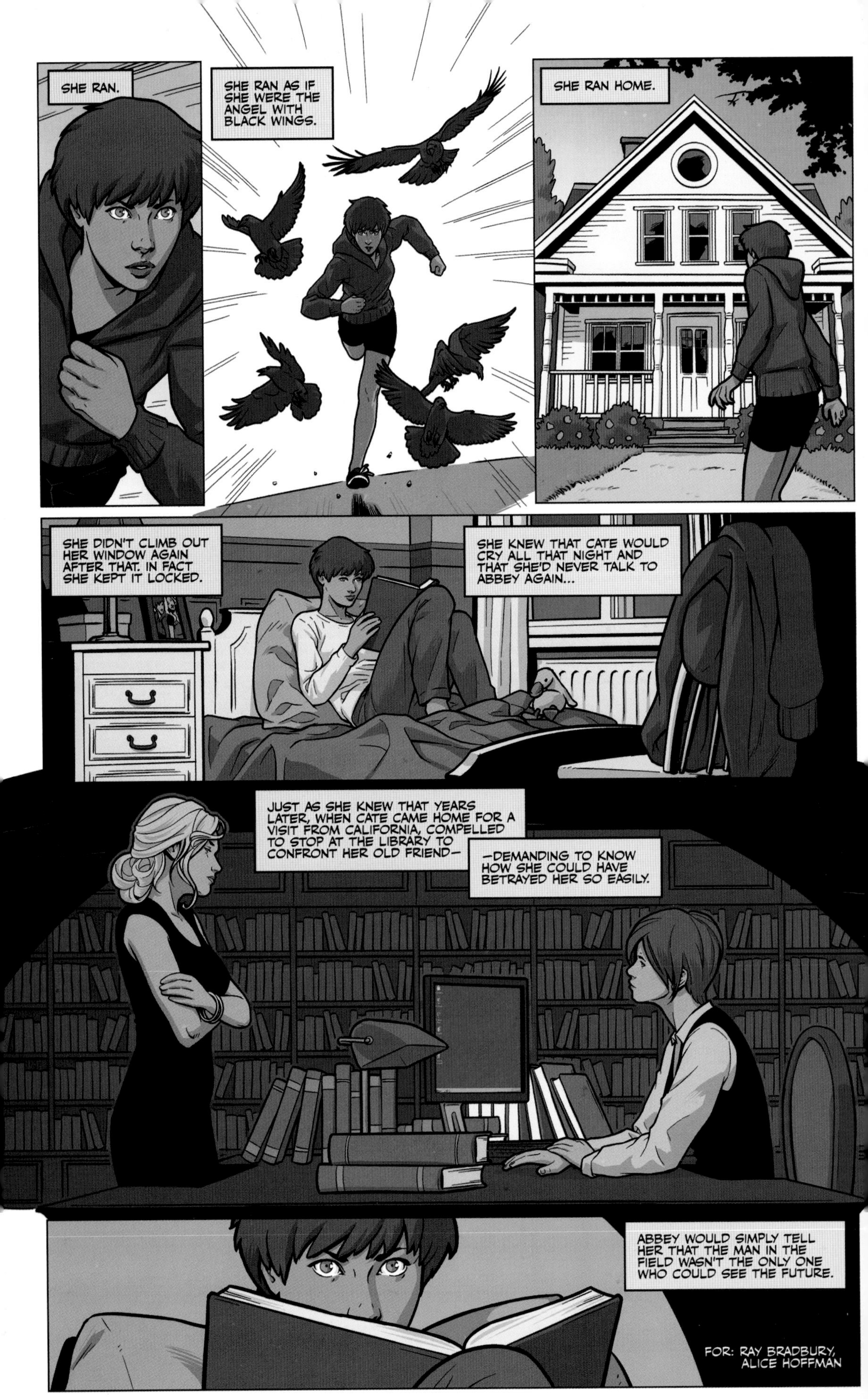
SHE RAN.
SHE RAN AS IF SHE WERE THE ANGEL WITH BLACK WINGS.
SHE RAN HOME.
SHE DIDN'T CLIMB OUT HER WINDOW AGAIN AFTER THAT. IN FACT SHE KEPT IT LOCKED.
SHE KNEW THAT CATE WOULD CRY ALL THAT NIGHT AND THAT SHE'D NEVER TALK TO ABBEY AGAIN...
JUST AS SHE KNEW THAT YEARS LATER, WHEN CATE CAME HOME FOR A VISIT FROM CALIFORNIA, COMPELLED TO STOP AT THE LIBRARY TO CONFRONT HER OLD FRIEND—
—DEMANDING TO KNOW HOW SHE COULD HAVE BETRAYED HER SO EASILY.
ABBEY WOULD SIMPLY TELL HER THAT THE MAN IN THE FIELD WASN'T THE ONLY ONE WHO COULD SEE THE FUTURE.
FOR: RAY BRADBURY, ALICE HOFFMAN

ABOUT "CONJURE"

Ray Bradbury's masterwork, *Fahrenheit 451*, a hymn to books and to the power of literature, is a classic work of American Fiction, and one of the most important books of our lifetime. In a series of novels, short stories and linked short stories, Bradbury has created his own genre, one that has greatly influenced American Literature. Due to his work, magic is no longer corralled into genre writing. It is everywhere in American fiction. Critics may call it magic realism, but it's simply what Ray Bradbury has been doing from the start.

Bradbury's themes of innocence and experience echo a world made up of equal parts of dark and light, where characters yearn for both the future and the past and where loss is inevitable. Bradbury has given readers a singular vision of small-town American life, one in which a dark thread is pulled through the grass. Bradbury's blend of suburban magic rejoices in the American dream, but it also presents the twilight world of darker possibilities, the opposing nightmare.

In my story "Conjure," many of Ray's themes surface—two friends who must step into the future and leave their childhoods behind, like it or not; a summer that will never be forgotten; a stranger who comes to town with a dark past and perhaps an even darker future; a huge love of the library; and ultimately, personal salvation through books. Of course I'm quite certain that *Something Wicked This Way Comes* saves my characters from a terrible fate, echoing my own life. Had I not discovered Ray Bradbury's books, I most certainly would not have become the writer I am today.

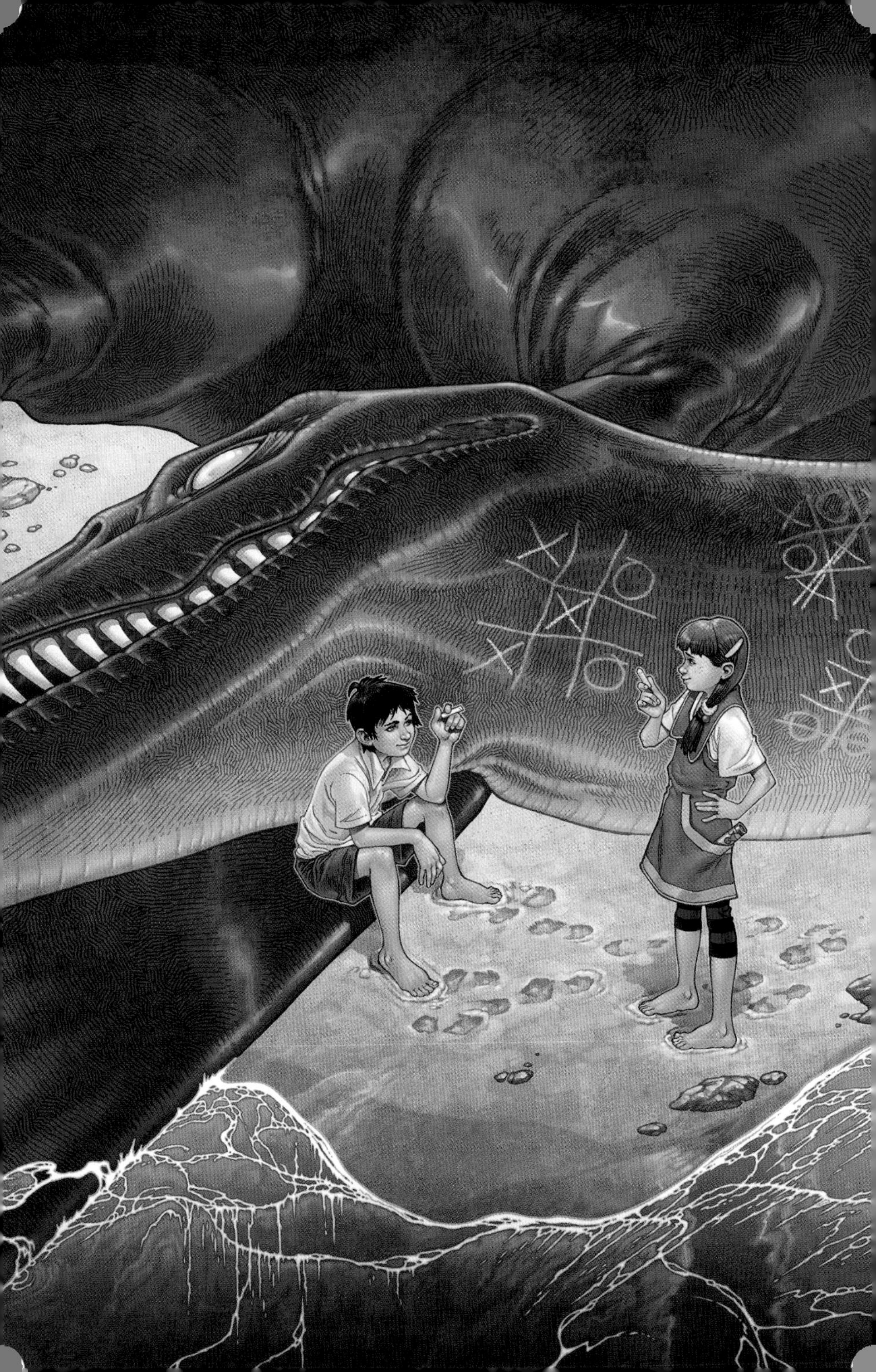

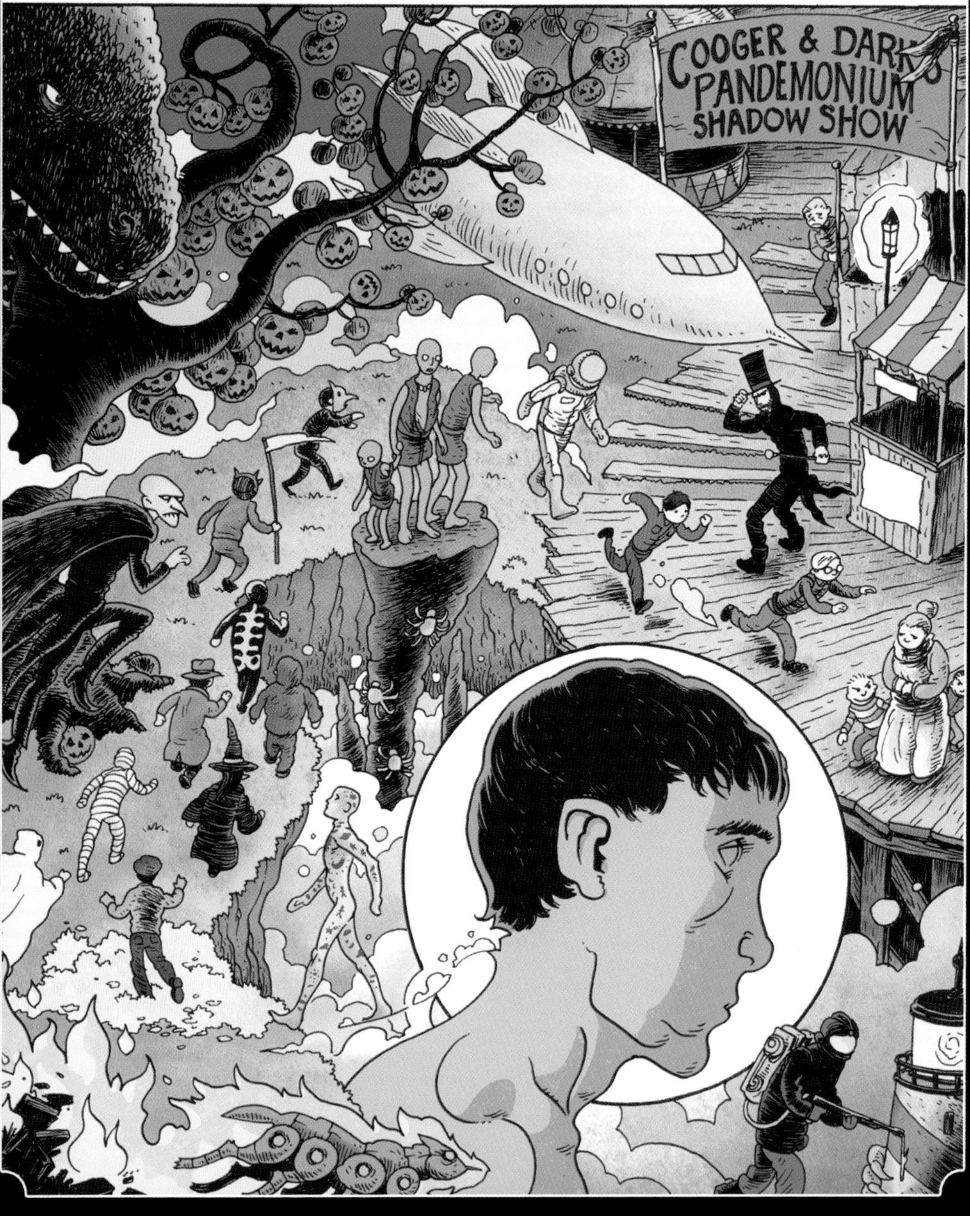
COOGER & DARK'S
PANDEMONIUM
SHADOW SHOW

art by CHARLES PAUL WILSON III

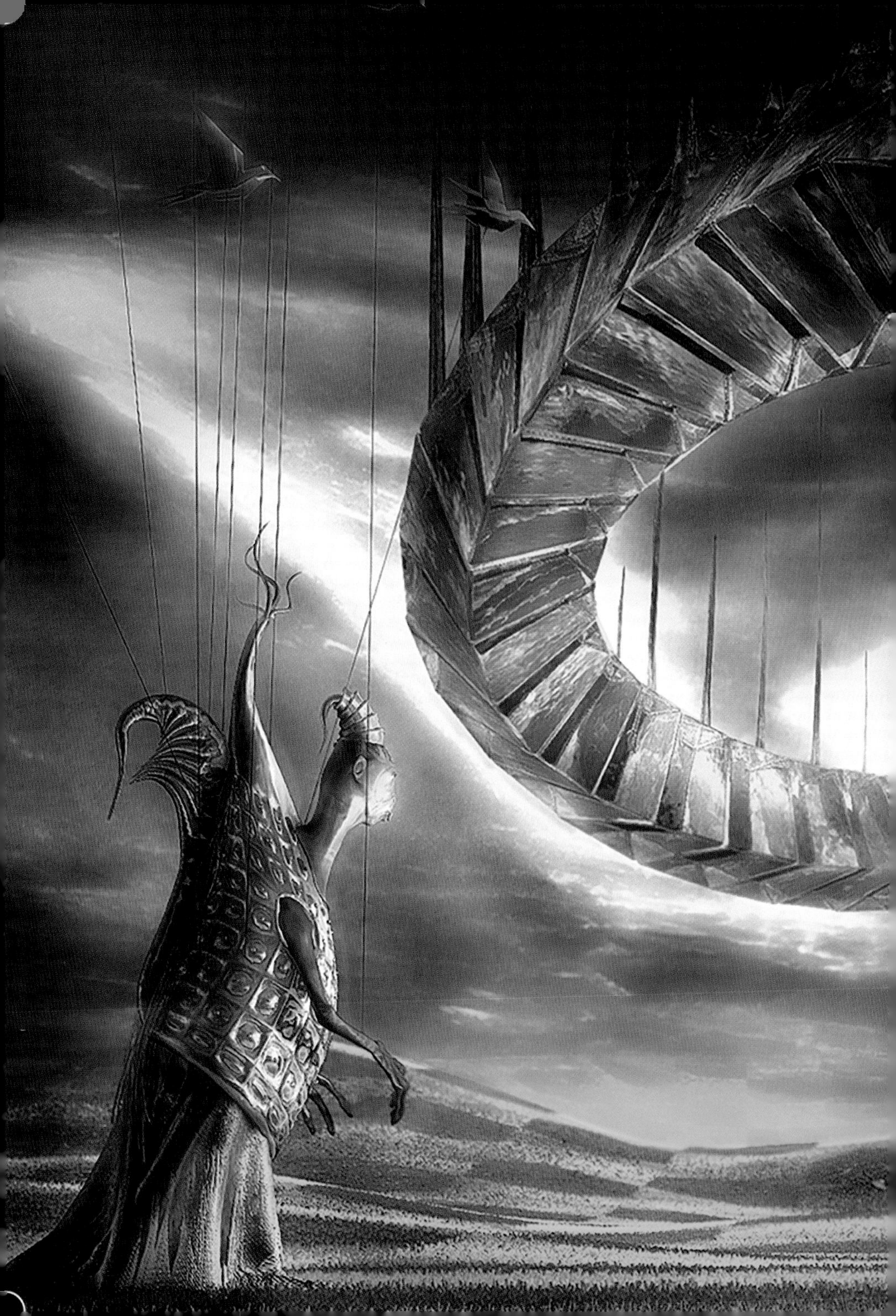

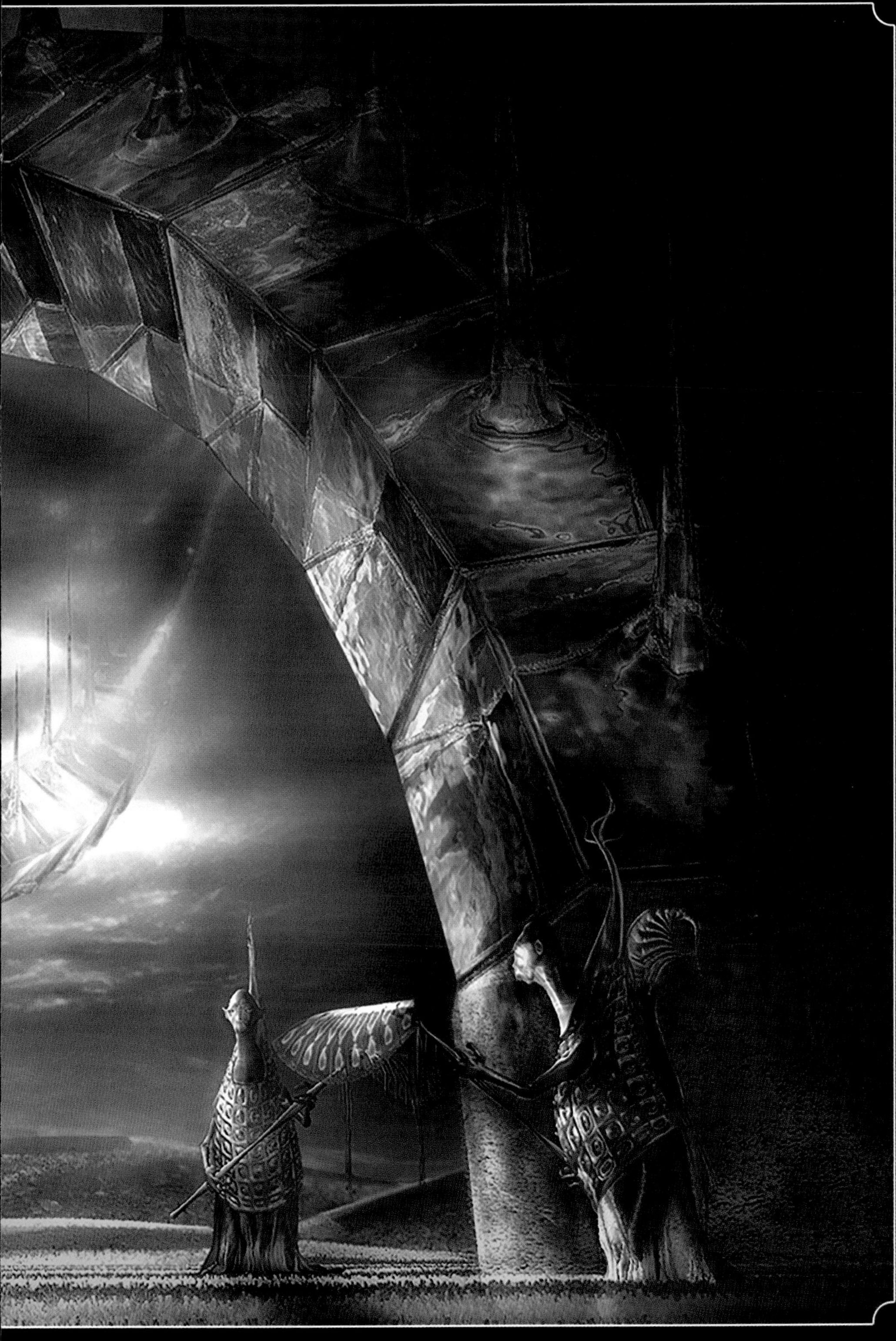

art by HUBERT J. DANIEL

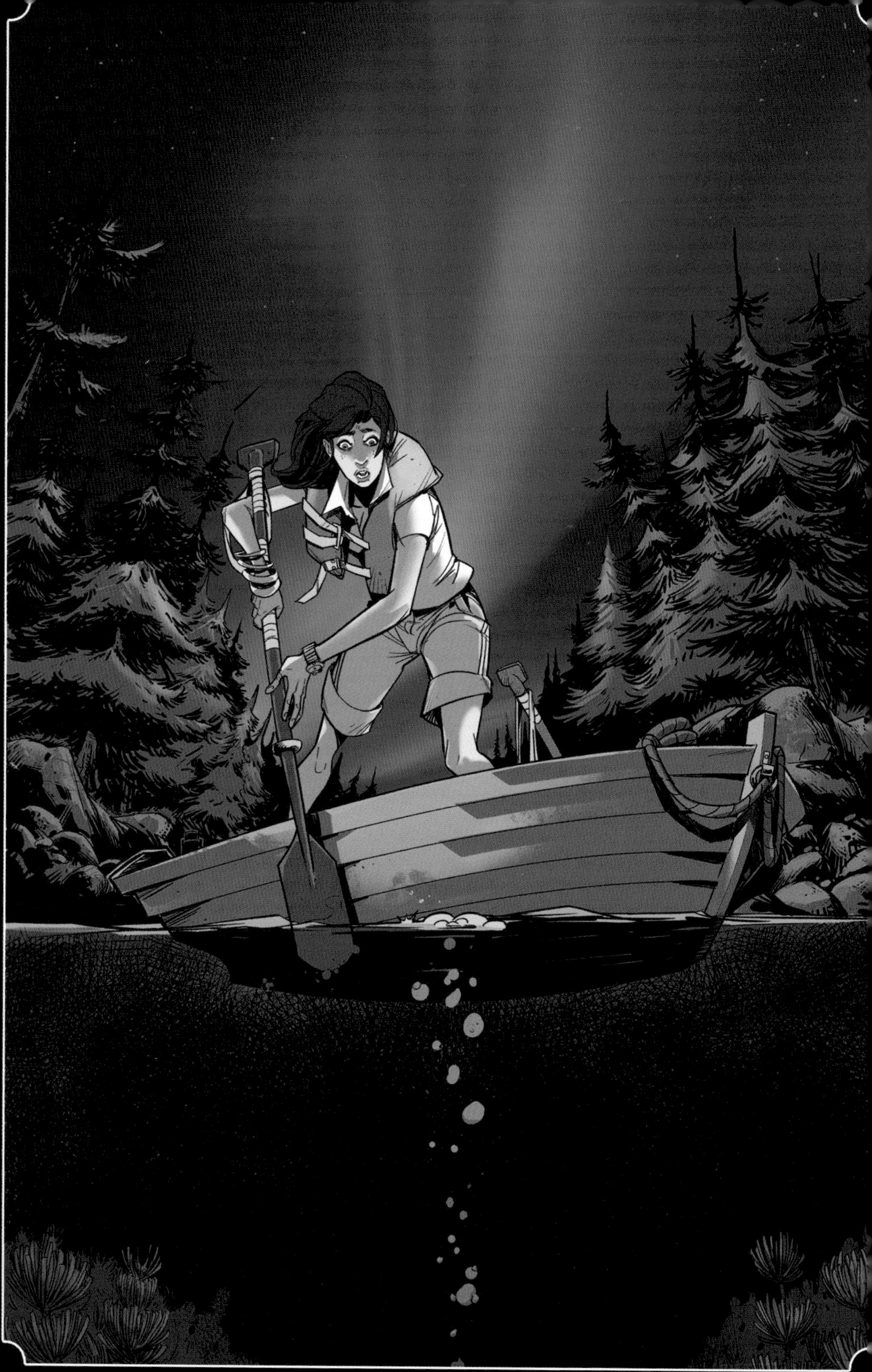

art by CHRISTIAN WILDGOOSE

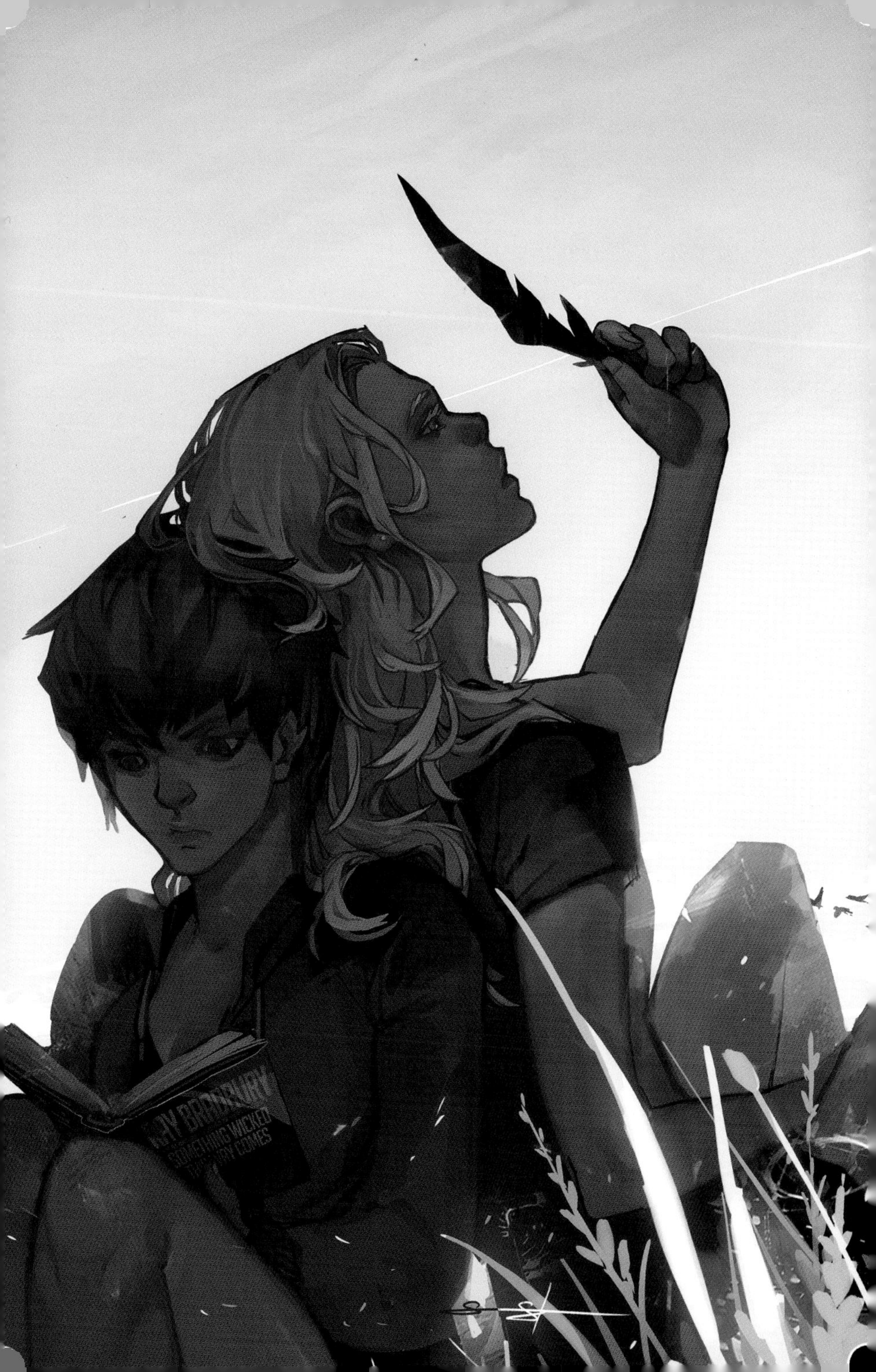

BRADBURY
SOMETHING WICKED
WAY COMES

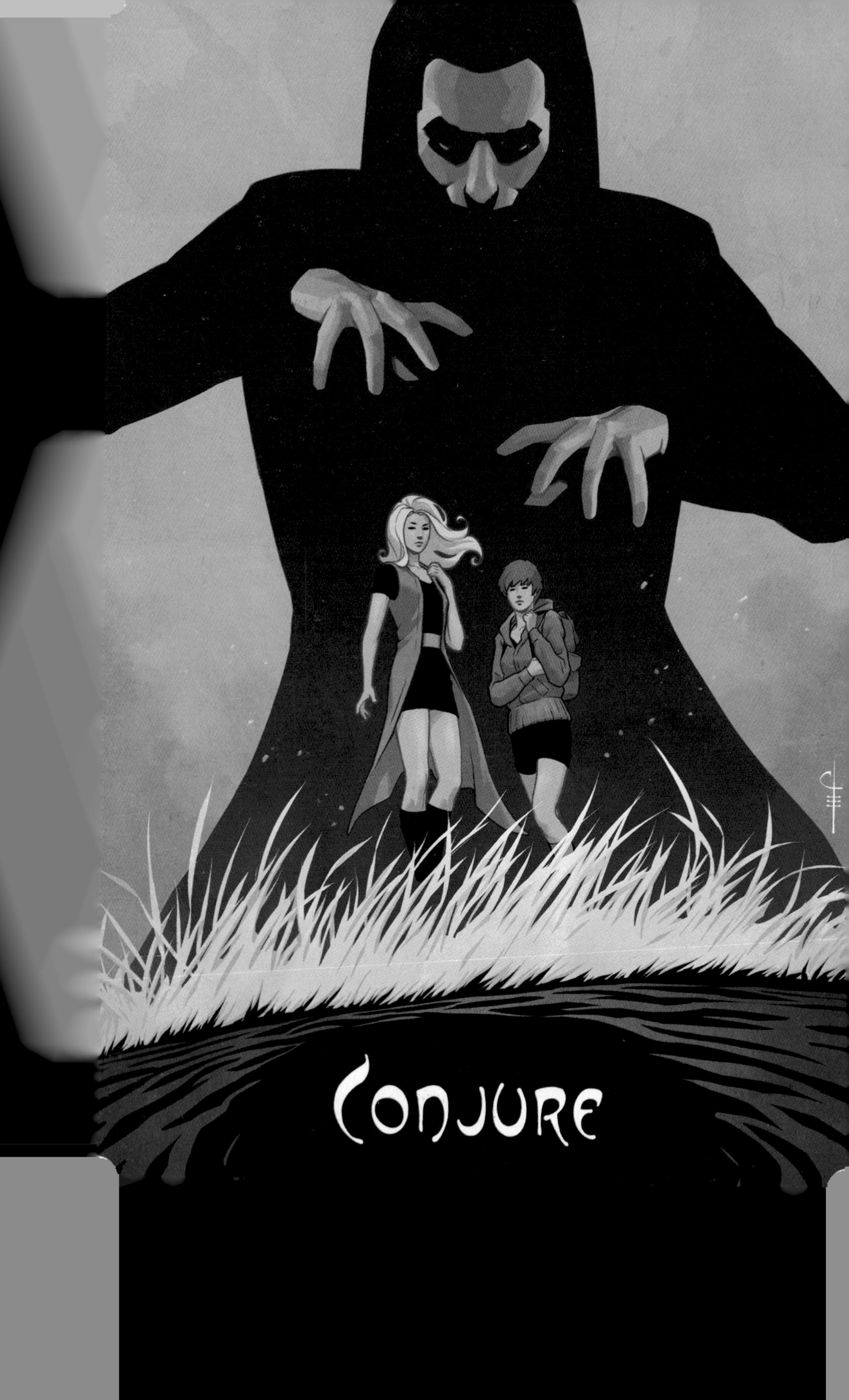
CONJURE